THE DESIGN AND IMPLEMENT~

MULTIMEDIA

SOFTWARE

WITH EXAMPLES IN JAVA™

DAVID BERNSTEIN
JAMES MADISON UNIVERSITY

JONES & BARTLETT
LEARNING

World Headquarters

Jones & Bartlett Learning
40 Tall Pine Drive
Sudbury, MA 01776
978-443-5000
info@jblearning.com
www.jblearning.com

Jones & Bartlett Learning
Canada
6339 Ormindale Way
Mississauga, Ontario L5V 1J2
Canada

Jones & Bartlett Learning
International
Barb House, Barb Mews
London W6 7PA
United Kingdom

Jones & Bartlett Learning books and products are available through most bookstores and online booksellers. To contact Jones & Bartlett Learning directly, call 800-832-0034, fax 978-443-8000, or visit our website, www.jblearning.com.

Substantial discounts on bulk quantities of Jones & Bartlett Learning publications are available to corporations, professional associations, and other qualified organizations. For details and specific discount information, contact the special sales department at Jones & Bartlett Learning via the above contact information or send an email to specialsales@jblearning.com.

Production Credits
Publisher: David Pallai
Senior Acquisitions Editor: Timothy Anderson
Editorial Assistant: Melissa Potter
Production Manager: Tracey Chapman
Production Assistant: Lindsey Jones
Senior Marketing Manager: Andrea DeFronzo
V.P., Manufacturing and Inventory Control: Therese Connell
Composition: Northeast Compositors, Inc.
Cover Design: Kristin E. Parker
Cover Image: © Wingedsmile/Dreamstime.com
Printing and Binding: Malloy, Inc.
Cover Printing: Malloy, Inc.

Library of Congress Cataloging-in-Publication Data
Bernstein, David, 1960 June 9-
   The design and implementation of multimedia software with examples in Java / David Bernstein.
      p. cm.
   Includes index.
   ISBN-13: 978-0-7637-7812-5 (pbk.)
   ISBN-10: 0-7637-7812-5 (ibid.)
   1. Interactive multimedia. 2. Software engineering. I. Title.
   QA76.76.I59B47 2010
   006.7—dc22
                              2010004749

6048
Printed in the United States of America
14 13 12 11 10   10 9 8 7 6 5 4 3 2 1

Preface

According to the *Oxford English Dictionary*, the word "multimedia" has been in use since 1962 and has been used in the computing domain since 1970. It has attracted people to (and in) computing since its first use. Thus, it is not surprising that there are a large number of books with the word "multimedia" in their titles. This particular book is intended for software engineers and object-oriented programmers who are interested in developing multimedia software. This particular book is intended for students and practitioners of software engineering and object-oriented programming who are interested in developing multimedia software. It can be used in a traditional lecture-based course, a project-based studio course, and a self-study "course." Each chapter has various kinds of exercises, some that require a careful reading of the text, some that require library research, some that require programming, and some that require design. A few of the exercises lead quite naturally to large-scale projects.

Necessary Background

The Design Implementation of Multimedia Software assumes that the reader has a general understanding of object-oriented design and programming. This includes an understanding of the fundamentals of object-oriented programming (OOP) like classes and objects, abstraction, encapsulation, information hiding, the use of interfaces and abstract classes, specialization and inheritance, overriding and overloading, and polymorphism. This also includes a basic understanding of class, sequence, and state diagrams in the Unified Modeling Language (UML). (Don't be too concerned if you do not have any experience with UML. You should be able to learn what you need very quickly if you understand the fundamentals of OOP.) Readers should also have an understanding of some of the more common design patterns and experience with software requirement specifications (SRSs) and top-down design as they are used (though somewhat loosely) throughout this book.

Though the principles in this book are not language-specific, all of the examples are in Java™. Hence, readers should be fairly familiar with the Java programming language. This includes an understanding of the basics (like Java's data types, operators, control structures, and parameter passing) as well as Java's packaging and exception-handling mechanisms and the way it defines different levels of visibility and resolves polymorphism. In addition, readers of this book should be fairly familiar with Java's collection framework and have a basic understanding of Java's threading mechanism. Readers who are familiar with developing graphical user interfaces in Java using Swing will be able to build more elegant apps than those who are not. However, no knowledge of Swing is required. This preface includes a set of exercises that you can use to determine whether you have the necessary Java background.

Approach to Problem Solving

The approach to problem solving used throughout this book (which is discussed more fully in Chapter 1) is one that is used in a variety of different disciplines, including artificial intelligence, software engineering, operations research, and urban planning. Put succinctly, this book treats problem solving as a process that involves the identification of goals/objectives/constraints, the generation of alternatives, the evaluation of alternatives, and the selection of an alternative. In any given problem-solving situation, these steps may occur in any order and may occur more than zero or more times.

Structure of This Book

This book is divided into three parts. Part I contains introductory material; it begins with a consideration of multimedia, then considers event-based programming, and finally develops an architecture for the applications and applets that are to follow. Part II is devoted to visual content; it considers both sampled content and described content. For both, it distinguishes between static and dynamic content. Part III is devoted to auditory content; it too considers both sampled and described content.

Icons, Typefaces, and Typesetting Conventions

A number of icons, typefaces, and typesetting conventions are used throughout this book to make it more readable. They are summarized in the following sections.

Typefaces and Adornments

In the body of the text, `the teletype font` is used to denote a piece of code (e.g., a Java class, a variable), **bold** is used to denote emphasis, and *italics* is used to highlight a piece of text (e.g., an important term that is being used for the first time). Mathematics is typeset in a special font as in the following example: $x \neq y$.

The UML diagrams in this book use a sans serif font. Abstract classes and methods in a UML diagram are denoted with a *slanted sans serif font*.

Quote Marks

There are two different kinds of quote marks, single and double, and they can look very different in different fonts. In code examples, the Java language specification is followed. Hence, `String` literals are enclosed in double quotes and `char` literals are enclosed in single quotes as in the following example:

```
char    c = 'a';
String  s = "Apple";
```

In the body of the text, double quotes are used for quotations and when referring to a word or phrase. For example, the word "application" is referred to in this sentence. Single quotes, on the other hand, are used to indicate that a word or phrase is being used loosely or colloquially. For example, this book contains many 'cool' examples. In the body of the text, opening and closing quotes use different glyphs.

Asides

An *aside* is a short discussion that is somewhat off-topic. Asides have a dialogue bubble in the margin and are typeset in sans serif font. For example:

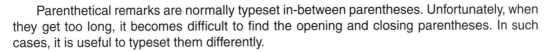

An Aside: Parenthetical Remarks

Parenthetical remarks are normally typeset in-between parentheses. Unfortunately, when they get too long, it becomes difficult to find the opening and closing parentheses. In such cases, it is useful to typeset them differently.

Definitions

Definitions that are particularly important are set apart from normal body text and the word/phrase being defined is *italicized*. They are numbered by section to make them easy to find. For example:

Definition 0.1 *Important definitions* are definitions that are essential to the discussion that follows.

Less important words/phrases are normally defined in the body of a paragraph. In such cases, the word/phrase of interest will be *italicized*.

Requirements

Requirements are the specification of a software product's features, capabilities, and interfaces. An icon is placed in the margin to make them easy to see and they are numbered by section to make them easy to find. For example:

F0.1 Functional requirements are behavioral requirements. They specify how the software product must map inputs to outputs.

N0.2 Nonfunctional requirements contain properties that the software product must have. Examples include quality, performance, and security requirements.

They are numbered and preceded by either an "F" to indicate a functional requirement or an "N" to indicate a nonfunctional requirement.

Alternatives

Software design involves problem solving, and problem solving involves the generation of alternatives. Hence, this book often presents several different alternative solutions to the same problem. To help make them easier to see, each alternative has an icon in the margin. Since software design often involves top-down refinement (as discussed more fully in Chapter 1), the icon indicates the alternative's level of abstraction.

 This is an example of the start of a high-level design alternative. That is, an alternative that involves a high-level of abstraction (or, alternatively, a low-level of resolution). The icon is supposed to convey the notion of a forest (as in the expression, "being able to see the forest for the trees"). High-level design alternatives are sometimes called architectural alternatives.

 This is an example of the start of a mid-level design alternative. Mid-level alternatives are fairly abstract, but not as abstract as high-level alternatives. (Of course, one can disagree about levels of abstraction. What is a mid-level alternative to one person might be a low-level alternative to another.) The icon is supposed to convey the notion of a tree (which is at a higher level of detail/resolution than a forest). Note that the tree icon/analogy is unrelated to the graph—theoretic notion of a tree.

 This is an example of the start of a low-level design alternative. Low-level alternatives are fairly concrete, but are not yet at the level of the code. The icon is supposed to convey the notion of a branch (which is at a higher level of detail than a tree). At this level of abstraction, one focuses on a part of a single tree, ignoring the rest of the tree and the other trees in the forest. Note that the branch icon/analogy is unrelated to what is sometimes called branching in code/algorithms (e.g., if statements).

 This is an example of the start of an alternative implementation. Implementation alternatives are at the level of the code and involve a significant amount of detail. The icon is supposed to convey the notion of a leaf (which is at a higher level of detail than a branch). At this level of abstraction, one focuses on a small aspect of a particular tree.

Numbering

Definitions, equations, figures, requirements, and tables are all numbered using a two-part scheme, $C.I$, where C denotes the chapter number and I denotes the item number. The item number is reset at the start of each chapter. So, for example, Figure 4.2 is the second figure in Chapter 4. This system makes it easier to find an item from one chapter that is cross referenced to in another chapter.

Code

As mentioned previously, code is typeset in a sans serif font. Code that involves more than a single expression is almost always set apart from the body of the text and placed inside of a box. A distinction is made between 'bad' code (i.e., code that contains mistakes/faults/defects) and 'good' code.

'Good' code that is an integral part of the system being designed and implemented in the book is placed inside of a box. For example:

```
public int getNextIndex()
{
  return ++index;
}
```

'Good' code that is not used elsewhere in the book (i.e., code that is part of a local example or discussion) has an icon in the margin. The icon indicates that this code is not actually used. For example:

```
public void wasteTime()
{
  int     i;

  ++i;
}
```

'Bad' code also has an icon in the margin. In this case, the icon indicates that the code should not even be typed. For example:

```
public int problem()
{
  double     x, y;

  x = 5.0;
  y = '7.3';
  return location;
}
```

Code may extend across multiple pages. When code extends to the next page, the bottom of the box is omitted. When code extends from the previous page, the top of the box is omitted.

To save space, most code fragments in the book do not include comments. The actual code is fully-commented using the `javadoc` standard.

Acknowledgments

This book has benefited greatly from the feedback provided by students in CS349 at James Madison University. Especially important were the questions and comments provided by Chris Ashworth, Stephen Ayers, Victoria Barrow, Michael Beaumont, David Burgess, Brad Campbell, Mitchell Charchalis, Chris Dilbeck, Kevin Eckerman, Charlie Fairchild, Justin Fielder,

Dan Funk, Brandon Gauthier, Kelly Harris, David Hazel, Glen Henderson, Jon Herman, Troy Herndon, Dan Hodos, Josh Houck, Evan Jacobs, Sammy James, Matt Jennings, Leigh Johann, Tomomi Kotera, Zane Kreider, Ryan Lanman, Rob MacHardy, Kendal Miller, Brian Minter, Rob Offutt, Sam Patteson, Will Pope, Zach Rezin, Adrian Romano, Claire Rooney, Doug Roper, Chris Rothgeb, A. J. Schuster, Brian Singer, Ryan Slominski, Alex Srisuwan, Jerry Timbrook, Kevin Tougher, Ritul Walia, Jeff Ward, Ken White, David Winfield, Andrew Wynham, and Kevin Yarmosh.

Four students deserve special acknowledgments for the work they did proofreading the text and debugging the code: Seth Fowler, Kris Kalish, John Magnotti, and Karl Ridgeway.

I would also like to thank Jones and Bartlett Acquisitions Editor, Tim Anderson; Editorial Assistant, Melissa Potter; and Managing Editor, Tracey Chapman and their staff for their help and support during this project.

EXERCISES

I've included some exercises covering the background needed for this text.

1. In Java, how would you instantiate an object of the class `SoundStage`?

2. In Java, how do you call the parent's constructor in a constructor of a derived class?

3. In Java, explain the difference between an interface and an abstract class.

4. In Java, what are the differences between static methods and other methods?

5. Your company has just purchased a partial implementation of an e-mail system called JMUumble. In this system, arriving messages are handled by a `PostOffice` object. Depending on how the system is configured at runtime, one or more objects might need to know when a message arrives. Several such classes have been implemented: `ScreenFlasher` makes the entire screen flash so that you always know when a message has arrived, `PopularityTimer` starts a clock that shows the amount of time since the most recent message arrived, and `Mumbler` uses speech generation to read the name of the person who sent the message. Use the observer pattern to develop a class model of this system (in UML). You do not need to include the attributes of each class, only the operations/methods. Include comments that describe each operation/method.

6. Modify the following implementation of the `GateListenerDatabase` class so that it uses type-safe collections (and is, itself, type-safe):

```java
import java.util.*;

/**
 * A database of GateListenerRecord objects
 *
 */
public class GateListenerDatabase
{
    private Hashtable                  db;
```

```java
/**
 * Construct a new GateListenerDatabase
 */
public GateListenerDatabase()
{
    db = new Hashtable();
}



/**
 * Add a GateListenerRecord to the database
 *
 * @param glr   The record to add
 * @return      true if successful and false otherwise
 */
public boolean add(GateListenerRecord glr)
{
    boolean           added;
    GateListenerRecord old;
    String            key;


    added = false;

    key = glr.getHost()+":"+glr.getPort();
    old = (GateListenerRecord)(db.get(key));

    if (old != null)
    {
        added = false;
    }
    else
    {
        added = true;
        db.put(key, glr);
    }
    return added;
}


/**
 * Drop a GateListenerRecord from the database
 *
 * @param glr   The record to drop
 * @return      true if successful and false otherwise
 */
```

```
    public boolean drop(GateListenerRecord glr)
    {
        boolean    dropped;
        Object     old;
        String     key;

        key = glr.getHost()+":"+glr.getPort();
        old = db.remove(key);

        dropped = true;
        if (old == null) dropped = false;

        return dropped;
    }



    /**
     * Returns an Enumeration containing all of the GateListenerRecord
     * Objects in the database
     *
     * @return  The Enumeration of records
     */
    public Enumeration getAll()
    {
        return db.elements();
    }
}
```

7. Modify your answer to Exercise 6 so that it is impossible to construct more than one instance of a GateListenerDatabase. Use the singleton pattern.

Contents

List of Figures

List of Tables

I

Introduction

Part I contains introductory material. It begins, in Chapter 1, with an introduction to software design, multimedia, and the physics of waves. Then, in Chapter 2, it continues with an introduction to event-driven programming and why it is important for multimedia software. Finally, Chapter 3 includes a discussion of the differences between applications and applets and develops the unified framework that is used throughout the remainder of this book.

Background

1

The title of this book is likely to be of interest to more people than the book itself. The **title** will attract a lot of attention because an enormous number of people are interested in multimedia, and many of them are interested in using multimedia software to design and create multimedia content. The **book** will be of interest only to people who want to design multimedia software. This chapter is about the difference between the two.

1.1 Software Design

This book is about *software design*. Following Fox (2006), this means that this book is about the process of specifying the nature and composition of a software system that satisfies client needs and desires, subject to constraints. However, this book is not about all aspects of software design. To understand what it is and isn't about, it is essential to distinguish between two different software design activities.

....

Definition 1.1 *Software Product Design* is the process of specifying software product features, capabilities, and interfaces to satisfy client needs and desires.

....

....

Definition 1.2 *Software Engineering Design* is the process of specifying programs and subsystems, and their constituent parts and workings, to meet software product specifications.

....

Perhaps the easiest way to explain the difference is to consider an example—the design of a role-playing game. The product design team would decide how the user controls play, when games can be saved and how the user does so, when scores are presented, the way in which scores are presented to the user (e.g., visual or auditory), how the game transitions between levels, etc. The engineering design team would decide how the player's location is managed, how artifacts (e.g., weapons, treasure) are managed (e.g., carried by the player, state changes), how health/power/etc. levels are stored and changed, etc.

This book is concerned exclusively with software engineering design. Hence, for simplicity, this book uses the shorter terms "software design" and "design" in place of the more correct "software engineering design." With that in mind, it is now possible to consider software engineering design (and, hence, what this book is about) in more detail.

1.1.1 Engineering Design and Systems Theory

The software design community (especially the object-oriented software design community) has borrowed many terms and ideas from systems theorists. Hence it is difficult to understand the (object-oriented) software design literature without at least understanding the meanings of these terms.

....

Definition 1.3 A *system* is a set of entities (including their attributes) and the relationships between them.

....

As a result, a system has parts. What distinguishes a set of parts from a system is that the system includes the connections/relationships between the parts.

Every system can be defined in an enormous (perhaps infinite) number of ways. In any given situation, one tries to use the definition that is most appropriate. This involves deciding that some things are important and others can be ignored, a process that is known as *abstraction*. So, what often distinguishes these different definitions is their level of detail. The *resolution* (or level of detail) of a system is gauged in relation to its parts and to other systems. With that in mind, several other terms must be defined.

....

Definition 1.4 The *environment* is the set of all other systems.

....

The environment is also known as the *context* or the *domain*.

....

Definition 1.5 A *subsystem* is a part of the whole system that, in and of itself, displays a richness of interrelationships.

....

Obviously, there is no hard-and-fast rule for determining when a particular set of parts has relationships that are rich enough to make them qualify as a subsystem.

....

Definition 1.6 *Elements* (or *atoms*) are the smallest parts of the system.

....

Elements/atoms are often described as the *black boxes* that one can't 'see inside.'[1]

Some systems are 'real' and some are 'conceptual.' That is, some systems include entities that exist in space and time (and can be 'pointed to'), and some include entities that are purely conceptual. This distinction will be made clearer in the discussion of semiotics in Section 1.1.5 on page 7. Needless to say, the 'real world' is full of systems, including cells, tables, plants, automobiles, the human body, and the solar system.

Many theorists believe that different systems can be arranged hierarchically based on their complexity. Boulding (1956), for example, created such a hierarchy that he thought of as a "skeleton of science." While the different hierarchies that have been proposed are quite interesting, they are not necessary for what is to follow and, hence, are not considered here.

---

[1] The term "atom" is, of course, a misnomer given what we now know about particle physics. It continues to be used for historical reasons.

1.1.2 Engineering Design and Problem Solving

Since software engineering design is the "process of specifying...subsystems...to meet...specifications" it involves problem solving. Problem solving has been studied in a number of different disciplines, including architecture, computer science, economics, engineering, operations research, philosophy, and urban planning.

While there are a large number of disagreements in the literature, most people agree that problem solving involves the following activities:

- The identification of goals, objectives, and constraints
- The generation of alternatives
- The evaluation of alternatives
- The selection of an alternative

Most of the disagreements revolve around the order in which these activities are (and/or should be) performed. For example, in the urban planning literature, a distinction is made between the rational process at one extreme (in which the steps are performed in the order listed and a complete set of alternatives is generated and evaluated) and successive limited comparisons (in which means and ends are not distinct and many alternatives are omitted). As another example, in the software engineering literature, a distinction is made between heavyweight processes and agile processes.

This book does not take a particular position on how people do, or should, solve problems. It does, however, approach the different problems that it solves by specifying requirements, considering alternatives, and selecting one of the alternatives.

1.1.3 Object-Oriented Design

When engineering design is *data driven* the focus is on first identifying the important data and then identifying the processes that manipulate these data. When engineering design is *function driven* the focus is on first identifying the important processes and then identifying the data that are manipulated by these processes.

Object-oriented engineering design, which is used in this book, is often said to be *responsibility driven*. That is, object-oriented engineering design involves thinking about real-world entities/concepts and their responsibilities. Hence, unlike data-driven and function-driven design, object-oriented design involves the consideration of data and functions simultaneously. That is, when one thinks about the entities one considers both their characteristics (i.e., the data) and their capabilities (i.e., the functions/processes).

A common way to start the object-oriented engineering design process is to identify important concepts. This includes looking for things such as physical objects, places, organizations, events, records, containers, roles of people, descriptions, specifications, rules, and processes. Again, since object-oriented engineering design is a responsibility-driven process, this involves describing these entities in terms of both their attributes and their behaviors. Obviously, this process always involves some amount of abstraction (i.e., focusing on the important characteristics of the problem at hand and ignoring other characteristics).

The next step in the object-oriented engineering design process is to identify the important associations between concepts. This includes looking for associations such as part of (physical or logical), contained in (physical or logical), description of, member of, uses/manages/controls, communicates with, related to, owned by, and near/far from/above/below/etc.

It should be apparent that the result of these two steps in the object-oriented engineering design process is a conceptual system. In other words, the output of these two steps is a set of entities (including their characteristics and behaviors) and the relationships between them. Once the conceptual system has been described, the next step in the process is to create the necessary program units.

....

Definition 1.7 *Encapsulation* is the process of combining the attributes and behaviors that define a concept into a program unit.

....

In most object-oriented programming languages (including Java) the resulting program unit is called a *class*. So, to create a class one must list the attributes (that collectively define the state of each element) and the behaviors of the elements. A particular instance of a class is called an *object*.

1.1.4   Object-Oriented Design and Set Theory

In mathematics, there are two common methods for defining a set. Most people have seen and used both, though many are unaware that they have done so.

The first, the *extensive* definition, is a list of all of the elements in the set. So, for example, one can define the set S as follows:

$$S = \{1, 2, 3, 4\}. \tag{1.1}$$

That is, S contains the elements 1, 2, 3, and 4.

The second, the *intensive* definition, is a description of the elements in the set. So, for example, one can define the set T as follows:

$$T = \{x : 0 < x < 5, x \text{ is an integer}\}. \tag{1.2}$$

That is, T is the set of values x, such that x is greater than 0, and x is less than 5, and x is an integer.

The important point here is that, while the sets S and T contain the same elements, they were defined in very different ways. S was defined by exhaustively listing its members whereas T was defined by describing its members. The relationship to object-oriented design should be clear—a class is an intensive definition of a set, and an object (of class C) is a member of the set (defined by C). An object is said to be an *instance* of a class.[2]

With this in mind, it is easy to distinguish between attributes of the set (which are usually called *static* attributes or class variables) and attributes of each member of the set

---

[2]In common usage, the word "class" is used in two different, but related, ways. That is, the word "class" is used to mean both the definition of the set and the set itself.

(which are usually called non-static attributes or instance variables). For example, consider a bank of progressive slot machines at a casino. Each slot machine has its own attributes (e.g., the amount of money that has been wagered thus far) but the set of slot machines also has attributes (e.g., the current jackpot that, though changing over time, is common to all of the slot machines in the bank).

Not surprisingly, it is also worthwhile to distinguish between behaviors of the set (i.e., static methods) and behaviors of each element (i.e., non-static methods). Static methods can be called without first creating an instance of the class (but, obviously, cannot use non-static attributes).

1.1.5 Object-Oriented Design and Semiotics

Semiotics is usually said to be the study of signs.

....

Definition 1.8 A *sign* is anything that someone interprets as signifying something.

....

In other words, a sign is anything that refers to or stands for something other than itself. Since object-oriented design involves abstraction it is clearly related to signs.

....

Definition 1.9 A *token* is a sign that represents by way of its particular place in time and space.

....

By definition, every token is unique and every token can, in some sense, be 'pointed to.'

....

Definition 1.10 A *type* is a sign that represents a class or set.

....

Thus, types are real but cannot be 'pointed to.'

The distinction between an object and a class is clearly related to the distinction between a token and a type. It is very important to keep this distinction in mind when studying the design of multimedia software. It is also important to understand the two different parts of a sign. Specifically, a sign is composed of a *signifier* (the form that the sign takes) and the *signified* (the concept it represents). For the purposes of this book, the form of the sign is something that can be sensed using one of the five traditional senses (i.e., taste, touch, sound, sight, and smell).[3]

1.2 Multimedia

It is difficult to discuss multimedia software in a meaningful way without first defining the word "multimedia." Surprisingly, especially given how frequently the term is used, this is not a simple task.

---

[3]Semioticians do not, in general, limit the signifier to something that can be sensed. This assumption makes it much easier to understand the distinction between the signifier and the signified and is sufficient for the purposes of this book.

1.2.1   Etymology

One natural way to begin to define a word is to consider its etymology (i.e., its derivation or origins). In this case,

multi is from the Latin word "multus," which means "numerous"; and

media is from the Latin word "medium," which means "center."

Thus, on the surface, the word "multimedia" seems to mean "multiple centers."[4]

However, if one looks a little deeper, one can see that the word "medium" (and its plural "media") are used in a variety of different ways in English. In physics, a medium is a sequence of interacting particles (e.g., air is a medium through which sound is transmitted). In biology, a medium is the substance in which an organism lives (e.g., agar in a petri dish). In chemistry, a medium is a substance used for filtering (e.g., filter paper). In communications, a medium is a means of mass communication (e.g., radio and television are both media). In computer engineering, a medium is a device/object on which data are stored (e.g., a magnetic disk). Finally, in art, the word "medium" is used to refer to both the materials used in a technique (e.g., oils vs. watercolors) and solvents (e.g., paint thinner).

In these cases, the word "medium" seems to be used in the sense of the words "intermediary" or "means." Thus, it seems that a reasonable definition of the word "multimedia" is "involving multiple methods, means, or intermediaries."

1.2.2   Common Usage

Things get even more confusing if one looks to the popular press for help. As the term is commonly used, "multimedia software" involves (presumably more than one of) the following items:

- Text
- Graphics
- Images
- Animation
- Video
- Sounds
- Music
- Audio

Indeed, before you started reading this book, you probably would have used the above terms to describe multimedia software. Unfortunately, these terms neither have generally accepted definitions nor are particularly useful when designing software. This is easiest to see using

---

[4]It's not clear that the phrase "multiple centers" is any more informative than the word "centers," since the word "centers" is already plural. In other words, one can argue that the word "multimedia" is redundant and that the word "media" should suffice. This book ignores this issue completely and uses "multimedia" because of its popularity.

some of the concepts from systems theory and semiotics discussed in Sections 1.1.1 and 1.1.5, respectively.

First, some of these terms are sense-specific and some are not. For example, most people would agree that images and sounds are each associated with a particular sense (vision and hearing, respectively). However, text is not associated with a particular sense since it can either be seen or heard. In other words, all images have a visual signifier, all sounds have an auditory signifier, but words/text can have either a visual or auditory signifier.

Second, even if one thinks of text as having only a visual signifier, the term "text" is defined at a different level of abstraction from images. The term "image" refers to a type and a particular image is a token. However, the term "text" is a type and a particular piece of text, for example the word "dog," is also a type. A token doesn't exist until a particular instance of the word "dog" can be pointed to (set in a particular font, at a particular size, in a particular color, etc.).[5]

Third, some of the distinctions that are being made are either unclear or not agreed upon. For example, many people use the terms "image" and "graphic" interchangeably, whereas other people use the term "image" as shorthand for the phrase "raster/bitmap image" and the term "graphic" as shorthand for the phrase "vector graphic." As another example, for some people a video is sensed only visually, but for others a video can contain a sound track. As a final example, the terms "sounds," "music," and "audio" are used in any of a number of different ways.

Fourth, some important distinctions are ignored and, as a result, things are grouped together that are, in fact, very different. For example, the term "music" is often used as shorthand for both the phrase "recorded music" and the phrase "musical score."

Though it isn't often discussed, these problems/inconsistencies make it very difficult to design multimedia software. Specifically, it is very difficult to use object-oriented design when one can neither describe the important entities/concepts nor classify them. Hence, a better definition is needed.

1.2.3 Creating a Better Definition

This book needs a definition of the term "multimedia" that is useful in software engineering design. In other words, this book needs a definition that helps in the creation of software systems and subsystems that meet product specifications. To that end, the right way to create such a definition is to look at the various types of content and try to identify their important characteristics.

Clearly, one important characteristic of content is the sense used to perceive it. Specifically, some content is visual (e.g., images, graphics, animations, and video) and some is *auditory* (e.g., sounds, music, and audio).[6] However, it is clear that the sense used is not enough to define the medium since it does not enable us to distinguish between, for example, images and animations. That is, the term "multimedia" is not synonymous with the term "multisensory." Hence, one must consider other characteristics as well.

---

[5]The same is true if one thinks of text as having only an auditory signifier.

[6]In principle, one could include taste, touch, and smell as well but, since there are very few output devices that target these senses, this book ignores them.

A second important characteristic is the temporal nature of the content. Specifically, some content does not change over time (e.g., images) and some does (e.g., animations). In other words, some content is *static* and some content is dynamic.

While both of these two characteristics are **necessary** to distinguish different types of content, they are not **sufficient**. For example, they do not let us distinguish vector graphics from bitmap images and they do not let us distinguish recorded music from generated music. Hence, a third important characteristic is the way the content is represented. Some content is sampled before it is 'stored' and/or 'presented' (e.g., bitmap images, recorded music, recorded speech, flip-chart video, bitmapped fonts) and some content is described before it is 'stored' and 'presented' (e.g., vector graphics, musical scores, generated speech, animations, outline fonts).

These characteristics allow one to completely categorize all of the different types of content considered in this book. This means that it is now possible to create the definitions used throughout the remainder of this book.[7] Specifically:

....

Definition 1.11   A *medium* is a means of representing, storing, transmitting, or presenting information that is perceived using a particular sense.

....

The word "media" is simply the plural form of the noun "medium." The word "multimedia" is the adjectival form of the word "media."[8] Thus,

....

Definition 1.12 *Multimedia software* is software that uses more than one medium.

....

Combining the two definitions, multimedia software uses one or more means of representing, storing, transmitting, or presenting information that is perceived using one or more senses. In practice, very few multimedia software products target the senses of taste, touch, or smell. Hence, most multimedia software presents auditory information or visual information (or both).

1.3   A Brief Introduction to Waves

Since multimedia software presents visual and auditory information, Chapters 4 and 10 discuss how these kinds of information are perceived, respectively, beginning with the physics of sound and light. To understand the physics of sound and light it is first necessary to understand waves. Hence, this section provides a brief introduction to waves.

---

[7]At a more detailed level, one could use storage and/or transport characteristics to distinguish between different types of content. As discussed in Section 1.4 on page 16, this book is not concerned with storage or transmission issues and, hence, need not worry about such low-level characterizations.

[8]It is important not to confuse the term "multimedia" with the term "hypermedia." The term "hypermedia" usually refers to linked media/content.

1.3.1   Mechanical Waves

A mechanical *pulse* is a single disturbance that moves through a sequence of interacting particles (called a *medium*).[9] A mechanical *periodic wave* is a periodic (i.e., evenly 'timed/spaced') disturbance that moves through a medium, transporting energy as it moves.

It is important to remember that the individual particles do not move very far. Each particle oscillates around its equilibrium position; its average position does not change. As a particle interacts with its neighbors it transfers some of its energy to them, causing them to oscillate. As this process continues, the energy is transported through the medium.

Your first meaningful exposure to this phenomenon was probably water waves. Hence, much of your intuition about waves comes from your experience with water waves. However, a better place to start is with waves in a spring. A spring is a medium consisting of individual coils. Springs are interesting because there are two ways to generate waves in a spring, both of which become important in the discussions that follow.

First, suppose that the wave is generated by moving the left end of the spring 'back and forth' in the horizontal direction. This creates a series of compressions (areas in which the particles are closer than in equilibrium) and *rarefactions* (areas in which the particles are farther apart than in equilibrium). A 'snapshot' of a spring being moved 'back and forth' might look like the illustration in Figure 1.1.

Moving the spring 'back and forth' in this way generates a *longitudinal* wave; the particles (in this case, the coils) move parallel to the direction in which the energy is transferred. In other words, the particles move parallel to the direction in which the wave moves (i.e., both the particles and the wave move 'back and forth').

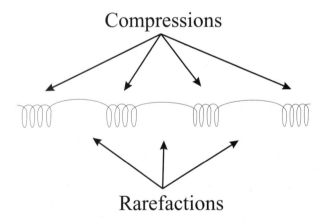

Figure 1.1   A Longitudinal Wave

---

[9]As discussed in Section 1.2 on page 7, the word "medium" is used in a variety of different ways in different disciplines. We use it only to mean a sequence of interacting particles when discussing waves. Elsewhere, we use it in the sense of Definition 1.11 on the page before.

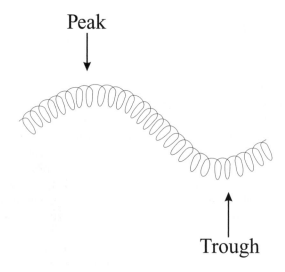

Figure 1.2   A Transverse Wave

Now suppose that the wave is generated by moving the left end of the spring 'up and down' in the vertical direction. This creates a series of *peaks* (areas in which the particles are 'higher' than in equilibrium) and *troughs* (areas in which the particles are 'lower' than in equilibrium). A 'snapshot' of a spring being moved 'up and down' might look like the illustration in Figure 1.2.

Moving the spring 'up and down' in this way generates a *transverse* wave; the particles move perpendicular to the direction in which the energy is transferred. In other words, the particles move perpendicular to the direction in which the wave moves (i.e., the particles move 'up and down' but the wave moves 'back and forth').

1.3.2 Waves in the Position Domain

Though the two kinds of waves, longitudinal and transverse, are physically very different, one can abstract away from those differences fairly easily by introducing the notion of the amplitude of a wave.

For a longitudinal wave in a spring, the amplitude is related to the number of coils per unit length. However, to 'center' the amplitude, one subtracts off the number of coils per unit length when the spring is in equilibrium (i.e., resting). This is illustrated in Figure 1.3 on the following page in which the spring is shown while being moved 'back and forth' and while at rest.

The dotted rectangle in Figure 1.3 on the next page indicates the fixed unit of length used to measure the amplitude, and the vertical line indicates the position at which the amplitude is being measured. At the indicated position, there are two coils per unit length when the spring is at rest (i.e., in the bottom spring) and there are four coils per unit length in the wave (i.e., in the top spring). This means that the amplitude at this position is two. The rectangle and line are then moved slightly and the process is repeated, yielding the graph in Figure 1.4 on the following page.

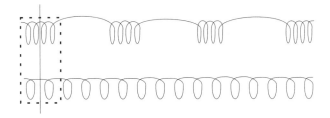

Figure 1.3 A Spring: Moving Longitudinally and at Rest

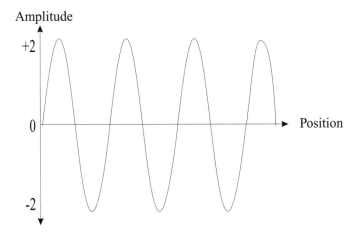

Figure 1.4 A Graph of Amplitude vs. Position for a Longitudinal Wave

For a transverse wave, the amplitude is related to the height of the coils. However, to 'center' the amplitude, one subtracts off the height of the coils when the spring is in equilibrium. This is illustrated in Figure 1.5 in which the spring is shown while being moved 'up and down' and while at rest.

The vertical line in Figure 1.5 indicates the position at which the amplitude is being measured. (When the coil in the spring at rest is below the coil in the wave, the amplitude is

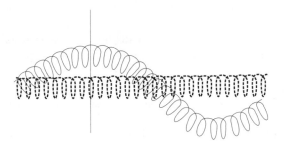

Figure 1.5 A Spring: Moving Transversely and at Rest

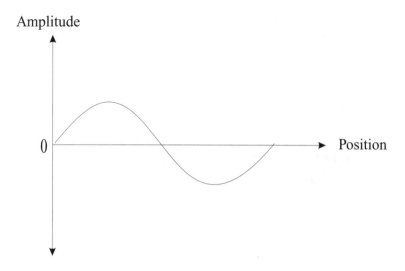

Figure 1.6   A Graph of Amplitude vs. Position for a Transverse Wave

positive; in the opposite situation the amplitude is negative.) The line is then moved slightly and the process is repeated, yielding the graph in Figure 1.6.

The wavelength of a periodic wave can be thought of as the distance one has to travel along the wave until it 'repeats'. The wavelength is usually measured in meters (or parts thereof) and denoted by λ.

When two waves meet while traveling through the same medium they are said to interfere with each other. The *principle of superposition* says that when two waves interfere, the resulting displacement of the medium at any location is the algebraic sum of the displacements of the individual waves at that same location. This leads us to distinguish between *constructive* interference (in which the displacements are both positive) and *destructive* interference (in which one displacement is positive when the other is negative).

1.3.3   Waves in the Time Domain

The graphs discussed thus far involve the amplitude of the wave versus the position along the wave. That is, they involved picking a point in time and measuring the amplitude of the wave at each position along the wave. This approach considers the wave in the position domain.

Alternatively, since a wave varies periodically in time as well as space, one could have picked a particular position along the wave and measured the amplitude at that position over time. This approach leads to a graph of the amplitude versus time as shown in Figure 1.7 on the next page. This approach considers the wave in the *time domain*.

In the time domain, a *cycle* is a portion of a wave from rest to crest to rest to trough to rest, and the *period* is the time required for a cycle (measured in seconds per cycle). The period can also be thought of as the time one has to wait at a position in space for the pattern to repeat.

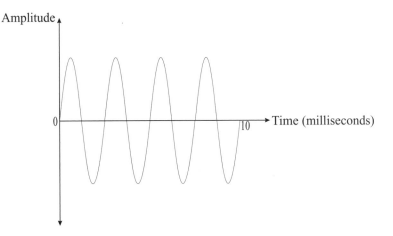

Figure 1.7   A Graph of Amplitude vs. Time

The *frequency*, denoted by f, is the reciprocal of the period and, hence, is measured in cycles per second (i.e., *hertz*). The *speed* of a wave, denoted by v, is the product of its wavelength and frequency.[10] That is:

$$v = \lambda f. \tag{1.3}$$

The speed (or velocity) of an object normally refers to its change in position over time. For waves, one has to choose a particular point on the wave. The easiest way to do this is to use a particular crest.

1.3.4   Waves in the Frequency Domain

While the position and time domains are often both useful and convenient, there are times when they are somewhat awkward to use. An alternative approach is to consider the *frequency domain*.

Figure 1.8 on the following page illustrates a 400 Hz periodic wave in both the time domain (at the top) and the frequency domain (at the bottom). This particular example is called a *line spectrum* because the wave is strictly periodic. Quasiperiodic waves have *harmonic spectra* and aperiodic waves have *continuous spectra*.

Converting from the time domain to the frequency domain often involves the use of the Fourier transform. This approach is named after the mathematician who discovered that:

- All periodic waves may be expressed as the sum of a series of sinusoidal waves
- These waves are all integer multiples (called *harmonics*) of the fundamental frequency
- Each harmonic has its own amplitude and phase

---

[10]Given the speed of light, one can easily calculate the wavelength of an electromagnetic wave from its frequency, and vice versa.

A 400 Hz Periodic Wave

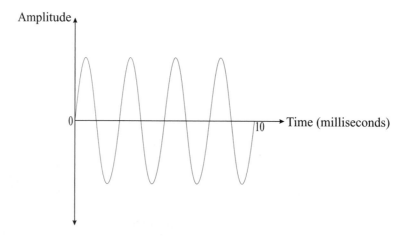

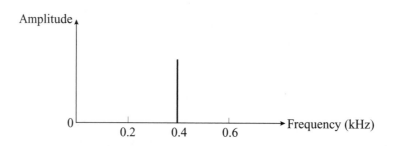

Figure 1.8 A Wave in the Time and Frequency Domains

Fourier analysis is used to determine the component frequencies of a complicated wave. The way in which this is accomplished is beyond the scope of this book. However, the fact that a complicated wave can be represented as a sum of sinusoidal waves is relevant in several settings.

1.4 The Focus of This Book

Broadly, this book is about the design of multimedia software. That is, it is a book about the design of software that either represents/stores/transmits/presents information that is perceived using more than one sense or represents/stores/transmits/presents information that is perceived using one sense in multiple different ways.

Since it is a book about engineering design (and not product design), it does not consider:

- Software product design (e.g., user interface design issues)
- Multimedia product design (e.g., usability issues)
- Content development (e.g., art, music, scripts)
- Delivery media (e.g., CD/DVD production)

that are part of the product design and/or product development process.

In addition, this book does not consider all aspects of the engineering design process. In particular, it does not consider low-level design issues. That is, it does not consider issues related to the storage, transmission, or presentation of multimedia content. So, for example, it does **not** consider the topics summarized in Table 1.1.

Storage Issues	Transmission Issues	Presentation Issues
Compression Algorithms	Bandwidth Requirements	Drawing and Filling Algorithms
File Formats	Latency Requirements	Signal Processing
Storage Devices		Output Devices

Table 1.1   Design Issues That Are **Not** Considered in This Book

Instead, this book is about higher-level engineering design. Returning to the definition of media, this means that this book is primarily concerned with representational issues. Specifically, this book is about:

- Characterizing content based on whether it is auditory or visual, static or dynamic, and sampled or described
- Designing software components that encapsulate different kinds of content

Since it uses an object-oriented approach, this book is about developing a well-designed class hierarchy that encapsulates various kinds of content.

1.5   Engineering Design Practices

The discussion thus far ignores the question of what it means for a class hierarchy to be well designed. Obviously, a complete answer to this question is beyond the scope of this book. Nonetheless, a brief summary is useful.

1.5.1   Characterizing Good Software Engineering Designs

Again following Fox (2006), a good software engineering design is:

1. *Adequate:* Meets all of the requirements and satisfies all of the constraints.

2. *Rugged:* Has a low probability of failure under normal conditions (i.e., is *reliable*), is able to operate under a wide variety of conditions (i.e., is *robust*), and minimizes the damage that results from failure (i.e., is *safe*).

3. Easy to repair and enhance.

4. Easy to understand/document and use.

In addition, a good software design has components/classes that are easy to reuse. That is, the components/classes should be *composable* (i.e., should aid in the construction of new systems), should localize small changes, and should confine problems.

1.5.2   Software Engineering Design Practices

There are several things that designers can do to help develop good engineering designs.

One of the most important practices is *information hiding*; that is, hiding the internal details of a class from all other classes. Information hiding helps prevent damage from errant external code since you can't hurt what you can't see. It also helps to make components easier to understand by shielding the user from the details (i.e., increasing the level of abstraction). Finally, it simplifies modification and repair since changes to the internal details should not have any impact on other classes.

Another important practice is the minimization of coupling between classes. Clearly, completely decoupled classes are more likely to be reused because they can be used in isolation. As the amount of coupling increases, classes become more difficult to understand, more difficult to debug, and more difficult to change.

Perhaps the most important practice is the maximization of cohesion. That is, the parts of a class should be closely related to each other. Or, in other words, a class should have a single, clear responsibility. The biggest benefit of cohesion is that it makes classes easier to understand (like a well-written paragraph).

EXERCISES

1. Suppose you were given the job of designing a multimedia software system for providing flight information to passengers at an airport. What would you need to decide during the product design phase and what would you need to decide during the engineering design phase?

2. The term "system" is often used very casually, often as an alternative to the term "thing." Carefully define the term "system."

3. What does the phrase "elements/atoms in a system are treated as black boxes" mean?

4. What makes a particular system complex (rather than simple)?

5. Define the terms "object" and "class." How does one create a class in Java? How does one create an object in Java?

6. Carefully define the term "encapsulation."

7. Discuss two benefits of information hiding.

8. Discuss a 'real life' problem that you have solved. Carefully describe the alternatives you generated and how you evaluated them.

9. Choose a popular multimedia software system and identify the different media that it uses/supports.

10. The following two designs were created for a computer inventory system:

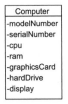

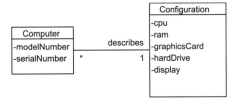

Which of the two is better? Why? (Your answer should be phrased in terms of the characteristics of good designs discussed in Section 1.5.1 on page 17.)

11. Carefully interpret/explain the following design of a 'phone book':

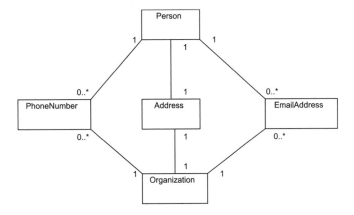

How can it be improved?

12. Create a new design for a 'phone book' that allows for people to be members of an organization. (Note: The organization should have one address and everybody associated with that organization should have that address. The organization may have a central phone number and e-mail address and everybody associated with the organization may have one as well.)

REFERENCES AND FURTHER READING ·······································

Boulding, K. E. 1956. General systems theory: The skeleton of science. *Management Science* 197–208.

Chapman, N. 2005. *Digital multimedia.* Hoboken, NJ: John Wiley and Sons.

Fox, C. 2006. *Introduction to software engineering design: Processes, principles and patterns with UML2.* Reading, MA: Addison-Wesley.

Savage, T. M., and K. E. Vogel. 2009. *An introduction to digital multimedia.* Sudbury, MA: Jones and Bartlett.

Serway, R. A., J. S. Faughn, C. Vuille, and C. A. Bennet. 2005. *College physics.* Boston: Brooks Cole.

Sommerville, I. 2006. *Software engineering.* Reading, MA: Addison-Wesley.

Steinmetz, R., and K. Nahrstedt. 2002. *Multimedia fundamentals volume 1: Media coding and content processing.* Upper Saddle River, NJ: Prentice Hall.

Tsui, F. 2007. *Essentials of software engineering.* Sudbury, MA: Jones and Bartlett.

Event-Driven Programming

2

Good designs are adequate, rugged, easy to repair/enhance, easy to understand/document, and have components that are easy to reuse. This book is predicated on the belief that object-oriented techniques help lead to designs with these properties. However, for multimedia software, object-oriented techniques on their own are often not enough. Hence, this chapter considers how an event-driven design can help ensure that multimedia software has these desirable properties.

2.1 Introduction

Most introductory programming and design courses focus on software products that follow a 'step-by-step' process. That is, the description/conceptualization of the products involves statements like "first this happens; then that happens; then, depending on the value of such and such, this or that happens; etc." A good example is a batch billing product that processes a collection of customer accounts and sends each customer a bill.

Unfortunately, most multimedia software products cannot be described/conceptualized in this way. There are two primary reasons for this.

- Most multimedia software products have a graphical user interface (GUI). As a result, the software needs to respond to various user actions (e.g., mouse clicks, key presses) that might occur in any order and at any time.
- Most multimedia software products need to do multiple things 'at the same time' (e.g., present visual and auditory content, present multiple tracks of auditory content). As a result, the software needs to be multi-threaded.

Together, these two properties make multimedia software products very different from 'step-by-step' software products. Most importantly, they make it very difficult to ensure that everything happens in the right order and at the right times. For example, when a user can click on the "Load" and "Play" buttons at any time, it is difficult to ensure that the loading process and the playing process happen in the right order and do not interfere with each other. As another example, when two animated characters are being processed in different threads, it is difficult to ensure that they interact properly.

2.2 Event-Driven Designs

One way to overcome these problems is to use an *event-driven* design.[1] In event-driven design one focuses on:

- The events that can occur (e.g., mouse clicks, timing signals, key presses)
- The classes that can generate events of different kinds (often called *event generators*)
- The classes that need to respond to events of different kinds (often called *event receivers*)

One does not focus on the order in which events occur or the order in which they must be processed. The *event queue* is responsible for ensuring that everything happens in the right order.

The event queue is a central repository for events. Event generators add events to the back of the queue (a process known as *posting*), and event receivers are sent events as they are removed from the front of the queue (a process that is known as *firing* or *dispatching*). Every object that generates events posts them to a single event queue, and that same event queue fires events to the objects that need to receive them. The events themselves are kept in a first-in-first-out collection to ensure that they are fired/dispatched in the proper order. The events in the queue at any point in time are said to be *pending*.

An important property of event-driven designs is that the generators do not communicate directly with the receivers. Hence, generators do not need to know about specific receivers, they only need to know about the event queue. Similarly, receivers do not need to know about specific generators, they only need to know about the event queue. This effectively decouples the generators and receivers.

There are two important variants of this general design: *event listening* and *event bubbling*. Event listening makes use of the observer pattern. In event bubbling there is a (usually predefined) hierarchy of objects that handle events. This book focuses almost exclusively on event listening.[2]

2.3 The Event Queue and Dispatch Thread in Java

In Java, events are managed by a single `EventQueue` object.[3] The current `EventQueue` object can be obtained using the `getSystemEventQueue()` method in the `Toolkit` class.

The `EventQueue` object fires events using the `dispatchEvent()` method. The actual mechanism used by the `EventQueue` is implementation-dependent. For example, some implementations coalesce multiple events of the same type and attributes into a single event and others do not. However, the Java specification does make several important guarantees. First, the events

---

[1]Many authors prefer the term "event-driven (or event-based) architecture." This book does not distinguish between designs and architectures. For the purposes of this book, an architecture is just a higher-level (i.e., more abstract) design.

[2]Java actually uses both. Swing 'widgets' use event listening whereas AWT 'widgets' use event bubbling. This book only uses Swing 'widgets' and, hence, focuses on event listening.

[3]It is actually possible to temporarily replace the default `EventQueue` by calling its `push()` method. It can then be reinstated by calling its `pop()` method. This is rarely necessary.

will be dispatched in a first-in-first-out manner. Second, the events will be dispatched sequentially (i.e., multiple events will not be dispatched 'at the same time') and will not overlap (i.e., one event will be completely processed before the next is fired/dispatched).

Events are dispatched in a single *event dispatch thread*. One can determine if the current thread is the event dispatch thread with a call to the static method `EventQueue.isDispatchThread()`.[4] Tasks that execute in the event dispatch thread are expected to "finish quickly." A task that doesn't finish quickly "hogs" the event dispatch thread and causes events to back up in the queue. Tasks that can't satisfy this requirement should use a helper thread.[5]

There are two closely related ways to execute statements in the event dispatch thread. They both involve static methods in the `SwingUtilities` class that must be passed an object that implements the `Runnable` interface. The difference between the two is their blocking behavior. The `invokeAndWait()` method in the `SwingUtilities` class blocks until all pending events have been processed.[6] This method must not be called from the event dispatch thread. The `invokeLater()` method in the `SwingUtilities` class adds the call to the `Runnable` object's `run()` method to the end of the event queue and returns immediately.

2.4 GUIs and GUI Events

Though there are no complicated GUIs in this book, it is impossible to build interesting multimedia software products in Java without using GUI 'widgets.' GUIs also provide an interesting example of the use of event-driven programming. Hence, it is useful to consider the basics of GUIs in Java.

For historical reasons, Java has two different sets of GUI widgets. One set is part of the Abstract Windowing Toolkit (AWT) and the other set is called Swing.[7] This book focuses on the Swing widgets. A Swing widget is generally characterized as either a *component* or a *container*.[8] Not surprisingly given the names, containers 'hold' components.

2.4.1 Components

Probably the simplest Swing component is the `JLabel` that displays a `String`, an `Icon`, or both. The alignment of a `JLabel` object's content can be controlled with the `setHorizontalAlignment()` and `setVerticalAlignment()` methods, both of which must be

---

[4]The `EventQueue` can, and often does, start other 'helper' threads. This makes it a little difficult to determine when the JVM will terminate. See Section 3.1 on page 43 and the Java documentation for details.

[5]Java now includes the `SwingWorker` class that can be used for this purpose.

[6]Note that this method throws `InterruptedException`. So, if you need to actually know whether the code executed completely or not, you must catch this exception and handle it appropriately.

[7]There are many differences between the AWT widgets (which are *heavyweight*) and the Swing widgets (which are *lightweight*). Before you build a significant GUI-based software product you should learn about the advantages and disadvantages of each.

[8]Actually, Swing uses the composite pattern and, as a result, almost all containers are themselves components. However, for the purposes of this book, it is convenient to treat the two sets as distinct.

passed an `int` value (defined in `SwingConstants`). In the following fragment, a `JLabel` is created that displays the `String` named `s` centered horizontally within its bounds.

```
label = new JLabel(s, SwingConstants.CENTER);
```

A `JButton` is one of the simplest components that allows for user interaction. It is, essentially, a GUI component that behaves like a key on the keyboard. When you press the mouse button while the pointer is over the `JButton` it appears to move into the screen, and when you release the mouse button the `JButton` appears to move out of the screen. Like a `JLabel`, it can contain a `String`, an `Icon`, or both. In the following fragment, a `JButton` is created that contains the `String` in the constant named `CHANGE`.

```
button = new JButton(CHANGE);
```

Swing has many other components including `JCheckBox`, `JList`, `JCheckBox`, `JSlider`, `JSpinner`, `JTextArea`, and `JTextField`. Each of these classes is a descendent of the abstract `JComponent` class. The interested reader should consult the Java documentation or a book on GUI development for more information.

2.4.2 Containers

Swing distinguishes between *top-level containers* and ordinary containers. The top-level container that is easiest to understand is the `JFrame`, which is an encapsulation of a *window*—a rectangular portion of the 'display' that can (usually) be moved, iconified, closed, etc. As illustrated in the following fragment, it is very easy to construct a `JFrame` and set its size.

```
window = new JFrame();
window.setSize(600,400);
```

Though top-level containers are, in fact, containers, they should not be used in that way. Instead, one should get the *root pane* (which is, itself, a container) from the top-level container and use it. To that end, all top-level containers implement the `RootPaneContainer` interface that includes a `getRootPane()` method that returns a `JRootPane`. In fact, for reasons that are beyond the scope of this book, one should not even use the root pane directly; rather one should use the *content pane* (that is inside of the root pane) that can be obtained using the `getContentPane()` method of the `JRootPane` (or the `getContentPane()` method of the `RootPaneContainer`).[9]

---

[9]Classes that implement the `RootPaneContainer` interface also have methods for obtaining other parts of the top-level container. They are not needed for the purposes of this book.

The JPanel class is an encapsulation of a generic container in Swing. Every top-level Swing container uses a JPanel object as its content pane. So, continuing the fragment above, one can get the content pane as follows:

```
contentPane = (JPanel)window.getContentPane();
```

2.4.3 Layout

Layout is the process of positioning and sizing the components in a container. The components that are added to a JPanel are normally positioned and sized using a LayoutManager. This book uses a simpler, though less flexible, approach called *absolute layout*. That is, this book explicitly sets the position and size of each component, both of which are measured in pixels. The position $(0,0)$ is at the upper-left corner. The x-coordinate increases from left to right and the y-coordinate increases from top to bottom (unlike traditional Cartesian coordinates).

To use absolute layout (sometimes called *null layout*) one must tell the container not to use a LayoutManager. Continuing the fragment above, this involves the following call to the setLayout() method:

```
contentPane.setLayout(null);
```

One must then set the position and size of each component and add it to the container. The position and size can be set using the component's setBounds() method, which must be passed the horizontal and vertical position of the upper-left corner of the component and its width and height. The component can be added to the container using the container's add() method. For the JLabel named label, this involves statements like the following:

```
label.setBounds(50,50,500,100);
contentPane.add(label);
```

Similarly, for the JButton named button, this involves statements like the following:

```
button.setBounds(450,300,100,50);
contentPane.add(button);
```

2.4.4 A Simple Example with a GUI

A good way to understand these ideas is to consider an example. To that end, consider the following software product that displays a random message in a 'window.'

```java
import java.util.*;
import javax.swing.*;

public class BadRandomMessageApplication
{
    // The pseudo-random number generator
    private static Random        rng = new Random();

    // The messages
    private static final String[] MESSAGES = {
        "What a great book.","Bring on the exercises.",
        "Author, author!","I hope it never ends."};

    public static void main(String[] args) throws Exception
    {
        JFrame               window;
        JLabel               label;
        JPanel               contentPane;
        String               s;

        // Select a message at random
        s = createRandomMessage();

        // Construct the "window"
        window = new JFrame();
        window.setSize(600,400);
        window.setDefaultCloseOperation(JFrame.EXIT_ON_CLOSE);

        // Get the container for all content
        contentPane = (JPanel)window.getContentPane();
        contentPane.setLayout(null);

        // Add a component to the container
        label = new JLabel(s, SwingConstants.CENTER);
        label.setBounds(50,50,500,100);
        contentPane.add(label);

        // Make the "window" visible
        window.setVisible(true);
    }
```

```
    private static String createRandomMessage()
    {
        return  MESSAGES[rng.nextInt(MESSAGES.length)];
    }
}
```

The `main()` method first selects a message at random, constructs a 'window,' and gets the container that will hold all of the components. It then creates a single component (in this case, a `JLabel` that contains the message), sets the bounds of the component (in pixels), and adds it to the container. Finally, it makes the 'window' visible.

If you (compile and) execute this code, you will probably get lucky—it will probably execute correctly. However, you might get unlucky. This is because the `main()` method manipulates elements of the GUI outside of the event dispatch thread (i.e., in the main thread).

As discussed above, one can correct this problem using the `invokeAndWait()` method in the `SwingUtilities` class. To do so, one must first indicate that the class implements the `Runnable` interface.

```
public class       BadRandomMessageSwingApplication
      implements Runnable
```

Next, the code that manipulates GUI elements must be moved into the `run()` method.

```
    public void run()
    {
        JFrame                window;
        JPanel                contentPane;
        String                s;

        // Select a message at random
        s = createRandomMessage();

        // Construct the "window"
        window = new JFrame();
        window.setDefaultCloseOperation(JFrame.DISPOSE_ON_CLOSE);
        window.setSize(600,400);

        // Get the container for all content
        contentPane = (JPanel)window.getContentPane();
        contentPane.setLayout(null);

        // Add a component to the container
        label = new JLabel(s, SwingConstants.CENTER);
        label.setBounds(50,50,500,100);
```

```
      contentPane.add(label);

      // Make the "window" visible
      window.setVisible(true);
   }
```

Finally, the `main()` method must be changed so that it executes the code in the `run()` method in the event dispatch thread. Specifically, one must construct an instance of the 'main' class (which is a `Runnable`) and pass it to the `invokeAndWait()` method.

```
   public static void main(String[] args) throws Exception
   {
      SwingUtilities.invokeAndWait(
                  new BadRandomMessageSwingApplication());
   }
```

2.4.5   GUI Event Handling

GUI events can often be considered at different levels of abstraction. One usually distinguishes between low-level events and high-level events.

Consider what happens at a low level when a button is used. First a `mouseEntered()` message is generated, then a `mousePressed()` message is generated, then a `mouseReleased()` message is generated.[10] All of these messages are relevant to the button itself. When the `mouseEntered()` message is generated the button needs to render itself in a way that indicates that it has the focus. When the `mousePressed()` message is generated the button needs to render itself in a way that makes it appear to be pressed. When the `mouseReleased()` message is generated the button needs to render itself in a way that indicates it isn't being pressed.

Now, consider what happens at a high level. The object that needs to respond to the button press does not need to know about the rendering of the button. It only needs to know that the button was pressed. So, the button generates a high-level event that the event queue fires to the objects that need to receive it (i.e., the listeners/observers).

In particular, `JButton` objects generate `ActionEvent` objects that are fired to objects that implement the `ActionListener` interface and register themselves with the JButton. An object that wants to register itself with a `JButton` need only call its `addActionListener()` method. A class that wants to implement the `ActionListener` interface need only have an `actionPerformed()` method.

Swing has many low-level events, including `MouseEvent` and `KeyEvent`. Swing also has many high-level events, including `ActionEvent`, `ItemEvent`, `TextEvent`, and `WindowEvent`. Most of these classes have one or more corresponding listener interfaces.

---

[10]Actually, in Java, after this a `mouseClicked()` message is generated if the mouse was pressed and released while the mouse pointer was within the bounds of the button.

2.4.6   An Example with a GUI and Event Handling

It is now useful to consider software products that make use of some simple event handling. To that end, consider another software product that displays a random message. What distinguishes this example from the earlier example is that this one includes a button that the user can press to request that a new message be chosen and displayed. This class has a `String` 'constant' that contains the text on the button.

```
// String "constants"
private static final String   CHANGE = "Change";
```

This class also has logic for handling the button events. As mentioned above, objects that want to respond to button-presses must implement the `ActionListener` interface. In this case, the `actionPerformed()` method generates and displays a new message as follows:

```
public void actionPerformed(ActionEvent event)
{
    String       actionCommand;

    actionCommand = event.getActionCommand();
    if (actionCommand.equals(CHANGE))
    {
        label.setText(createRandomMessage());
    }
}
```

For robustness reasons, even though there is only one button, this method first determines which object generated the `ActionEvent`, getting the 'action command' (which, in this case, will be the text on the button) using the `getActionCommand()` method. It then checks to see whether the 'action command' is the constant `CHANGE`, and, if it is, selects a message at random and sets the text of the `JLabel` appropriately.

Of course, this class must declare that it implements the `ActionListener` interface. This is accomplished as follows:

```
public class       BadInteractiveRandomMessageSwingApplication
       implements ActionListener, Runnable
```

The `JButton` itself is added to the content pane just before the window is made visible in the `run()` method.

```
button = new JButton(CHANGE);
button.setBounds(450,300,100,50);
contentPane.add(button);
button.addActionListener(this);
```

The call to the JButton object's `addActionListener()` method makes the current instance of the 'main' class an `ActionListener` for `button`. As a result, when the user clicks on the "Change" button, the 'main' object's `actionPerformed()` method is called (in the event dispatch thread).

Note that when you test this software product you might notice that it is 'broken' in the sense that the message does not change every time you press the button. This is not a problem with the event handling but with the way messages are being generated. That is, this implementation does not check to make sure that the message being generated is not the same as the one that is currently being displayed. It should be obvious how this failing can be corrected.

2.5   Timed Events

Many of the events in multimedia software products are 'clock-based' in one fashion or another. These kinds of events can be categorized as follows:

> Events that occur at a particular point in time
>
> Events that occur after a particular interval of time
>
> Events that recur after a particular interval of time (called *fixed-delay* execution)
>
> Events that recur at a particular rate (called *fixed-rate* execution)

The differences between the first three should be clear; however, the difference between the last two is a little subtle.

In both of the last two the executions take place at (approximately) regular intervals. In fixed-delay execution, the next execution is scheduled relative to the actual time of the current execution. As a result, if the current execution is 'late,' the subsequent executions will also be 'late.' In fixed-rate execution, on the other hand, the time interval between executions is adjusted to keep the rate constant. Hence, if the current execution is 'late,' the subsequent execution will be 'rushed.'

2.5.1   Implementing a Metronome Class

As with other kinds of events, timed events involve a subject and an observer. As illustrated in Figure 2.1 on the next page, the `Metronome` class plays the role of the subject and objects that implement the `MetronomeListener` interface will play the role of the observer.

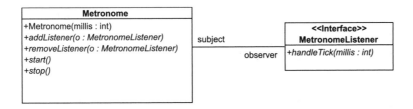

Figure 2.1 Design of a `Metronome`

The `MetronomeListener` interface is straightforward and is specified as follows:

```
package event;

public interface MetronomeListener
{
    public abstract void handleTick(int millis);
}
```

The interesting aspect of this design is the `Metronome` class.[11]

Since the `Metronome` class plays the role of the subject, it must manage a collection of `MetronomeListener` objects. Each time the `Metronome` ticks, the `handleTick()` method of all registered listeners are called.[12]

Given the discussion above, it is clear that the `handleTick()` method in a `MetronomeListener` should/must be called in the event dispatch thread. This complicates synchronization somewhat because one would like to be able to modify the collection of listeners in one thread of execution at the same time as the listeners are being notified in the event dispatch thread.

One obvious way to proceed is to use a thread-safe collection (i.e., a collection that can safely be modified and used in different threads). The shortcoming of this approach is that the notification process could be delayed by modifications to the collection of listeners.

The other obvious approach is to make a copy of the collection of listeners and use the copy for notification. The copy can either be made each time the collection is changed or each time the listeners are notified. Since notification happens frequently and is time sensitive, the

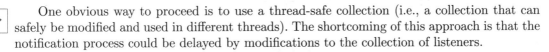

---

[11]The `Timer` class in the `javax.swing` package and the `Timer` class in the `java.util` package can also be used for this purpose. This book considers a custom class for several reasons. First, it is an instructive exercise. Second, the `javax.swing.Timer` class supports only fixed-delay execution and the `java.util.Timer` class does not make its call-backs in the event dispatch thread. Third, the `javax.swing.Timer` class is not available in all editions/versions/platforms of Java.

[12]Many Java classes use the `EventListenerList` class to manage observers. It is not used because it provides access to the array of observers and this can cause problems if one is not very careful. The `AWTEventMulticaster` class can also be used for this purpose. This book designs and implements a custom class because it is instructive to do so.

former alternative is preferred. So, each time a `MetronomeListener` is added or removed, it is added to an unsynchronized `ArrayList` and a copy is made.

```
public synchronized void addListener(MetronomeListener ml)
{
   listeners.add(ml);
   copyListeners();
}

private void copyListeners()
{
   copy = new MetronomeListener[listeners.size()];
   listeners.toArray(copy);
}

public synchronized void removeListener(MetronomeListener ml)
{
   listeners.remove(ml);
   copyListeners();
}
```

Then, when the `MetronomeListener` objects need to be notified, the copy is used to avoid any problems that might arise from concurrent modifications to the collection. However, one must still be very careful.

To understand why the copy must be used, consider the following bad implementation of the `notifyListeners()` method:

```
private synchronized void notifyListeners()
{
      int     n;
      MetronomeListener   listener;

      n = listeners.size();
      for (int i=n-1; i>=0; i--)
      {
        listener = listeners.get(i);
        if (listener != null) listener.handleTick(time);
      }
}
```

The problem with this approach is that, even though the addListener() and removeListener() methods are synchronized, a problem will arise if a listener modified the list of listeners (e.g., removes itself) in its handleTick() method.

Alternatively, one might use the copy as follows:

```
private synchronized void notifyListeners()
{
        int    n;
        MetronomeListener    listener;

        n = copy.length;
        for (int i=n-1; i>=0; i--)
        {
          listener = copy[i];
          if (listener != null) listener.handleTick(time);
        }
}
```

However, notice that the addListener() and removeListener() methods both change copy. As a result, there is still a problem if any of the listeners modify the list of listeners in handleTick().

Hence, it is important to recognize that there is an enormous difference between the above and the following:

```
private synchronized void notifyListeners()
{
        int     n;
        MetronomeListener     listener;
        MetronomeListener[]   alias;

        alias = copy;
        n = alias.length;
        for (int i=n-1; i>=0; i--)
        {
          listener = alias[i];
          if (listener != null) listener.handleTick(time);
        }
}
```

Now, even if copy changes, alias continues to be a reference to the original version. Hence, a listener can remove itself from the collection in its handleTick() method without causing any problems.

Another big problem still remains—the `handleTick()` method must be called in the event dispatch thread. This is accomplished using the static `invokeLater()` method in the `EventQueue` class. This method must be passed an object that implements the `Runnable` interface; the `MetronomeTickDispatcher` class is used for this purpose. This is a private inner class because there is no reason for it to be used by any other class.[13]

```java
private class MetronomeTickDispatcher implements Runnable
{
    private MetronomeListener[]    listeners;
    private int                    time;


    public void run()
    {
        int    n;

        n = listeners.length;
        for (int i=n-1; i>=0; i--)
        {
            if (listeners[i] != null)
                listeners[i].handleTick(time);
        }
    }

    public void setup(MetronomeListener[] listeners,
                      int time)
    {
        this.listeners = listeners;
        this.time      = time;
    }
}
```

The `run()` method, which is called in the event dispatch thread, simply calls the `handleTick()` method of each `MetronomeListener` in the (copy of the) collection. In other words, the correct implementation of the `notifyListeners()` method is as follows:

```java
protected synchronized void notifyListeners()
{
    // Setup the state of the MetronomeTickDispatcher
    dispatcher.setup(copy, time);

    // Cause the run() method of the dispatcher to be
```

---

[13]Alternatively, it could be a class with package visibility.

```
      // called in the GUI/event-dispatch thread
      EventQueue.invokeLater(dispatcher);
}
```

The Metronome class also implements the Runnable interface and has a Thread attribute named timerThread. The start() method constructs and starts the timerThread.

```
public void start()
{
   if (timerThread == null)
   {
      keepRunning = true;
      timerThread = new Thread(this);
      timerThread.start();
   }
}
```

This causes the run() method of the Metronome object to be called in the timerThread object's thread of execution.

The run() method, in turn, puts the thread of execution to sleep. When it wakes up, it calls the notifyListeners() method.

```
public void run()
{
   int        currentDelay;
   long       currentTick, drift;

   currentDelay = delay;
   if (adjusting) lastTick = System.currentTimeMillis();

   while (keepRunning)
   {
      try
      {
         timerThread.sleep(currentDelay);
         time += currentDelay * multiplier;

         if (adjusting)
         {
            // Compensate for any drift
            currentTick = System.currentTimeMillis();
            drift = (currentTick - lastTick) - currentDelay;
            currentDelay = (int)Math.max(0, delay-drift);
```

```
                    lastTick = currentTick;
            }
            notifyListeners();
        }
        catch (InterruptedException ie)
        {
            // stop() was called
        }
    }
    timerThread = null;
}
```

Note that this method reports the apparent elapsed time rather than the actual elapsed time. That is, the elapsed time is increased by the delay times a multiplier. This allows one to 'trick' the listeners into thinking that time is passing faster than it actually is (which might be used, for example, to provide 'fast-forward' functionality).

2.5.2   A Simple Example with Timed Events

As an example of a software product with timed events, consider a simple stopwatch that displays the elapsed time in a JLabel. It has two JButton objects, one that starts the elapsed time indicator and another that stops it.

```java
import java.util.*;
import java.awt.event.*;
import javax.swing.*;

import event.*;

public class      StopWatchSwingApplication
        implements ActionListener, MetronomeListener, Runnable
{
    private JLabel                      label;
    private Metronome                   metronome;

    private static final String         START = "Start";
    private static final String         STOP  = "Stop";

    public static void main(String[] args) throws Exception
    {
        SwingUtilities.invokeAndWait(
                    new StopWatchSwingApplication());
    }
```

```
}
```

The `run()` method constructs and adds a `JLabel` to display the elapsed time and two `JButton` objects that can be used to start and stop the app. It also constructs a `Metronome` and make this a listener.

```
public void run()
{
    JButton                 start, stop;
    JFrame                  window;
    JPanel                  contentPane;

    window = new JFrame();
    window.setDefaultCloseOperation(JFrame.DISPOSE_ON_CLOSE);
    window.setSize(600,400);

    contentPane = (JPanel)window.getContentPane();
    contentPane.setLayout(null);

    label       = new JLabel("0");
    label.setBounds(250,100,100,100);
    contentPane.add(label);

    start = new JButton(START);
    start.setBounds(50,300,100,50);
    start.addActionListener(this);
    contentPane.add(start);


    stop  = new JButton(STOP);
    stop.setBounds(450,300,100,50);
    stop.addActionListener(this);
    contentPane.add(stop);


    metronome = new Metronome(1000, true);
    metronome.addListener(this);

    window.setVisible(true);
}
```

The `handleTick()` method sets the text on the `JLabel`. Since this method is called (in the event dispatch thread) every second (i.e., every 1000 milliseconds), it increases the label by 1 each time it is called.

```
public void handleTick(int millis)
{
    label.setText(""+millis/1000);
}
```

Finally, the `actionPerformed()` method responds to `JButton` clicks by starting and stopping the `Metronome` as appropriate.

```
public void actionPerformed(ActionEvent event)
{
    String    actionCommand;

    actionCommand = event.getActionCommand();
    if      (actionCommand.equals(START))
    {
        label.setText("0");
        metronome.reset();
        metronome.start();
    }
    else if (actionCommand.equals(STOP))
    {
        metronome.stop();
    }
}
```

EXERCISES

1. Why must the `main()` method in a Java application be declared `static`? Why isn't the `init()` method in a Java applet declared `static`?

2. `BadRandomMessageSwingApplication` and `BadRandomMessageJApplet` contain a significant amount of duplicate code. Why is this a problem in practice?

3. Explain how event-driven designs reduce coupling. How does this result in classes that are more likely to be reused?

4. Though it is not discussed above, the containers and components in Java make use of the composite pattern. That is, containers are, themselves, components. Why might this be useful?

5. Provide an example of each of the four different kinds of 'clock-based' events.

6. Given the following attributes:

```
private JButton                 toggle;
private JLabel                  light;

private static final String     OFF   = "Off";
private static final String     ON    = "On";
private static final String     SPACE = " ";
```

complete the following fragment so that `toggle` is 100 pixels by 50 pixels with its upper-left corner at (50, 100) and `light` is 100 pixels by 50 pixels with its upper-left corner at (250, 100).

```
JPanel                    contentPane;

contentPane = (JPanel)rootPaneContainer.getContentPane();
contentPane.setLayout(null);


toggle      = new JButton();
toggle.setText(ON);


light       = new JLabel();
light.setText(SPACE);
light.setBackground(Color.BLACK);
light.setOpaque(true);
```

7. What code do you need to add (to your answer to Exercise 6 above) so that the object referred to by `this` can respond when `toggle` is pressed?

8. Complete the following method so that the `light` will switch between black (when off) and white (when on). Specifically, when the "On" button is pressed the background color of `light` should be set to `Color.WHITE` and the text of `toggle` should be set to `OFF`. On the other hand, when the "Off" button is pressed the background color of `light` should be set to `Color.BLACK` and the text of `toggle` should be set to `ON`.

```
    public void actionPerformed(ActionEvent event)
    {
       String   actionCommand;

       actionCommand = event.getActionCommand();




    }
```

9. Given the following attributes:

```
    private int                    count, direction;
    private JLabel                 label;
    private Metronome          metronome;
    private String                 message;
    private String[]               padding;

    private static final int       LENGTH = 40;
```

the following code initializes the **padding** array so that element i contains i spaces, and creates a JLabel that contains **message** preceded by zero spaces:

```
        JPanel                     contentPane;
        String                     temp;

        contentPane = (JPanel)rootPaneContainer.getContentPane();
        contentPane.setLayout(null);

        message      = "Multimedia";

        count      = 0;
        direction  = 1;

        padding      = new String[LENGTH];
        for (int i=0; i<LENGTH; i++)
        {
           temp = "";
           for (int j=0; j<i; j++)
           {
              temp += " ";
           }
```

```
        padding[i] = new String(temp);
    }

    label       = new JLabel();
    label.setText(padding[count] + message);
```

What code do you need to add so that `label` is 400 pixels by 50 pixels with its upper-left corner at (100, 100)?

10. What code do you need to add (to your answer to Exercise 9 above) to construct the `Metronome` named `metronome` and have it tick 10 times per second? What code do you need to add so that the object referred to by `this` can respond to the events generated by `metronome`?

11. Complete the following method so that `message` will appear to bounce back and forth in `label`. (Hint: You should use the `padding` array to prepend the appropriate number of spaces to `message`.)

```
    public void handleTick(int millis)
    {
        count = count + direction;




    }
```

12. You may have noticed that classes that extend `MultimediaApplet` are all quite similar, as are the classes that extend `MultimediaApplication`. As a result, it is fairly easy to automate the writing of source code for such classes. Write a console application named `Builder` that, given the name of a `MultimediaApp`, creates two files, one containing the source code for a `MultimediaApplication` that uses the `MultimediaApp` and one containing the source code for a `MultimediaApplet` that uses the `MultimediaApp`.

REFERENCES AND FURTHER READING

Gosling, J., B. Joy, G. Steele, and G. Bracha. 2005. *Java language specification.* Upper Saddle River, NJ: Prentice-Hall.

Horstman, C. 2007. *Big Java.* Hoboken, NJ: John Wiley and Sons.

Taylor, H., A. Yochem, L. Phillips, and F. Martinez. 2009. *Event-driven architecture.* Reading, MA: Addison-Wesley.

Programs

3

Thus far this book has not used the word "program" and, instead, has used the phrase "software product." This chapter explores a (somewhat) formal definition of the word "program," considers different types of Java programs, and discusses a way to unify different types of Java programs (which is especially important in the context of multimedia software products).

3.1 Java Programs

For the purposes of this book, a program (in an object-oriented programming language) is defined as follows:

....

Definition 3.1 A *program* in an object-oriented programming language is a group of cooperating classes with a well-defined *entry point* (i.e., a method that should be executed first) and, perhaps, a reentry point and/or an exit point.

....

In Java there are several different kinds of programs. On 'desktop' and 'laptop' computers, the two most common programs are applications and applets.[1]

	Environment	Top-Level Container	Entry Point
Application	Operating System	JFrame	main()
Applet	Browser	JApplet	init() then start()

Table 3.1 Java Programs with GUIs

The differences between applications and applets are summarized in Table 3.1. In short, they differ in the way they are executed and in the top-level container they use. Applications run in a virtual machine directly under the operating system, and are normally executed by clicking on them (or using the `java` command) which causes the operating system to call the `main()` method. An application's principle top-level container is normally a `JFrame` object (though it may use multiple `JFrame` and/or `JDialog` objects). Applets, on the other hand, normally run in a virtual machine inside of a WWW browser.[2] They are executed when the browser loads an HTML page that contains an `<applet>` element. When such a page is first

---

[1]There are several other Java programs. For example, midlets are programs that run on mobile information devices and servlets are programs that run on/in HTTP servers.

[2]Applets can actually run inside of a variety of different desktop/laptop programs. For simplicity, this book focuses on the most common situation. When run inside of a browser, applets are generally limited/restricted in a variety of ways. For example, applets in a browser typically can't read or write files on the client, run executables on the client, or communicate with any machine other than the originating host.

loaded, the applet's `init()` and `start()` methods are called. An applet's top-level container is normally a `JApplet` object.

When an application is started the `main()` method is executed in a non-daemon thread that this book refers to as the main thread. A single-threaded application terminates when the `System.exit()` method is called, in response to a platform-specific event such as a `SIGINT` or a `Ctrl-C`, or when the main thread 'drops out of' the `main()` method.[3] A multi-threaded application terminates when the `System.exit()` method is called, in response to a platform-specific event, or when all non-daemon threads have died.[4] Note that all GUI applications are, intrinsically, multi-threaded since they have both a main thread and an event dispatch thread.

When an HTML page containing an `<applet>` element is loaded into a browser for the first time, the appropriate object (i.e., the descendent of the `Applet` class referred to in the `<applet>` element) is constructed and its `init()` and `start()` methods are called in a thread other than the event dispatch thread. Then, each time the user leaves the page containing the applet, the `stop()` method is called (again, not in the event dispatch thread). Similarly, each time the user reloads the page containing the applet, the `start()` method is called. When the browser is shut down, the `destroy()` method is called (again, not in the event dispatch thread). As with GUI applications, all applets are multithreaded (since all applets have a GUI even if they don't use it in any meaningful way).

To further understand the differences and similarities between applications and applets, it is helpful to consider a simple example of each.

3.1.1   Applications

Chapter 2 contains a simple application (consisting of one class) that displays a random message when a button is pressed. This application is reproduced here (in its entirety) for convenience.

```
import java.awt.event.*;
import java.util.*;
import javax.swing.*;


public class        BadInteractiveRandomMessageSwingApplication
        implements ActionListener, Runnable
{
```

---

[3]This is actually referred to as an *orderly* termination. An application can also by terminated *abruptly* by calling the `Runtime.halt()` method in the `Runtime` class.

[4]The `addShutdownHook()` method in the `RunTime` class can be used to perform specific tasks during the termination process. To do so, one creates a *shutdown hook* (a `Thread` object that has not been started) and passes it to the `Runtime` object (obtained by a call to the static method `Runtime.getRuntime()`). At the onset of the termination process, each of the shutdown hooks is started. Unfortunately, the shutdown hooks are started in no particular order. So, if you need to have the shutdown tasks performed in a particular order they should be performed by a single shutdown hook. Some people argue that shutdown tasks should be performed in the `finalize()` method of each object. It is certainly possible to do it this way since, after all of the shutdown hooks have died, the `finalize()` method will be called on all objects that have not had their `finalize()` method called previously (i.e., after they were garbage collected). However, it is very difficult to write `finalize()` methods that behave correctly.

```java
// Attributes
private JLabel                  label;

// The pseudo-random number generator
private static Random           rng = new Random();

// String "constants"
private static final String     CHANGE = "Change";

// The messages
private static final String[] MESSAGES = {
   "What a great book.","Bring on the exercises.",
   "Author, author!","I hope it never ends."};

public static void main(String[] args) throws Exception
{
   SwingUtilities.invokeAndWait(
           new BadInteractiveRandomMessageSwingApplication());
}

public void actionPerformed(ActionEvent event)
{
   String       actionCommand;

   actionCommand = event.getActionCommand();
   if (actionCommand.equals(CHANGE))
   {
      label.setText(createRandomMessage());
   }
}

private static String createRandomMessage()
{
   return  MESSAGES[rng.nextInt(MESSAGES.length)];
}

public void run()
{
   JButton                  button;
   JFrame                   window;
   JPanel                   contentPane;
   String                   s;

   // Select a message at random
   s = createRandomMessage();

   // Construct the "window"
```

```
        window = new JFrame();
        window.setSize(600,400);
        window.setDefaultCloseOperation(JFrame.DISPOSE_ON_CLOSE);

        // Get the container for all content
        contentPane = (JPanel)window.getContentPane();
        contentPane.setLayout(null);

        // Add the message component to the container
        label = new JLabel(s, SwingConstants.CENTER);
        label.setBounds(50,50,500,100);
        contentPane.add(label);

        // Add the button to the container
        button = new JButton(CHANGE);
        button.setBounds(450,300,100,50);
        contentPane.add(button);
        button.addActionListener(this);

        // Make the "window" visible
        window.setVisible(true);
    }
}
```

Recall that the run() method in this class adds a JButton to the JFrame and makes the application object an ActionListener. When the JButton is pressed, the actionPerformed() method is called, and it changes the message on the JLabel.

3.1.2 Applets

Now, consider a specialization of the JApplet class with the same functionality as the application above. This class has the following overall structure:

```
import java.awt.event.*;
import java.util.*;
import javax.swing.*;

public class       BadInteractiveRandomMessageJApplet
        extends     JApplet
        implements ActionListener
{
    // Attributes
    private JLabel                     label;
```

```
// The pseudo-random number generator
private static Random        rng = new Random();

// String "constants"
private static final String   CHANGE = "Change";

// The messages
private static final String[] MESSAGES = {
    "What a great book.","Bring on the exercises.",
    "Author, author!","I hope it never ends."};

private static String createRandomMessage()
{
    return  MESSAGES[rng.nextInt(MESSAGES.length)];
}
}
```

As with the application, this applet implements the `ActionListener` interface and, hence, has an `actionPerformed()` method.

```
public void actionPerformed(ActionEvent event)
{
    String       actionCommand;

    actionCommand = event.getActionCommand();
    if (actionCommand.equals(CHANGE))
    {
        label.setText(createRandomMessage());
    }
}
```

Since the constructor is not called in the event dispatch thread, it does nothing.

```
public BadInteractiveRandomMessageJApplet()
{
    super();
}
```

Tasks performed in the `run()` method of the application are, instead, performed in the `init()` method in the applet. In particular, the `init()` method generates a message at random, gets the container that will hold the content, and then adds the component to the container. Note that there is no need to construct a 'window' because the JApplet is a RootPaneContainer.

```
    public void init()
    {
        JButton                 button;
        JPanel                  contentPane;
        String                  s;

        // Select a message at random
        s = createRandomMessage();

        // Get the container for all content
        contentPane = (JPanel)getContentPane();
        contentPane.setLayout(null);

        // Add a component to the container
        label = new JLabel(s, SwingConstants.CENTER);
        label.setBounds(50,50,500,100);
        contentPane.add(label);

        // Add the button to the container
        button = new JButton(CHANGE);
        button.setBounds(450,300,100,50);
        button.addActionListener(this);
        contentPane.add(button);
    }
```

3.2   A Unified Approach for Multimedia

In general, there are good reasons for distinguishing between different kinds of programs. However, this distinction can be awkward in some domains. It is particularly awkward for multimedia programmers, who must frequently create applications and applets that provide the same functionality.

 One way to deal with this situation is to develop distinct applications and applets that share classes. Indeed, as you can see from the example above, this is not difficult because the general structure of applets and applications are very similar. However, the details are different enough that there is no easy way to create an applet and an application with the same functionality without copying and pasting code from one method in one class to another method in another class. Hence, this approach leads to a large amount of code duplication.

 Alternatively, one could create a unified system that, to the extent possible, makes it possible to use the same 'glue code' (i.e., code that connects the various cooperating classes)

in applets and applications. Though this approach adds a little complexity, the reduction in code duplication makes it worth pursuing.

A unified system of this kind must satisfy the following requirements:

F3.1 Applets and applications must have a common programming interface.

F3.2 Applets and applications must have a common lifecycle.

F3.3 Applets and applications must have a common way to obtain start-up parameters.

N3.4 Transition methods in both applets and applications must be called in the event dispatch thread.

This section develops such a system, and the resulting classes are used throughout the remainder of this book. As a result, every software product developed in this book can be delivered as both an application and an applet with no additional effort.

3.2.1 Unifying Applications and Applets

There are several different ways to satisfy these requirements. Each has advantages and disadvantages.

One obvious way to proceed is to create an abstract JApplication class that has access to a RootPaneContainer of some kind, most likely a JFrame. So that it behaves like a JApplet, a JApplication must have an init() method that is called in the event dispatch thread. To make this happen, it must implement the Runnable interface and call init() from run() (which will, itself, be called in the event dispatch thread after the driver calls the invokeAndWait() method in the SwingUtilities class). This is illustrated in Figure 3.1 on the next page.

The run() method in the JApplication class is implemented as follows:

```
public final void run()
{
    constructMainWindow();
    init();
    mainWindow.setVisible(true);
}
```

The constructMainWindow() method in the JApplication class constructs a JFrame, sets its properties, and sets the properties of the content pane. Note that this JFrame does not allow the user to resize it. This is both for convenience and to make it consistent with the main container in a JApplet (which cannot be resized).

```
mainWindow = new JFrame();
mainWindow.setTitle("James Madison University");
```

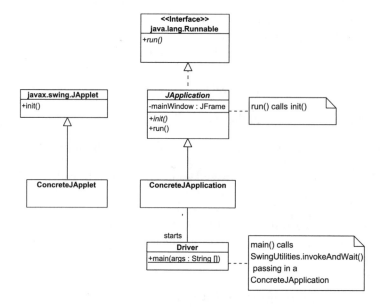

Figure 3.1 Initial Design of a JApplication Class

```
    mainWindow.setResizable(false);

    contentPane = (JPanel)mainWindow.getContentPane();
    contentPane.setLayout(null);
    contentPane.setDoubleBuffered(false);
```

The init() method is abstract so that it must be implemented by all concrete specializations.

```
    public abstract void init();
```

With this one can now create a JApplication and JApplet with the same functionality that are almost identical. To illustrate this, again consider an application that displays a random message.

```
import java.util.*;
import javax.swing.*;

import app.JApplication;

public class       BadRandomMessageJApplication
        extends    JApplication
{
```

```java
   // Attributes
   private JLabel                    label;

   // The pseudo-random number generator
   private static Random             rng = new Random();

   // The messages
   private static final String[] MESSAGES = {
      "What a great book.","Bring on the exercises.",
      "Author, author!","I hope it never ends."};

   public static void main(String[] args) throws Exception
   {
      SwingUtilities.invokeAndWait(
         new BadRandomMessageJApplication(600,400));
   }

   public BadRandomMessageJApplication(int width, int height)
   {
      super(width, height);
   }

   private static String createRandomMessage()
   {
      return  MESSAGES[rng.nextInt(MESSAGES.length)];
   }

   public void init()
   {
      JPanel                  contentPane;
      String                  s;

      // Select a message at random
      s = createRandomMessage();

      // Get the container for all content
      contentPane = (JPanel)getContentPane();
      contentPane.setLayout(null);

      // Add a component to the container
      label = new JLabel(s,SwingConstants.CENTER);
      label.setBounds(50,50,500,100);
      contentPane.add(label);
   }
}
```

As should be apparent, this application is almost identical to the previous applet. Hence, at first glance, this would seem to be a good design. Unfortunately, upon further consideration, it becomes clear that this design does not satisfy all of the specified requirements (and has some other shortcomings as well).

Requirement F3.3 on page 49 is not satisfied because the `RootPaneContainer` for an applet (which is the `JApplet` itself) has access to the start-up parameters (which are included in the HTML and passed by the browser), whereas the `RootPaneContainer` for an application (which is likely to be a `JFrame`) does not (which are passed to the `main()` method by the operating system). To help solve this problem it makes sense to add a `MultimediaRootPaneContainer` interface that extends the `RootPaneContainer` interface by adding such a method.

```
package app;

import javax.swing.*;

public interface MultimediaRootPaneContainer
        extends    RootPaneContainer
{

    public abstract String getParameter(String name);
}
```

While it is not obvious, Requirement N3.4 on page 49 is also not satisfied by this design. It turns out that the transition methods (i.e., the `init()`, `start()`, `stop()` and `destroy()` methods) in a `JApplet` are not called in the event dispatch thread.[5] Hence, one should not manipulate GUI components in these methods.

The other big problem with this design is that it encourages code duplication. In particular, if you write a `JApplet` and `JApplication` with the same functionality, they will have an enormous amount of duplicate code. Thus, while this design makes it easy to create a `JApplet` and `JApplication` that have the same functionality, they will be very difficult to maintain.

 A better design, which uses the decorator pattern, is illustrated in Figure 3.2 on the following page. This design includes a `MultimediaApplet` class that extends the `JApplet` class and a `MultimediaApplication` class that extends the `JApplication` class. This design also includes an interface that describes the requirements of applications and applets.

Since both "application" and "applet" begin with "app," it makes sense to call this interface `MultimediaApp`. Obviously, this interface must include the transition methods. In addition, it must include a way to inform the delegate about which `RootPaneContainer` it should use to get the content pane.

---

[5]The Java documentation states that these methods **must not be** called in the event dispatch thread. Unfortunately, this dictum is not obeyed by all 'browsers.' Hence, the code that follows assumes they **may** be called in the event dispatch thread. That is, the code that follows includes logic that prevents the problems that would arise if the transition methods were called in the event dispatch thread.

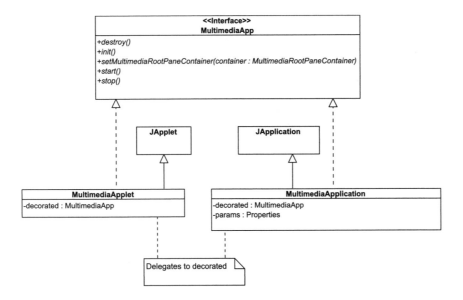

Figure 3.2 Initial Design of a `MultimediaApp`

```java
package app;

import javax.swing.*;

public interface MultimediaApp
{
    public abstract void destroy();

    public abstract void init();

    public abstract void setMultimediaRootPaneContainer(
                    MultimediaRootPaneContainer container);

    public abstract void start();

    public abstract void stop();
}
```

Since one may not always want to implement all of the transition methods, it is convenient to have an `AbstractMultimediaApp` class that has empty implementations.

```
package app;

import javax.swing.*;

public abstract class     AbstractMultimediaApp
                implements MultimediaApp
{
    protected MultimediaRootPaneContainer rootPaneContainer;

    public void destroy()
    {
    }

    public void init()
    {
    }

    public void setMultimediaRootPaneContainer(
                            MultimediaRootPaneContainer container)
    {
        rootPaneContainer = container;
    }

    public void start()
    {
    }

    public void stop()
    {
    }
}
```

The MultimediaApplet has the following structure:

```
package app;

import java.awt.*;
import javax.swing.*;

public abstract class     MultimediaApplet
                extends    JApplet
                implements MultimediaRootPaneContainer
{
```

```
    private MultimediaApp           app;

    public MultimediaApplet(MultimediaApp app)
    {
        super();

        this.app = app;
        setLayout(null);
        app.setMultimediaRootPaneContainer(this);
    }

    protected MultimediaApp getMultimediaApp()
    {
        return app;
    }
}
```

To satisfy Requirement N3.4 on page 49, the `MultimediaApplet` class delegates all calls to its transition methods, performing the delegation in the event dispatch thread. This is accomplished using the `invokeAndWait()` method in the `SwingUtilities` class,

```
    public void destroy()
    {
        if (SwingUtilities.isEventDispatchThread()) app.destroy();
        else
        {
            try {SwingUtilities.invokeAndWait(new DestroyRunnable());}
            catch (Exception e) {}
        }
    }

    public void init()
    {
        if (SwingUtilities.isEventDispatchThread()) app.init();
        else
        {
            try {SwingUtilities.invokeAndWait(new InitRunnable());}
            catch (Exception e) {}
        }
    }

    public void start()
    {
        if (SwingUtilities.isEventDispatchThread()) app.start();
        else
```

```
        {
            try {SwingUtilities.invokeAndWait(new StartRunnable());}
            catch (Exception e) {}
        }
    }

    public void stop()
    {
        if (SwingUtilities.isEventDispatchThread()) app.stop();
        else
        {
            try {SwingUtilities.invokeAndWait(new StopRunnable());}
            catch (Exception e) {}
        }
    }
}
```

and an inner class for each of the transition methods.

```
    private class DestroyRunnable implements Runnable
    {
        public void run()
        {
            app.destroy();
        }
    }

    private class InitRunnable implements Runnable
    {
        public void run()
        {
            app.init();
        }
    }

    private class StartRunnable implements Runnable
    {
        public void run()
        {
            app.start();
        }
    }

    private class StopRunnable implements Runnable
    {
        public void run()
```

```
            {
                app.stop();
            }
        }
    }
```

Since the `invokeAndWait()` method should never be called in the event dispatch thread, each of the transition methods first checks to see whether it is (mistakenly) being called in that thread. (Since these methods are called infrequently, the overhead of these checks is not significant.)

To reduce code duplication, one should move all of the logic that is in an application/applet to a delegate that implements the `MultimediaApp` interface. For the example above, this involves the creation of a `RandomMessageApp` that contains all of the common code from the applet and application above.

```java
import java.util.*;
import javax.swing.*;

import app.*;

public class   RandomMessageApp
       extends AbstractMultimediaApp
{
    // Attributes
    private JLabel                 label;

    // The pseudo-random number generator
    private static Random          rng = new Random();

    // The messages
    private static final String[] MESSAGES = {
        "What a great book.","Bring on the exercises.",
        "Author, author!","I hope it never ends."};

    private static String createRandomMessage()
    {
        return  MESSAGES[rng.nextInt(MESSAGES.length)];
    }

    public void init()
    {
        JPanel                     contentPane;
        String                     s;

        // Select a message at random
        s = createRandomMessage();
```

```
            // Get the container for all content
            contentPane = (JPanel)rootPaneContainer.getContentPane();
            contentPane.setLayout(null);


            // Add a component to the container
            label = new JLabel(s, SwingConstants.CENTER);
            label.setBounds(50,50,500,100);
            contentPane.add(label);
        }
    }
```

It is then trivial to create a specialization of MultimediaApplet that decorates this RandomMessageApp.

```
import app.*;

public class     RandomMessageMultimediaApplet
        extends   MultimediaApplet
{
    public RandomMessageMultimediaApplet()
    {
        super(new RandomMessageApp());
    }
}
```

Before a comparable application can be created, it is necessary to create a specialization of the JApplication class that delegates to a MultimediaApp. This class has the following structure:

```
package app;

import java.awt.*;
import java.awt.event.*;
import java.util.*;
import javax.swing.*;

public abstract class     MultimediaApplication
                extends     JApplication
                implements MultimediaRootPaneContainer
{
    private   MultimediaApp app;
    private   Properties     params;
```

```
    public MultimediaApplication(String[] args,
                                 MultimediaApp app,
                                 int width, int height)
    {
        super(width, height);

        this.app    = app;
        app.setMultimediaRootPaneContainer(this);

        params      = new Properties();
        for (int i=0; i<args.length; i++)
        {
            params.put(Integer.toString(i), args[i]);
        }
    }

    protected MultimediaApp getMultimediaApp()
    {
        return app;
    }

    public String getParameter(String name)
    {
        return params.getProperty(name);
    }
}
```

The transition methods are implemented as follows:

```
    public void destroy()
    {
        app.destroy();
    }

    public void init()
    {
        app.init();
    }

    public void start()
    {
        app.start();
    }
```

```
    public void stop()
    {
       app.stop();
    }
```

Unlike the MultimediaApplet class, this class does not have to use the invokeAndWait() method in the SwingUtilities class. This is because of the way the JApplication class is implemented. Specifically, the transition methods in the JApplication class are always called in the event dispatch thread.

It is now trivial to create a specialization of MultimediaApplication that decorates this RandomMessageApp.

```
import app.*;

import java.util.*;
import javax.swing.*;

public class      RandomMessageMultimediaApplication
      extends     MultimediaApplication
{
    public static void main(String[] args) throws Exception
    {
       SwingUtilities.invokeAndWait(
          new RandomMessageMultimediaApplication(args, 600, 400));
    }

    public RandomMessageMultimediaApplication(String[] args,
                                      int width, int height)
    {
       super(args, new RandomMessageApp(), width, height);
    }
}
```

At this point, the only difference between MultimediaApplication objects and MultimediaApplet objects is the transition methods other than init(). Recall that a MultimediaApplet (which is a JApplet) has its transition methods called by the browser when the page containing the JApplet is loaded/unloaded (see the discussion on page 44). Ideally, the transition methods in MultimediaApplication objects would be called at corresponding times. This can be accomplished by making JApplication a WindowListener on its main window.

To do so, the following is added to the `constructMainWindow()` method:

```
mainWindow.setDefaultCloseOperation(
                        JFrame.DO_NOTHING_ON_CLOSE);
mainWindow.addWindowListener(this);
```

The first statement instructs the main window to do nothing when the "close" button is clicked. The second statement registers the `JApplication` as a `WindowListener`.

Now, it is necessary to actually implement the `WindowListener` interface. When a `windowOpened()` message is generated, the `start()` method must be called.

```
public void windowOpened(WindowEvent event)
{
    resize();
    start();
}
```

The same is true when a `windowDeiconfied()` message is generated.

```
public void windowDeiconified(WindowEvent event)
{
    start();
}
```

When a `windowIconified()` message is generated, the `stop()` method must be called.

```
public void windowIconified(WindowEvent event)
{
    stop();
}
```

When a `windowClosing()` message is generated, the `exit()` method must be called.

```
public void windowClosing(WindowEvent event)
{
    exit();
}
```

The `exit()` method asks the user to confirm and then calls the `stop()` method.

```
private void exit()
{
    int        response;

    response = JOptionPane.showConfirmDialog(mainWindow,
                          "Exit this application?",
                          "Exit?",
                          JOptionPane.YES_NO_OPTION);

    if (response == JOptionPane.YES_OPTION)
    {
        mainWindow.setVisible(false);
        stop();
        mainWindow.dispose();
    }
}
```

Finally, when a `windowClosed()` message is generated (which happens after the `windowClosing()` message is generated and the `stop()` method is called), the `destroy()` method is called.

```
public void windowClosed(WindowEvent event)
{
    destroy();
    System.exit(0);
}
```

    The final design is summarized in Figure 3.3 on the following page. A `MultimediaApplet` is just a `JApplet` that delegates transition method calls to its `MultimediaApp` in the event dispatch thread. The parent class implements the methods in `MultimediaRootPaneContainer`. A `MultimediaApplication` is a `WindowListener` for a `JFrame` that it constructs. It responds to window events by delegating to its `MultimediaApp` in the event dispatch thread. Its `JFrame` implements the `RootPaneContainer` interface and it implements the `getParameter()` method in the `MultimediaRootPaneContainer` interface using a `Properties` object that it fills with the command-line arguments that are passed into its constructor.

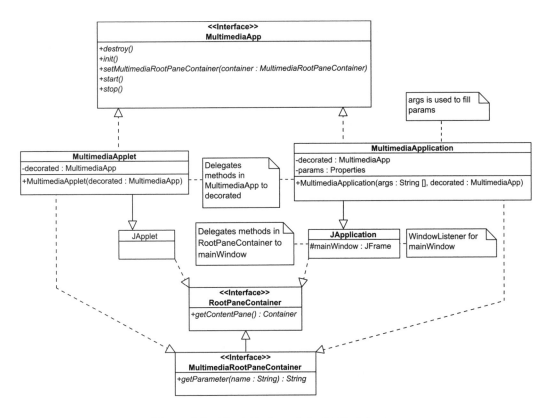

Figure 3.3 Final Design of the Unified System

3.2.2 Program Resources

Most multimedia programs, be they applications or applets, need to 'load' resources of various kinds (e.g., artwork, preferences) at runtime. While this is not a problem conceptually, it can be somewhat problematic in practice because of the different ways in which applets and applications can be 'organized' (e.g., in a `.jar` file, in a packaged set of classes, in an unpackaged set of classes) and 'delivered/installed' (e.g., by an HTTP server, by an installer, as files on a CD/DVD). Hence, in practice, it can be very difficult for a program to know where resources are. Fortunately, with a little bit of effort, one can find resources in the same way that the Java interpreter does.

The Java interpreter obtains the byte codes that constitute a class using a `class loader`.[6] Obviously, the class loader must be able to find the byte codes regardless of how the applet/application is 'organized' and 'delivered/installed.' Fortunately, this same logic can be used to load resources. To do so, one must first understand a little about reflection.

---

[6]In fact, the Java interpreter uses three different kinds of class loaders. The bootstrap class loader loads system classes (e.g., from `rt.jar`), the extension class loader loads standard extensions, and the system/application class loader loads application classes (e.g., from the `classpath`).

Every interface, class, and object in Java has an associated `Class` object that can be used to obtain information about that interface's/class's/object's attributes, methods, etc. This information is encapsulated as `Constructor`, `Field`, `Method`, and `Type` objects. These objects can be used for a variety of purposes. The `ResourceFinder` class that follows uses the `getResource()` and `getResourceAsStream()` methods in `Class` objects.

Since, in the future, it might be desirable to create pools of `ResourceFinder` objects, this class uses the factory method pattern as follows:

```java
package io;

import java.io.*;
import java.net.*;
import java.util.*;


public class ResourceFinder
{
    private Class                    c;

    private ResourceFinder()
    {
       c = this.getClass();
    }

    private ResourceFinder(Object o)
    {
       // Get the Class for the Object that wants the resource
       c = o.getClass();
    }

    public static ResourceFinder createInstance()
    {
       return new ResourceFinder();
    }

    public static ResourceFinder createInstance(Object o)
    {
       return new ResourceFinder(o);
    }
}
```

When constructed, a `ResourceFinder` object can be 'told' to use either its class loader (by calling the default factory method) or another object's class loader (by calling the explicit-value factory method).

The findInputStream() method in the ResourceFinder class uses the appropriate Class object (with the help of the class loader) to get a resource as an InputStream.

```
public InputStream findInputStream(String name)
{
    InputStream    is;

    is    = c.getResourceAsStream(name);

    return is;
}
```

The resource can then be read from this InputStream.

In some situations, it may be more useful to have a 'pointer' to the resource, rather than an InputStream. In such situations, one can use a *uniform resource locator* (URL). URLs are encapsulated by the URL class and can be obtained (among other ways) using the getResource() method in the Class class.

```
public URL findURL(String name)
{
    URL                url;

    url    = c.getResource(name);

    return url;
}
```

3.2.3 A Simple Example Revisited

It is now useful to reconsider the stopwatch application from Chapter 2. Specifically, it is useful to create a MultimediaApp with the same functionality of that application. This class has the following structure:

```
import java.util.*;
import java.awt.event.*;
import javax.swing.*;

import app.*;
import event.*;

public class        StopWatchApp
```

```
        extends     AbstractMultimediaApp
        implements ActionListener, MetronomeListener
{
    private boolean                running;
    private JLabel                 label;
    private Metronome              metronome;

    private static final String    START = "Start";
    private static final String    STOP  = "Stop";
}
```

Much of this class is unchanged from the earlier example.

```
    public void actionPerformed(ActionEvent event)
    {
        String    actionCommand;

        actionCommand = event.getActionCommand();
        if      (actionCommand.equals(START))
        {
            label.setText("0");
            metronome.reset();
            metronome.start();
            running = true;
        }
        else if (actionCommand.equals(STOP))
        {
            metronome.stop();
            running = false;
        }
    }


    public void handleTick(int millis)
    {
        label.setText(""+millis/1000);
    }
```

The primary difference between the two is that the code in the run() method in the application is in the init() method in the app.

```
    public void init()
    {
        JButton                    start, stop;
```

```
    JPanel                      contentPane;

    running = false;

    contentPane = (JPanel)rootPaneContainer.getContentPane();
    contentPane.setLayout(null);

    label      = new JLabel("0");
    label.setBounds(250,100,100,100);
    contentPane.add(label);

    start = new JButton(START);
    start.setBounds(50,300,100,50);
    start.addActionListener(this);
    contentPane.add(start);


    stop  = new JButton(STOP);
    stop.setBounds(450,300,100,50);
    stop.addActionListener(this);
    contentPane.add(stop);

    metronome = new Metronome(1000, true);
    metronome.addListener(this);
}
```

The app also includes `start()` and `stop()` methods.

```
public void start()
{
    if (running) metronome.start();
}

public void stop()
{
    if (running) metronome.stop();
}
```

The `MultimediaApplication` that uses this app is then very simple.

```
import app.*;

import javax.swing.*;
```

```
public class      StopWatchMultimediaApplication
      extends     MultimediaApplication
{
    public static void main(String[] args) throws Exception
    {
      SwingUtilities.invokeAndWait(
         new StopWatchMultimediaApplication(args, 600,400));
    }

    public StopWatchMultimediaApplication(String[] args,
                                     int width, int height)
    {
      super(args, new StopWatchApp(), width, height);
    }
}
```

The `MultimediaApplet` that uses this app is also very simple.

```
import app.*;

public class      StopWatchMultimediaApplet
      extends     MultimediaApplet
{
    public StopWatchMultimediaApplet()
    {
      super(new StopWatchApp());
    }
}
```

EXERCISES ··

1. Using your answers to Exercises 6, 7, and 8 on page 39, create a class named `OnOffApp` that extends `AbstractMultimediaApp`. (Note: Remember that it must implement the `ActionListener` interface.)

2. Create a class named `OnOffApplication` that extends `MultimediaApplication` and uses `OnOffApp`.

3. Create a class named `OnOffApplet` that extends `MultimediaApplet` and uses `OnOffApp`.

4. Using your answers to Exercises 9 on page 40, 10 on page 41, and 11 on page 41, create a class named `TextBounceApp` that extends `AbstractMultimediaApp`. (Note: Remember that it must explicitly implement an interface.)

5. Modify your answer to Exercise 4 above so that `message` is initialized to the parameter named `"0"`.

6. Create a class named `TextBounceApplication` that extends `MultimediaApplication` and uses `TextBounceApp`.

7. Create a class named `TextbounceApplet` that extends `MultimediaApplet` and uses `TextBounceApp`.

8. Write a command-line application named `Builder` that, given the name of an app, creates the source code for both an applet and an application that uses the app (each of which should be in an appropriately named file). It must also create an HTML file that can be used to load the applet in a WWW browser. The command-line parameters should include the name of the app and the width and the height (in pixels).

REFERENCES AND FURTHER READING ···

Boese, E. S. 2010. *An introduction to programming with Java applets.* Sudbury, MA: Jones and Bartlett.

Horstmann, C. S., and G. Cornell. 2002. *Core Java: Volume I—fundamentals.* Palo Alto, CA: Sun Microsystems Press.

Horstmann, C. S., and G. Cornell. 2002. *Core Java: Volume II—advanced features.* Palo Alto, CA: Sun Microsystems Press.

II

Visual Content

Part II deals with visual content. It begins, in Chapter 4, with a general discussion of the physics, biology, and psychology of vision. It then considers static visual content (i.e., visual content that does not change over time); Chapter 5 is concerned with sampled static content, Chapter 6 is concerned with described static content, and Chapter 7 is concerned with a system that handles both. It next considers dynamic visual content, covering sampled dynamic content in Chapter 8 and described dynamic content in Chapter 9.

Visual Content

4

This chapter provides a brief overview of the science(s) of vision. That is, it considers how physics, biology, and psychology all play a role in our perception of visual content. It begins with a consideration of the physics of light. It then considers the biology of vision and the psychology of visual perception. Finally, it considers visual output devices, and how they can be used to present visual content.

4.1 Light

Loosely, the term "visible light" refers to electromagnetic waves with particular wavelengths. More formally, visible light is the portion of the *electromagnetic (EM) spectrum* with wavelengths ranging from about 380 nanometers to 740 nanometers (where 1 nm = 10^{-9} m). Aside from the wavelengths, there's nothing that distinguishes visible light from other parts of the electromagnetic spectrum.

As is true of all waves (see Section 1.3), EM waves are produced by a source of some kind. What makes EM waves unique is that sources of EM waves create both electric and magnetic fields, and the fields it produces are perpendicular to each other. As illustrated in Figure 4.1, these fields travel away from the source, and both are perpendicular to the direction of travel. That is, EM waves are *transverse waves* (which is why light can be *polarized*). An EM wave carries no mass but does carry energy. The energy of an EM wave is stored in the electric and magnetic fields, and is proportional to the frequency of the wave. While sound waves require

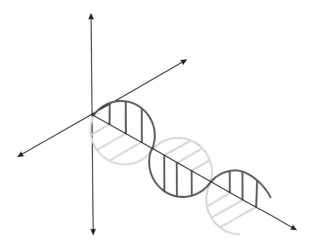

Figure 4.1 An Electromagnetic Wave

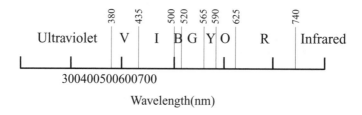

Figure 4.2   The Visible Spectrum

a medium for transmission (recall the tag line from the 1979 movie *Alien*—"In space no one can hear you scream"), EM waves can travel through a vacuum.

....

Definition 4.1 A *spectral color* is light of a single wavelength in the visible portion of the EM spectrum.

....

As illustrated in Figure 4.2, the visible portion of the EM spectrum is commonly divided into seven bands named red, orange, yellow, green, blue, indigo, and violet (listed in decreasing wavelength). While one can produce spectral colors using specialized hardware (for example, a helium-neon laser produces light with a wavelength of 632 nm), it is very difficult to reproduce spectral colors using conventional techniques (even photographic techniques). So it is important to remember that most reproductions of spectral colors should be considered approximate, at best. It is also important to remember that the bands given in Figure 4.2 are also approximate.

Light from common objects (whether they are sources of light or objects that reflect light) consists of a range of different wavelengths (and, hence, frequencies). For example, a bright red tomato might reflect light of all wavelengths between 590 nm and 720 nm. Hence, light is often characterized using a *spectral power distribution* that provides the power of the light at each wavelength in the visible spectrum. When light has only discrete wavelengths (e.g., light from a mercury vapor lamp or a low-pressure sodium lamp) it is said to have a *line spectrum*. Otherwise (e.g., light from an incandescent lightbulb) it is said to have a *continuous spectrum*. The spectral power distribution of light can be measured using a spectroscope.

4.2   Vision

Humans sense light using an organ called the eye and interpret the sensation using the brain. Both the eye and the brain are very complex organs. Hence, neither the sensing of light nor its interpretation are completely understood.

For the purposes of this book, the simplified illustration of the eye in Figure 4.3 on the next page will suffice. Light enters the eye through the *cornea*, is focused by the *lens*, and stimulates photoreceptors in the *retina*. When the lens does not focus the rays of light entering the pupil properly a single 'point' is sensed by multiple photoreceptors on the retina.

The retina contains two different kinds of photoreceptors: *rods* and *cones*. Photoreceptors are also classified as either *on*, *off*, or *on–off*, depending on whether they respond to the presence of light, the absence of light, or both. As light passes through these photoreceptors, some of it is absorbed by photopigments that generate electric current.

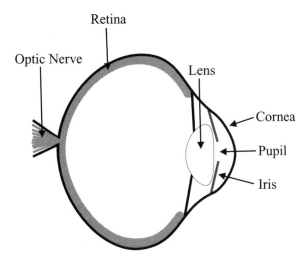

Figure 4.3   The Human Eye

A human eye has about 100 million rods, each of which is small and contains the photopigment rhodopsin. Rods are very sensitive and, hence, generate current under very low illumination levels. However, multiple rods are connected to one neuron in the retina. Hence, humans have poor visual acuity under low illumination levels. On the other hand, a human eye contains only about 6 million cones. Cones are less sensitive to light, and only operate under higher illumination levels. Hence, humans have poor color perception under low illumination levels.

In the periphery of the retina, rods and cones are intermixed. However, the *fovea*, a small portion of the retina, contains no rods and about 50,000 cones (each of which is connected to multiple neurons). Hence, it is hard for humans to see dim objects when they look directly at them. The density of cones relative to rods decreases as the distance to the fovea increases.

There are three kinds of cones, distinguished by the photopigment they contain. They are referred to as ρ-cones, γ-cones, and β-cones.[1] β-cones (about 2% of the cones) are sensitive to wavelengths between 400 nm and 550 nm, but are most sensitive to a wavelength of about 450 nm (what is usually called blue). γ-cones (about 32% of the cones) are sensitive to wavelengths between 420 nm and 660 nm, but are most sensitive to a wavelength of about 540 nm (what is usually called green). Finally, ρ-cones (about 64% of the cones) are sensitive to wavelengths between 400 nm and 700 nm, but are most sensitive to a wavelength of about 580 nm (what is usually called red).

Data from the eye is transmitted to the brain along the *optic nerve*, which consists of about 1 million individual nerve fibers. It is commonly believed that the optic nerve transmits information in multiple streams. One stream is used to transmit the signals that control eye movements, a second is used to transmit information that is highly variable over time but not space, and a third is used to transmit information that is highly variable over space but not time.

---

[1]Some authors use the terms "S-cones," "M-cones," and "L-cones" to indicate that they are most sensitive to short, middle, and long wavelengths, respectively.

The largest part of the information transmitted from the retina arrives at the portion of the occipital lobe of the brain called the *primary visual cortex*, which contains about 150 million neurons. In addition, about 20 other areas in the cortex seem to receive visual input.

4.3   Visual Perception

The data that is received by the brain is perceived in a variety of different ways.

4.3.1   Brightness

The processing of the output from the rods impacts one's perception of luminance or *brightness*. That is, an increase in output from the rods is perceived as an increase in brightness. So, light waves with a higher amplitude (e.g., from a 100-watt lightbulb) cause the rods to generate stronger signals and are perceived as being bright. On the other hand, light waves with a lower amplitude (e.g., from a 40-watt lightbulb) cause the rods to generate weaker signals and are perceived as being dim.

Interestingly, perceived brightness is not linear, it is approximately logarithmic. So, a doubling of output from the rods does not lead to a perceived doubling of the brightness. Instead, the output from the rods must increase by an order of magnitude to yield a perceived doubling in brightness.

4.3.2   Color

The processing of the output from the cones results in one's perception of color. However, the way in which this output is processed is not obvious. Most importantly, the cones do not capture the spectral power distribution of the light. Hence, the data processed by the brain is just the total levels of activity sensed by the three types of cones. This means that if several waves with different wavelengths were to interfere with each other and then enter the pupil, only one color would be perceived.[2]

This idea can be formalized using the notion of an integral.[3] Specifically, if the spectral power distribution of the light passing through the pupil is given by P and the sensitivity of the three types of cones are given by s_ρ, s_γ, s_β, then the brain processes the following values:

$$R = \int P(\lambda)s_\rho(\lambda)d\lambda \tag{4.1}$$

$$G = \int P(\lambda)s_\gamma(\lambda)d\lambda \tag{4.2}$$

$$B = \int P(\lambda)s_\beta(\lambda)d\lambda \tag{4.3}$$

---

[2]As discussed in Section 10.3 on page 292, this is very different from the way we perceive sound.

[3]If you don't know calculus, you can think of the integral, $\int$, as a sum, $\sum$.

where R, G, and B denote the total activity captured in the red, green, and blue ranges, respectively.

This observation led researchers to theorize that light with different spectral power distributions might be perceived as the same color (called *metameric substitution*) and this theory has been validated in a variety of color-matching experiments. In essence, what happens in these experiments is that subjects are shown light from two objects side by side. One object consists of three sources that have independent spectra (e.g., a red, green, and blue lamp). The other object generates the color to be matched. What these experiments reveal is that different combinations of R, G, and B can be perceived as the same color. In fact, the average person can perceive only between 7 million and 10 million colors. Experiments have also shown that increasing or decreasing the power of R, G, and B by the same factor changes the overall perceived brightness (as discussed in Section 4.3.2 on the page before) but not the perceived color. In other words, the perceived color (sometimes called the *chromaticity*) depends on the relative magnitudes of R, G, and B, not on their absolute numerical values.

One of the difficulties that arises when studying and discussing the perception of color is that colors are difficult to describe. To help remedy this, several different schemes have been proposed and used over the years.

One approach is to create a color atlas. That is, to give colors names or positions. The first such system was probably Isaac Newton's color wheel, which had the spectral colors on the outside edge and decreased the saturation along the radius (that is, the saturation was lower toward the center and higher toward the outer edge). The Munsell system is very similar, but divides the circle into 100 different hues. A final example is the commercial Pantone system. All of these approaches are inflexible, don't scale well, and are hard to work with (e.g., it is difficult to mix colors).

The most popular approach is to use three perceptual attributes of color: the hue, the saturation (sometimes called the chroma), and the *lightness* (sometimes called the *luminance* or *intensity*). Hue refers to where the color appears on a color wheel (i.e., the position of the dominant spectral color when placed on a circle; in degrees or radians). Saturation refers to the purity (i.e., does it have white or black mixed in with it?). In other words, the saturation is determined by the ratio of monochromatic to colorless light (or how gray the color is). Finally, the lightness refers to where the color stands, in terms of overall intensity, on a scale from black to white.

One nice thing about describing colors in this way is that it leads to the notion of *color harmonies*. For example, a collection of colors is monochromatic when they are all of the same (or nearly the same) hue. Two colors are *complements* when the distance between them is approximately 180°. Finally, three colors are said to form a triad if the distance between two consecutive colors is approximately 120°.

4.3.3 Depth and Distance

The retina is a 2-dimensional array of sensors; it does not collect any 3-dimensional data. In addition, the eye does not have a sensor that measures depth/distance. Hence, all perception of depth and distance is inferred by the brain.

For objects that are close to the viewer, the two eyes collect data from a slightly different position and a slightly different angle. This leads to what is called a *retinal disparity*. The brain can use this disparity directly to infer depth.

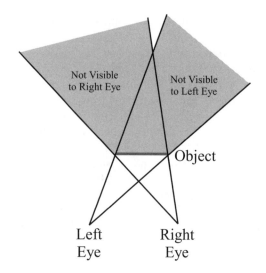

Figure 4.4   Occluded and Half-Occluded Regions

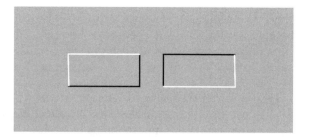

Figure 4.5   Shadows and Depth

In addition, the retinal disparity can be used as an indirect depth cue. When a foreground object is fairly close to the viewer, different background objects are visible to each eye. This is illustrated in Figure 4.4. If object A occludes object B, then A must be closer to the viewer than B. In addition, as object A is moved closer to the viewer, the half-occlusion region (i.e., the region that is occluded for only one eye) gets larger. Hence, both occluded regions and half-occluded regions enable us to perceive depth.

Size is also used as a depth/distance cue. For example, since automobiles are known to be approximately the same size, if the brain receives data on two differently sized automobiles, it infers that the smaller automobile is farther away.

Finally, shadows are used as a depth/distance cue. It is known that the position of an object relative to a light source has an impact on the shadows that it casts. As a result, the brain uses the relative lightness and darkness of a scene to infer depth. This is illustrated in Figure 4.5. The only difference between the two rectangles is the colors used to draw the four sides. In one, the left and top are white and the bottom and left are black. In the other, the

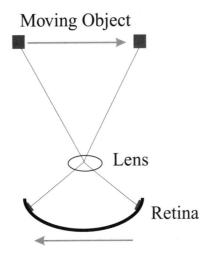

Figure 4.6 Motion Causing Sequential Firing of Receptors

colors are reversed. The dark lines are being perceived as shadows and, hence, the rectangle is perceived as being raised or lowered.[4]

4.3.4 Motion

One way the brain infers motion is from the signals received by on and off photoreceptors. As an object moves, a sequence of on and off photoreceptors fire as illustrated in Figure 4.6. These signals are then used to infer motion. It is important to note that, since each photoreceptor takes some amount of time to react, the brain is receiving a **sample** of all of the data that are actually available. As a result, people can not perceive temporal signals higher than about 60 Hz.

The brain also infers motion from head and eye movements, but there are two alternative explanations for how. Originally, evidence favored "inflow" theory, which posited that signals to move the eye go to the eye, and signals from the eye muscles and the retina go to the brain. The brain then uses the retinal data and the actual eye movement data to infer motion. Now, the evidence seems to support "outflow" theory, which says that signals to move the eye go both to the eye and the brain, and signals from the retina go to the brain. The brain then uses the retinal data and the eye movement commands to infer motion.

It is interesting to note that one's perception of velocity can be influenced by color and contrast. In fact, experiments have shown that, by properly choosing contrasts, moving objects can be made to appear to stand still.

---

[4]Most people perceive the left rectangle as raised and the right as lowered. Such people are 'assuming' that the light source is above and to the left of the rectangles.

4.4   Visual Output Devices

A visual output device is a machine that is capable of presenting visual information transmitted from a computer (i.e., making information stored in a computer perceivable to the human eye). This includes both devices that can create 'hardcopy' (e.g., put the information on a material like paper that reflects light) and those that create 'temporary' output (e.g., devices like monitors and displays that emit light). Several different aspects of visual output devices are worthy of discussion.

4.4.1   Display Spaces

Display spaces can be either discrete or continuous.

....

Definition 4.2 A visual output device with a discrete display space is called a *raster device*.

....

On the other hand:

....

Definition 4.3 A visual output device with a continuous display space is called a *vector device*.

....

The easiest way to understand the difference is with some examples.

Common raster devices include liquid crystal displays (LCDs), light-emitting diode (LED) displays, ink jet printers, and laser printers. Each of these devices works with a rectangular grid of 'dots' or *picture elements* (also known as *pixels*). An LCD consists of a rectangular grid of crystal molecules that can allow or prevent light from passing through, an LED display consists of a rectangular grid of semiconductor diodes that emit light, an ink jet printer sprays small dots of ink onto paper, and a laser printer fuses small dots of toner onto paper.

The most common vector device is the pen plotter. Less common vector devices include laser light projectors and oscilloscopes. These devices generate continuous 'lines' that are not composed of individual dots or pixels.

It is worth noting that some cathode ray tube (CRT) monitors are vector devices and some are raster devices. A discussion of the two may help clarify the difference between the two types of output devices. In a vector CRT, an electron beam is moved across the screen, which has a continuous coating of a phosphorescent material (a material that exhibits sustained, perhaps for a short time, glowing without further stimulus). For example, the original 1979 version of the Atari video game *Asteroids* used such a device. In a raster CRT, far and away the more common of the two, an electron beam lights dots in a fixed position on the phosphor coating. When the phosphors are hit by electrons (that pass through a mask) they fluoresce (i.e., emit light).

4.4.2   Coordinate Systems

The easiest way to identify points is with a coordinate system.

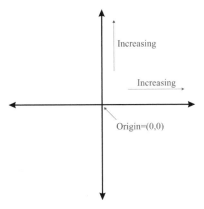

Figure 4.7 Cartesian Coordinates

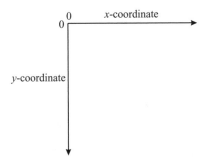

Figure 4.8 Output Device Coordinates

Definition 4.4 *Coordinates* are quantities (either linear or angular) that designate the position of a point in relation to a given reference frame.

The coordinate system that people are most familiar with is the 2-dimensional Cartesian system (named after Descartes) in which the *origin* is at the center, the basis consist of the horizontal and vertical axes, and positive values are in the 'northeast' quadrant. This is illustrated in Figure 4.7.

Many visual output devices use a rectangular coordinate system in which the origin is in the upper-left corner and positive values are in the 'southeast' quadrant. This is illustrated in Figure 4.8. The coordinate system used to represent visual content may or may not correspond to the coordinate system that is used by the output device. Hence, one often distinguishes between "user coordinates" and "device coordinates."

4.4.3 Aspect Ratio and Orientation

Most, though not all, visual output devices are rectangular. As a result, two terms have found their way into the nomenclature of visual output devices.

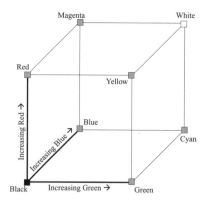

Figure 4.9   The RGB Cube

....

Definition 4.5 The *aspect ratio* of a rectangle is the ratio of the size of its larger side to the size of its smaller side.

....

For raster devices, the size can be measured either in pixels or in more traditional units of length (e.g., inches, centimeters). If the pixels are square, then the aspect ratio will be independent of the units. For vector devices, the size is almost always measured in traditional units.

Rectangles are often also said to have an orientation, either *portrait* or *landscape*. If you think about a rectangle on a wall, it has a portrait orientation if it is taller than it is wide (i.e., if the size in the up–down direction is larger than the size in the left–right direction). On the other hand, it has a landscape orientation if it is wider than it is tall. Since displays are normally used when they are parallel to a wall, it is quite natural to talk about their orientation, most of which have a landscape orientation. Printers, on the other hand, do not have a natural orientation, though the paper that they print on can be thought of as having one (i.e., by holding the paper in the air parallel to a wall).

4.4.4   Color Models and Color Spaces

The complete set of perceived colors that can be generated by an output device are called its color gamut. Most visual output devices use a tristimulus approach to generate different colors. This seems quite natural given that the perception of color results from the selective sensing of light in three different portions of the spectrum.

The red–green–blue (RGB) model makes direct use of the fact that people's eyes have ρ, γ, and β cones. The traditional RGB model begins with black and then adds red, green, and/or blue as shown in Figure 4.9. Hence, this is called an additive model. This is, obviously, the model used by most monitors/displays since they start with a black screen and then add different amounts of red, green, and blue light.

In the traditional cyan–magenta–yellow (CMY) model, one begins with white and then removes cyan, magenta, and/or yellow as shown in Figure 4.10. Hence, this is called a subtractive model. Not surprisingly, since paper starts out white and pigments are added that absorb different wavelengths of light, this is the kind of model that is normally used for printing. In

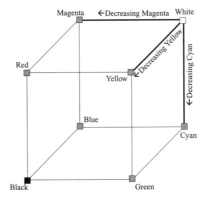

Figure 4.10 The CMY Cube

practice, many printers actually use a CMYK system that adds black (the "K") toner/ink. This is done simply because it is less expensive to use black toner/ink than it is to mix large amounts of cyan, magenta, and yellow toner/ink.

Both of these models have two serious limitations. Specifically,

- Some colors that people can perceive can only be generated using negative amounts of one component (e.g., red in the RGB model), which is not physically possible.
- They are both linear in their components and the cones in the eye do not respond in a linear fashion.

These limitations have led to the development of other models, most notable the CIEXYZ system. This model was created by the Commission Internationale d'Eclairage (CIE) and uses two color values and one luminance value. The details of the CIEXYZ model are not important for the purposes of this book, but are very important in many situations.

In Java, colors are encapsulated by the `Color` class, using an appropriate `ColorSpace`. A specific `Color` object consists of an array of (normalized) components; the meaning of each is defined in the `ColorSpace`. For example, in the HSV color space, each color consists of a hue, saturation, and value, whereas in the RGB color space, each color has a red component, a green component, and a blue component. Java supports a large number of different color spaces, including the sRGB standard, the CIEXYZ standard, and the Photo YCC standard.

4.5 Rendering

In art, rendering is the process by which a work of art is created. In cooking/industrial applications, rendering is the separation of fats from other organic materials. Not surprisingly, this book is more concerned with the former than the latter.

Definition 4.6 *Visual rendering* is the process of taking an internal representation of visual content and presenting it on a visual output device.

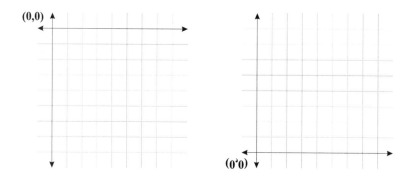

Figure 4.11   The Original and Translated Coordinate Systems

Depending on the internal representation and the output device, the rendering process may involve

- conversion of the color space, and/or
- rasterization or vectorization of the internal representation,

both of which can be very complicated. Fortunately, for the purposes of this book, each of these operations can be treated as a "black box." However, there are three other steps in the rendering process that this book is concerned with. That is,

- coordinate transformation,
- clipping, and
- composition.

The rendering process is managed/performed by a *rendering engine.* There are two different rendering engines in Java, encapsulated in the `Graphics` and `Graphics2D` classes.[5]

4.5.1 Coordinate Transformation

A *coordinate transformation* is any change made to a coordinate system. If you think of the coordinate system as a piece of graph paper, a coordinate transformation can be thought of as a movement of, or change to, the graph paper. The most common coordinate transformations are translation, rotation, scaling, and reflection.

....

Definition 4.7 A *translation* involves a horizontal and/or vertical displacement.

....

Returning to the graph paper analogy, a translation is a movement of the graph paper that does not change its orientation. One translation is illustrated in Figure 4.11. Translation can be used to reposition a (properly scaled) coordinate system. For example, one might translate a coordinate system so that all of the resulting coordinates are nonnegative.

_____

[5]The micro edition of Java supports only the `Graphics` class.

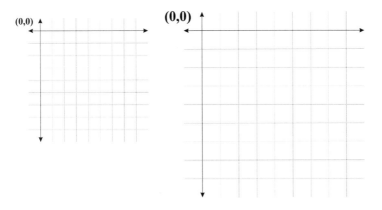

Figure 4.12 The Original and Scaled Coordinate Systems

Definition 4.8 A *scaling* is a multiplication of each of the coordinates by a particular value (which need not be the same in both dimensions).

If the piece of graph paper was made of rubber, a scaling would be a stretching of the graph paper. Figure 4.12 illustrates a scaling. Scaling can be used to make the coordinate system conform to the range of the visual content. As shown in Figure 4.12, you have to be careful when scaling the coordinate system since everything (e.g., text, line thickness) is scaled.

Definition 4.9 A *rotation* is an angular transformation of the coordinate system.

Figure 4.13 illustrates a 45° (i.e., $\pi/2$ radian) counterclockwise rotation around the origin. Coordinate systems are rarely rotated in practice (though, as discussed in Chapters 5 and 6, individual pieces of content are often rotated).

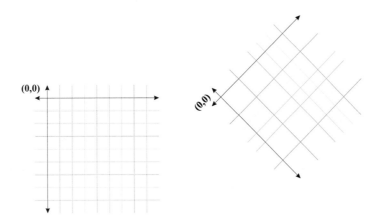

Figure 4.13 The Original and Rotated Coordinate Systems

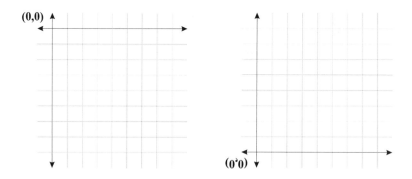

Figure 4.14   The Original and Reflected Coordinate Systems

Finally, a reflection is essentially a 'mirror image' around an arbitrary axis. A reflection around the x-axis is illustrated in Figure 4.14. The most common use of coordinate reflection is to change a computer graphics coordinate system to a Cartesian coordinate system.

In Java, these transforms, and others, are encapsulated by the `AffineTransform` class (which is considered at length in future chapters). As this book proceeds, it is important not to confuse transformations of the coordinate system with transformations of individual objects (which can be used, for example, to make objects appear to move).

4.5.2 Clipping

One does not always want to render the entirety of an internal representation of visual content. In such situations, one 'clips' the internal representation.

Definition 4.10 *Clipping* is the process of limiting the portion of the internal representation that will be rendered.

This book does not consider the details of how a rendering engine clips. Instead, it considers only how to specify the clipping area. In Java, both the `java.awt.Graphics` and `java.awt.Graphics2D` engines have a `setClip(int, int, int, int)` method that can be used to set the clipping rectangle.

4.5.3 Composition

In many situations, content is not presented on a blank display. In such situations, the rendering engine must combine the 'new' content with whatever is already being displayed.

Definition 4.11 *Composition* is the process of combining the content being presented (the source) with the background (the destination).

In addition to the obvious uses, composition can be used to achieve blending and transparency effects.

Rule	Definition
Destination	$C_d = C_d$
Destination Atop Source	$C_d = C_s(1 - \alpha_d) + C_d\alpha_s$
Destination Held Out By Source	$C_d = C_d(1 - \alpha_s)$
Destination In Source	$C_d = C_d\alpha_s$
Destination Over Source	$C_d = C_s(1 - \alpha_d) + C_d$
Source	$C_d = C_s$
Source Atop Destination	$C_d = C_s\alpha_d + C_d(1 - \alpha_s)$
Source Held Out By Destination	$C_d = C_s(1 - \alpha_d)$
Source In Destination	$C_d = C_s\alpha_d$
Source XOR Destination	$C_d = C_s(1 - \alpha_d) + C_d(1 - \alpha_s)$
Source Over Destination	$C_d = C_s + C_d(1 - \alpha_s)$

Table 4.1 Porter–Duff Rules

The most common composition approach is called *alpha blending*. Using this approach, every 'point' has four channels, one each for red, green, and blue, and one for alpha. The alpha channel is, essentially, a weighting factor. The way the weighting factor is applied depends on the compositing rule you use. The most common rule is the "Source Over Destination Rule" (which is one of several Porter–Duff rules). In this case, one has

$$
\begin{align}
R_d &= R_s + R_d(1 - \alpha_s) \tag{4.4} \\
G_d &= G_s + G_d(1 - \alpha_s) \tag{4.5} \\
B_d &= B_s + B_d(1 - \alpha_s) \tag{4.6} \\
\alpha_d &= \alpha_s + \alpha_d(1 - \alpha_s) \tag{4.7}
\end{align}
$$

where d and s represent the destination and source, respectively. Hence, when $\alpha_s = 1.0$ the source is totally opaque.

The Porter–Duff rules are summarized in Table 4.1 where C denotes an arbitrary channel (i.e., either the red, green, blue, or alpha value). You should be able to understand them with a little experimentation. In Java, the Porter–Duff rules are encapsulated in the `java.awt.AlphaComposite` class that implements the `java.awt.Composite` interface. The `java.awt.Graphics2D` engine can be instructed to use a particular composite using the `java.awt.Graphics2D.setComposite(java.awt.Composite)` method.

4.5.4 Obtaining a Rendering Engine

The way in which a rendering engine is constructed varies dramatically from platform to platform and language to language. Unfortunately, it even varies across different versions and editions of Java. For example, the micro edition and the standard edition of Java are very different in this respect. This book focuses on the standard edition of Java.

When a JComponent (see Section 2.4.1 on page 23) 'needs to be' rendered, its `paint()` method is called and is passed a rendering engine. A JComponent (or a specialization of a JComponent) then uses this rendering engine to render itself. Hence, to perform rendering in Java one needs to write a class that extends JComponent and implement the `paint(Graphics)` method. This is demonstrated in the following example:

```java
import java.awt.*;
import javax.swing.*;

public class BoringComponent extends JComponent
{
    public void paint(Graphics g)
    {
        Graphics2D            g2;

        // Cast the rendering engine appropriately
        g2 = (Graphics2D)g;


        // Put the rendering code here
    }
}
```

A JComponent that is added to the content pane of either a MultimediaApplet or a MultimediaApplication will be sent a paint() message whenever the content pane determines that some or all of the JComponent has become visible.

If, for some reason, one wants a JComponent to render itself in response to a particular event, one can instruct it to do so by calling its repaint() method. This will result in a call to the JComponent object's paint() in the event dispatch thread.

4.6 Designing a Visual Content System

Before turning to specific types of visual content, it is helpful to consider the design of a system for handling visual content in the abstract. The requirements for such a system are relatively straightforward—the system must be able to manage and render multiple different 'pieces' of visual content. Specifically, the system must

F4.1 Support the addition of visual content.

F4.2 Support the removal of visual content.

F4.3 Support 'front-to-back' ordering (i.e., z-ordering) of visual content.

F4.4 Support multiple different presentations of visual content at the same time.

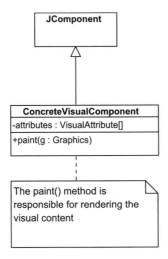

Figure 4.15   A Common Design

F4.5 Support the transformation of visual content.[6]

N4.6 Be thread safe.

4.6.1   Alternative Designs

One obvious, and very common, design is to create a `ConcreteVisualComponent` class that is responsible for rendering the visual content. As illustrated in Figure 4.15, this class must contain all of the attributes necessary to render all of the content. This includes such things as positions, colors, etc. The fundamental problem with this design is that the `ConcreteVisualComponent` class will almost never be cohesive. This is because, in most applications, it will be responsible for rendering both many different 'pieces' of visual content and many different types of visual content. In addition, this design can be difficult to implement because of the need to manage different visual attributes for different pieces and types of visual content. For example, some pieces of content may have multiple visual attributes (e.g., position, color, width) that need to be accounted for, and some may have only one (e.g., position).

A better design uses a specialization of the `JComponent` class that holds all of the pieces of visual content and delegates the work of rendering to them. This design is illustrated in Figure 4.16 on the following page. In this design, the `VisualContentCanvas` holds all of the content objects, which are exemplified by the `ConcreteContent` and `OtherConcreteContent` classes. Objects in both of these classes have the ability to render themselves using their own visual attributes. There are several advantages of this design. First, the `VisualContentCanvas` can be used in any number of different applications. Second, each `ConcreteContent` and

---

[6]While some types of programs do not need this functionality (e.g., in a simple photo album), many do. Hence, a general-purpose visual content system must include the ability to transform the content.

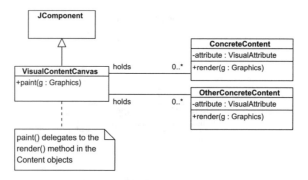

Figure 4.16   A Design with Coupling Problems

`OtherConcreteContent` object is responsible only for rendering itself and is, by definition, cohesive. The big shortcoming of this design is that the `VisualContentCanvas` class is too closely coupled to the `ConcreteContent` and `OtherConcreteContent` classes. As an example of the kinds of problems that this causes, observe that the `VisualContentCanvas` class would have to manage several different collections, one for each type of visual content.

 An even better design, illustrated in Figure 4.17, includes a `SimpleContent` interface that is implemented by the concrete content classes. The addition of this interface effectively decouples the `VisualContentCanvas` class from the concrete content classes. That is, the `VisualContentCanvas` need only know about the `SimpleContent` interface, and not the specific `ConcreteContent` classes that implement this interface. The only shortcoming of this design is that the `VisualContentCanvas` class is not cohesive. In particular, it is responsible for both managing the collection of `SimpleContent` objects (sometimes called 'model' responsibilities) and for the presentation functions (sometimes called 'view' responsibilities) that must be performed by all specializations of the `VisualComponent` class.

 This means that the design in Figure 4.17 can be improved by separating the two responsibilities in the `VisualContentCanvas` into different classes. In this design, illustrated in Figure

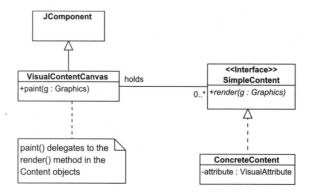

Figure 4.17   A Design That Eliminates the Coupling Problem

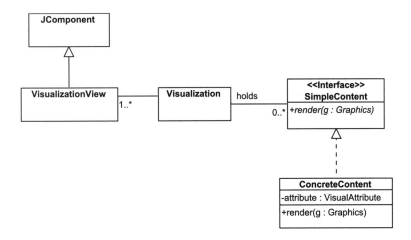

Figure 4.18   A Good Design That Satisfies Almost All Requirements

4.18, the `Visualization` class is responsible for managing the `SimpleContent` objects and the `VisualizationView` (which is a specialization of the `JComponent` class) is responsible for their presentation. In addition to making each class cohesive, this design also gives us the ability to have multiple 'views' associated with a single model, which gives us the ability to present the same visual content in multiple `VisualComponent` objects at the same time. That is, this design satisfies part of Requirement F4.4 on page 88. It does not, however, completely satisfy the requirement because the 'views' cannot have different capabilities/properties. To completely satisfy this requirement one must be able to 'enhance' objects in the `VisualizationView` class.

   One obvious way to 'enhance' `VisualizationView` objects is to create specializations of the `VisualizationView` class. For example, one might include `ScaledVisualizationView` and `PartialVisualizationView` classes in the system. This is illustrated in Figure 4.19 on the next page. While this is not a terrible design, it is less than ideal. In particular, it would be nice to be able to 'enhance' individual `VisualizationView` objects at runtime. For example, an application that supports picture-in-picture needs to be able to scale an existing `VisualizationView` object.

   One good way to do this is to use the strategy pattern. That is, one can have a class that contains the presentation logic but does not extend the `JComponent` class. Specifically, as illustrated in Figure 4.20 on the following page, the collection management functions are put in a `Visualization` class, the GUI functions are put in a `VisualizationView` class (that extends the `JComponent` class), and the presentation functions are put in classes that implement the `VisualizationRenderer` interface. This design includes three concrete strategies as examples. The `PlainVisualizationRenderer` class simply clears the background of the `VisualizationView` and then renders the `SimpleContent` objects contained in the `Visualization` object, the `ScaledVisualizationRenderer` class uses a coordinate transform to scale all of the visual content (e.g., for use in a 'picture-in-picture' application), and the `PartialVisualizationRenderer` translates the coordinate system (e.g., for use in a diptych application). The only real shortcoming of this design is that a `VisualizationView` object can use only a single strategy at a time. Thus, if one wanted to create an application that supports

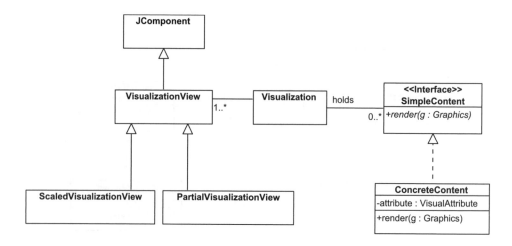

Figure 4.19 'Enhancing' the View with Specialization

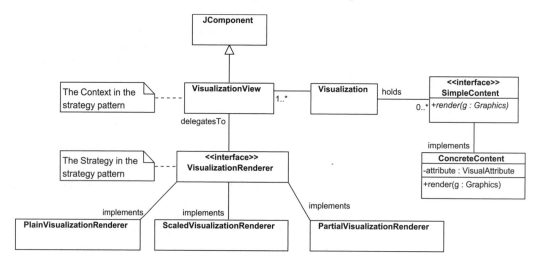

Figure 4.20 A Design That Uses the Strategy Pattern

zooming (which must be able to show part of a view and scale it at the same time), one would need to create a `ZoomingVisualizationRenderer` that includes the capabilities of both the `ScaledVisualizationRenderer` and the `PartialVisualizationRenderer`. This kind of code duplication can be avoided using the decorator pattern.

 A design that uses the decorator pattern in this way is illustrated in Figure 4.21. What's important about this design is that one could decorate a `PartialVisualizationRenderer` with a `ScaledVisualizationRenderer` and wind up with an object that provides all of the desired functionality.[7]

---

[7]Note that one could, in principle, use the decorator pattern without the strategy pattern. This is difficult to apply in this case because the `VisualizationView` class specializes a 'library' class (i.e., the `JComponent` class).

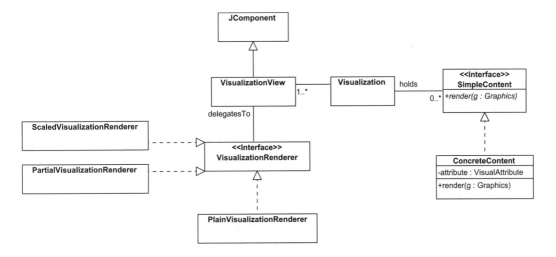

Figure 4.21 The Best Design

Implementing the Design

Implementing this design is relatively straightforward. A natural place to begin is with the SimpleContent interface in the visual.statik package.[8]

```
package visual.statik;

import java.awt.*;

public interface SimpleContent
{
    public abstract void render(Graphics g);
}
```

An Aside: Qualified Names

Though it isn't discussed often, it can be very difficult to find names that are both descriptive and short when designing large class hierarchies. This problem is exacerbated in domains, like multimedia, in which the specializations have a natural categorization.

Imagine you are designing a collection framework that is going to include multiple implementations of each collection. So, for example, you might have a List interface and one

---

While one could have decorators both extend and decorate VisualizationView objects, it is cumbersome to do so because of the number of methods in the JComponent class that must be delegated.

[8]visual.static can't be used because static is a reserved word in Java.

implementation that uses a linked data structure and another that uses a contiguous data structure. Similarly, you might have `Queue` and `Stack` interfaces and linked and contiguous implementations of them as well.

One possible naming convention is to use the data structure as a prefix. In this case you would have `LinkedList` and `ContiguousList` implement `List`, `LinkedQueue` and `ContiguousQueue` implement `Queue`, and `LinkedStack` and `ContiguousStack` implement `Stack`. Given that collection frameworks can be quite large, it probably also makes sense to put the different implementations in different packages. Then, you would have a `collections` package that contains the interfaces and two sub-packages, `collections.linked` and `collections.contiguous`, that contain the classes.

Alternatively, you could use the package name to fully qualify the class name. In this case you would have the same three packages organized the same way, but the classes would not include the prefixes. So, you would have `List`, `Queue`, and `Stack` interfaces in `collections`; `List`, `Queue`, and `Stack` classes in `linked`; and `List`, `Queue`, and `Stack` classes in `contiguous`.

If you want to use both implementations in the same class, the resulting code looks very similar in both cases. For example, consider the following side-by-side fragments:

```
import contiguous.ContiguousList;        import contiguous.List;
import linked.LinkedList;                import linked.List;


ContiguousList    receivable;            contiguous.List    receivable;
LinkedList        payable;               linked.List        payable;
payable    = new LinkedList();           payable    = new linked.List();
receivable = new ContiguousList();       receivable = new contiguous.List();
```

However, if you want to use only one implementation, say the linked implementation, the resulting code looks different with the two approaches. For example, consider the following side-by-side fragments:

```
import linked.LinkedList;                import linked.List;

LinkedList        payable;               List               payable;
payable    = new LinkedList();           payable    = new List();
```

Notice that the omission of the prefixes allows for a higher level of abstraction when desired. That is, one need not identify the data structure being used to implement the `List`. For this reason, this book does not use prefixes. Instead, when necessary, it uses fully qualified names in which the package name provides the same kind of information. So, for example, this book will have `visual.statik.sampled.Content` and `visual.statik.described.Content` classes.

The `Visualization` class has an ordered collection of `SimpleContent` objects[9] as well as an ordered collection of `VisualizationView` objects.

```
package visual;

import java.awt.*;
import java.awt.event.*;
import java.util.*;
import java.util.concurrent.CopyOnWriteArrayList;

import visual.statik.SimpleContent;

public class Visualization
{
    private   CopyOnWriteArrayList<SimpleContent>  content;
    private   LinkedList<VisualizationView>        views;

    public Visualization()
    {
        content = new CopyOnWriteArrayList<SimpleContent>();
        views   = new LinkedList<VisualizationView>();

        views.addFirst(createDefaultView());
    }
}
```

The collection of `SimpleContent` objects is ordered to satisfy Requirement F4.3 on page 88. The collection of `VisualizationView objects` is ordered so that the 'views' can be z-ordered as well, if necessary.

To satisfy Requirement N4.6, the collection of `SimpleContent` objects must be thread safe since it may be accessed from multiple threads (e.g., both the event dispatch thread and the main thread). The collection of `VisualizationView` objects, on the other hand, is only likely to be accessed from one thread since all such objects are likely to be created when the application is started.

To satisfy Requirements F4.1 and F4.2, the `Visualization` class has the ability to add a `SimpleContent` object, clear all `SimpleContent` objects, remove a `SimpleContent` object, and obtain an `Iterator`.

```
    public void add(SimpleContent r)
    {
        if (!content.contains(r))
```

---

[9]One might want to use a spatial data structure (e.g., a *quadtree*) for the collection of `SimpleContent` objects to facilitate spatial searches. See, for example, Samet (2006).

```
        {
            content.add(r);
            repaint();
        }
    }

    public void clear()
    {
        content.clear();
    }

    public Iterator<SimpleContent> iterator()
    {
        return content.iterator();
    }

    public void remove(SimpleContent r)
    {
        if (content.remove(r)) repaint();
    }
```

In addition, the Visualization class has the ability to move SimpleContent to the 'front' or the 'back', which controls whether they will be rendered last (and, hence, in front of all other SimpleContent) or first (and, hence, behind all other SimpleContent).

```
    public void toBack(SimpleContent r)
    {
        boolean         removed;

        removed = content.remove(r);
        if (removed)
        {
            content.add(r);
        }
    }

    public void toFront(SimpleContent r)
    {
        boolean         removed;

        removed = content.remove(r);
        if (removed)
```

```
    {
        content.add(0, r);
    }
}
```

The Visualization class also has methods for managing the VisualizationView objects. This includes the ability to add and remove a view, and obtain an Iterator for the collection of VisualizationView objects. In addition, this class includes convenience methods to get and set the 'main' VisualizationView (for those applications that don't need a collection of VisualizationView objects).

```java
public void addView(VisualizationView view)
{
    views.addLast(view);
}

public VisualizationView getView()
{
    return views.getFirst();
}

public Iterator<VisualizationView> getViews()
{
    return views.iterator();
}

public void removeView(VisualizationView view)
{
    views.remove(view);
}

public void setView(VisualizationView view)
{
    views.removeFirst();
    views.addFirst(view);
}
```

Finally, the repaint() method in this class is used to tell each VisualizationView to start the rendering process.

```
   protected  void repaint()
   {
      Iterator<VisualizationView>   i;
      VisualizationView             view;

      i = views.iterator();
      while (i.hasNext())
      {
         view = i.next();
         view.repaint();
      }
   }
}
```

The VisualizationView class maintains a reference to its associated Visualization.

```
package visual;

import java.awt.*;
import java.awt.event.*;
import java.util.*;
import javax.swing.*;

import visual.statik.*;

public class       VisualizationView
       extends     JComponent
       implements MouseListener
{
    protected Visualization          model;
    protected VisualizationRenderer renderer;

    public VisualizationView(Visualization          model,
                             VisualizationRenderer renderer)
    {
       super();
       this.model    = model;
       this.renderer = renderer;
    }
}
```

Its paint() method calls its preRendering(), render(), and postRendering() methods, in that order. These methods simply delegate to the VisualizationRenderer that contains the real presentation logic.

```java
public void setRenderer(VisualizationRenderer renderer)
{
   this.renderer = renderer;
}

protected void postRendering(Graphics g)
{
   renderer.postRendering(g, model, this);
}

protected void preRendering(Graphics g)
{
   renderer.preRendering(g, model, this);
}

protected void render(Graphics g)
{
   renderer.render(g, model, this);
}
```

The logic in the PlainVisualizationRenderer is very simple. The preRendering() method clears the background. The render() method then delegates to each of the SimpleContent objects in the associated Visualization.

```java
public void render(Graphics        g,
                   Visualization    model,
                   VisualizationView view)
{

   Iterator<SimpleContent>   iter;
   SimpleContent             c;

   iter = model.iterator();
   while (iter.hasNext())
   {
      c  = iter.next();
      if (c != null) c.render(g);
   }
}
```

As an example of both coordinate transformations and a use of the preRendering() and postRendering() methods, it is useful to implement two decorators of VisualizationRenderer objects: the ScaledVisualizationRenderer and PartialVisualizationRender classes discussed above.

The ScaledVisualizationRenderer class scales the coordinate system so that all of its content fits in a given amount of space. So, when constructed, it needs to be told the full/'true' size of the content.

```java
package visual;

import java.awt.*;
import java.util.*;

public class       ScaledVisualizationRenderer
        implements VisualizationRenderer
{
    private double                 height, scaleX, scaleY, width;
    private VisualizationRenderer  decorated;

    public ScaledVisualizationRenderer(VisualizationRenderer decorated,
                                       double width, double height)
    {
        this.decorated = decorated;
        this.width     = width;
        this.height    = height;
    }

    public void render(Graphics          g,
                       Visualization     model,
                       VisualizationView view)
    {
        decorated.render(g, model, view);
    }
}
```

Before rendering the actual content, the coordinate system must be scaled based on the 'true' size of the content and the size of the GUI component. Note that this scaling will change the aspect ratio if necessary.

```java
    public void preRendering(Graphics          g,
                             Visualization     model,
                             VisualizationView view)
    {
        Dimension          size;
```

```
    Graphics2D          g2;

    g2   = (Graphics2D)g;
    size = view.getSize();
    scaleX = size.getWidth()  / width;
    scaleY = size.getHeight() / height;

    g2.scale(scaleX, scaleY);

    decorated.preRendering(g, model, view);
}
```

Then, after rendering, the coordinate system must be returned to its original scaling. (Note that the preRendering() method saved the scaling it used so that it could be reversed in the postRendering() method.)

```
public void postRendering(Graphics          g,
                          Visualization     model,
                          VisualizationView view)
{
    Graphics2D   g2;

    g2 = (Graphics2D)g;
    g2.scale(1.0/scaleX, 1.0/scaleY);

    decorated.postRendering(g, model, view);
}
```

The PartialVisualizationRenderer class translates the coordinate system so that only some of its content is visible. So, when constructed, it needs to be told the size of the translation (i.e., the upper-left-most point that will be visible after the translation).

```
package visual;

import java.awt.*;
import java.util.*;

public class      PartialVisualizationRenderer
      implements VisualizationRenderer
{
    private double                   x, y;
    private VisualizationRenderer    decorated;
```

```
    public PartialVisualizationRenderer(VisualizationRenderer decorated,
                                        double x, double y)
    {
        this.decorated = decorated;
        this.x         = x;
        this.y         = y;
    }

    public void render(Graphics          g,
                       Visualization     model,
                       VisualizationView view)
    {
        decorated.render(g, model, view);
    }
}
```

Before rendering the actual content, the coordinate system must be translated as follows:

```
    public void preRendering(Graphics          g,
                             Visualization     model,
                             VisualizationView view)
    {
        Graphics2D   g2;

        g2 = (Graphics2D)g;
        g2.translate(-x, -y);
        decorated.preRendering(g, model, view);
    }
```

Then, after rendering, the coordinate system must be translated back as follows:

```
    public void postRendering(Graphics          g,
                              Visualization     model,
                              VisualizationView view)
    {
        Graphics2D   g2;

        g2 = (Graphics2D)g;
        g2.translate(x, y);
        decorated.postRendering(g, model, view);
    }
```

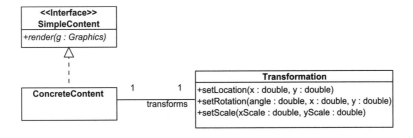

Figure 4.22   Adding Transformations Using a Helper

4.6.3   Adding Transformations

One thing is still missing from the above design—the ability to transform the visual content (i.e., functionality that satisfies Requirement F4.5 on page 89). As is always the case, there are several different ways to add this functionality to the existing design.

One alternative is to create a `Transformation` class that contains the attributes and methods necessary to transform one `SimpleContent` object into another. This is illustrated in Figure 4.22. The advantage of this design is that the classes are very cohesive. The shortcoming is conceptual—since `Transformation` objects are completely coupled to the `SimpleContent` objects that they operate on, there is no real reason to think of them as distinct objects. Indeed, this approach would necessitate passing both a `Transformation` and a `SimpleContent` object to any method that needed transformable content. Since this is both inconvenient and confusing, it seems better to try and encapsulate the necessary functionality in one place.

This leads to an obvious modification to the existing design—add the required methods to the `SimpleContent` interface. While this has some merit, some multimedia programs do not require transformations. Hence, this seems like 'overkill' and could be confusing in situations that do not require transformations.

Alternatively, one could create interfaces for each of the transformations as illustrated in Figure 4.23 on the following page. This seems pointless, however, since it is hard to imagine a multimedia program that would transform visual content without also rendering it.

Therefore, it makes much more sense to have each transformation interface extend the `SimpleContent` interface, as illustrated in Figure 4.24 on the next page. Since there are unlikely to be situations in which only one transformation is needed and since this makes it awkward to characterize objects that can be transformed in multiple ways, it makes much more sense to have a single `TransformableContent` interface. Given such an interface, there are two obvious alternatives to consider. In one, the content classes themselves implement this interface. In the other, the decorator pattern is used.

A design that uses the decorator pattern is illustrated in Figure 4.25. While the decorator pattern is very powerful and useful, it does not seem appropriate here. Specifically, it does not seem like there is any need to add capabilities to a particular content object rather than to the class of content objects. That is, in most multimedia programs either all content will

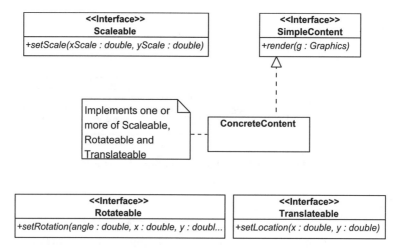

Figure 4.23   Adding Transformations Using Stand-Alone Interfaces

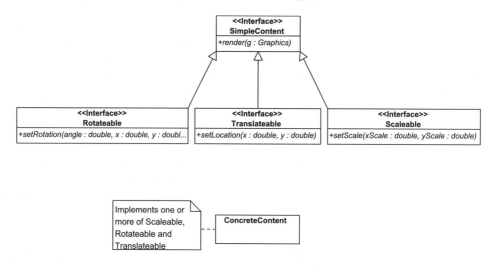

Figure 4.24   Adding Transformations Using Individual Interfaces

be transformable or none will. Hence, it seems more appropriate to use specialization, which leads to two final alternatives.

One way to use specialization is to have each type of content implement the `TransformableContent` interface as illustrated in Figure 4.26 on the following page. That is, one could add the necessary functionality to each class that implements the `TransformableContent` interface.

The other way to use specialization is to create an `AbstractTransformableContent` class that, if nothing else, maintains the necessary state variables. Since this design reduces code duplication and coupling with no loss of cohesiveness, it seems like the better of the two. Of course,

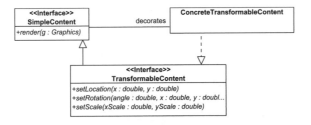

Figure 4.25   Adding Transformations Using the Decorator Pattern

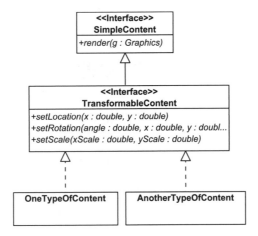

Figure 4.26   Adding Transformations Using Specialization

this naturally leads one to ask whether the `TransformableContent` interface is necessary. Since some types of content may not be able to extend the `AbstractTransformableContent` (e.g., because they extend another class), it makes sense to keep this interface. This leads to the design in Figure 4.27 on the next page.

The `TransformableContent` interface is, obviously, easy to implement.

```
package visual.statik;

import java.awt.*;
import java.awt.geom.*;

public interface TransformableContent extends SimpleContent
{
    public abstract void setLocation(double x, double y);

    public abstract void setRotation(double angle,
                                     double x, double y);
```

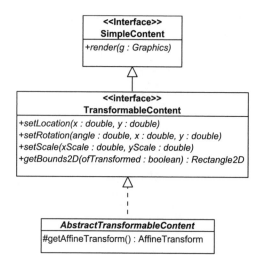

Figure 4.27   The Best Way to Add Transformations

```
    public abstract void setScale(double xScale, double yScale);

    public abstract Rectangle2D getBounds2D(boolean ofTransformed);
}
```

For convenience, the `AbstractTransformableContent` class includes a protected `getAffineTransform()` method that returns an `AffineTransform` object that encapsulates all of the transformation information. However, for efficiency reasons, one neither wants to create an `AffineTransform` object each time a transformation attribute is changed, nor keep it 'up-to-date.' Hence, `boolean` variables are used to keep track of whether the different state variables have changed since the last call to `getAffineTransform()`. This leads to an `AbstractTransformableContent` class with the following overall structure:

```
package visual.statik;

import java.awt.geom.*;

public abstract class AbstractTransformableContent
              implements TransformableContent
{
    protected boolean          relocated, rerotated, rescaled;
    protected double           angle;
    protected double           xScale, yScale;
    protected double           x, y;
    protected double           xRotation, yRotation;
```

```
public AbstractTransformableContent()
{
   setTransformationRequired(false);

   angle     = 0.0;
   xScale    = 1.0;
   yScale    = 1.0;
   x         = 0.0;
   y         = 0.0;
   xRotation = 0.0;
   yRotation = 0.0;
}
protected void setTransformationRequired(boolean required)
{
   relocated = required;
   rerotated = required;
   rescaled  = required;
}

protected boolean isTransformationRequired()
{
   return (relocated || rerotated || rescaled);
}
}
```

This class has the following getters:

```
public Rectangle2D getBounds2D()
{
   return getBounds2D(true);
}

public abstract Rectangle2D getBounds2D(boolean transformed);
```

and the following setters:

```
public void setLocation(double x, double y)
{
   this.x = x;
   this.y = y;
   relocated = true;
}
```

```
    public void setRotation(double angle, double x, double y)
    {
       this.angle = angle;
       xRotation  = x;
       yRotation  = y;
       rerotated  = true;
    }

    public void setScale(double xScale, double yScale)
    {
       this.xScale = xScale;
       this.yScale = yScale;
       rescaled    = true;
    }

    public void setScale(double scale)
    {
       setScale(scale, scale);
    }
```

The getAffineTransform() method creates an AffineTransform object that incorporates all of the transformation attributes that have changed since the last call. This is accomplished using the binary variables and the preConcatenate() method in the AffineTransform class as follows:

```
    protected AffineTransform getAffineTransform()
    {
       // We could use an object pool rather than local
       // variables.  Rough tests estimate that this method
       // would require 1/3 as much time with an object pool.
       AffineTransform     at, rotation, scaling, translation;
       Rectangle2D         bounds;

       // Start with the identity transform
       at = AffineTransform.getTranslateInstance(0.0, 0.0);

       if (rerotated)
       {
          bounds = getBounds2D(false);


          rotation = AffineTransform.getRotateInstance(angle,
                                         xRotation, yRotation);
          at.preConcatenate(rotation);
       }
```

```
    if (rescaled)
    {
        scaling = AffineTransform.getScaleInstance(xScale, yScale);
        at.preConcatenate(scaling);
    }

    if (relocated)
    {
        translation = AffineTransform.getTranslateInstance(x, y);
        at.preConcatenate(translation);
    }

    return at;
}
```

EXERCISES ··

1. Suppose one can produce 256 different amounts of light from each of a red, green, and blue source. How many different possible combinations of the three can one produce? What is interesting about this number given what you know about metameric substitution and the number of colors that people can perceive?

2. Suppose that you want to make one piece of visual content (e.g., a house) appear to be closer than another piece of visual content (e.g., a tree). Discuss three things that you can do (on a flat display in which all of the pixels are, actually, the same distance from the viewer) to make this happen? Will these same techniques work on a printer?

3. Understanding that the pixels on a display do not move, how can you make it appear that an object is moving across the screen? Will these same techniques work on a printer?

4. Define the term "translation" (as it relates to affine transforms).

5. Suppose you have a digital camera that has a sensor that is 2304×1728 pixels. What is the aspect ratio of this camera (in pixels)? How big will photographs be if they are printed on a laser printer with a resolution of 600 dots per inch (in both dimensions)?

6. Most high-definition television (HDTV) devices have a mode in which they display content using a rectangular grid of 1920×1080 pixels. How big are the pixels in a 1920×1080 HDTV that measures 32 inches on the diagonal? How big are the pixels in a 1920×1080 HDTV that measures 52 inches on the diagonal? Why will the image on the 52-inch HDTV be unpleasant if you sit 'too close'?

7. Why is it so common to use a color model in which red, green, and blue are the primary colors?

8. (*Library Research*) Explain how a black-and-white laser printer renders visual content.

9. Give two practical situations in which one might need to use clipping.

10. Suppose that the destination 'point' has the color $(R_d, G_d, B_d, \alpha_d) = (0.5, 0.0, 0.0, 0.0)$ and the source 'point' has the color $(R_s, G_s, B_s, \alpha_s) = (1.0, 1.0, 1.0, 1.0)$. What is the result of applying the source over destination rule to these points? Explain your answer. Specifically, describe (in words) the color of the source 'point,' destination 'point,' and the resulting 'point.'

11. Describe how the visual content system could support z-ordering without using an ordered collection of `SimpleContent` objects. What are the advantages and disadvantages of such an implementation?

12. Describe possible applications of a `ReflectedVisualizationRenderer`.

REFERENCES AND FURTHER READING

Gregory, R. L. 1997. *Eye and brain: The psychology of seeing.* Princeton, NJ: Princeton University Press.

Judd, D. B., and G. Wyszecki, 1975. *Color in business, science, and industry.* Hoboken, NJ: Wiley Interscience.

Samet, H. 2006. *Foundations of multidimensional and metric data structures.* Cambridge, MA: Morgan Kaufmann.

Serway, R. A., J. S. Faughn, C. Vuille, and C. A. Bennet. 2005. *College physics.* Boston: Brooks Cole.

Wandell, B. A. 1995. *Foundations of vision.* Sunderland, MA: Sinauer Associates.

Sampled Static Visual Content

5

The sampling of static visual content involves the sampling of both the color spectrum and space (usually in that order). The two are similar in that they both involve the discretization of continuous information. They are different in their dimensionality.

....

Definition 5.1 *Color sampling* is a process for converting from a continuous (infinite) set of colors to a discrete (finite) set of colors.

....

Such processes are sometimes called quantization schemes. The result of color sampling (i.e., the discrete set of colors) is often referred to as a *palette*, though one has to be somewhat careful because this term is sometimes used to describe the set of actual samples and other times is used to describe the set of all possible samples.

....

Definition 5.2 *Spatial sampling* is a process for discretizing space.

....

Hence, spatial sampling is sometimes called *spatial discretization*. Though there are many ways to perform spatial sampling, this book limits its attention to the plane and, in particular, with spatial sampling schemes that involve the use of a finite grid with cells of equal size. In essence, one places a regular grid on a planar surface and assigns a single color to each cell in the grid.

The result of color sampling and spatial sampling is a matrix/table of picture elements (or pixels), each of which contains a single color in the palette. Such a matrix/table is often called a *raster representation*. One example is illustrated in Figure 5.1 on the following page. In practice, sampled static visual content is usually created in one of two ways. In some cases, it is created using a *scanner* that samples from a source of some kind (e.g., a drawing or painting). In other cases, it is created on a computer by a person (who selects colors from a discrete set) using a pointing device of some kind (e.g., a mouse or a pen on a graphics tablet) that performs the spatial sampling. Two common examples of sampled static visual content are *bitmapped images* and *bitmapped fonts*.

This chapter begins with a small taste of what is to follow. It then discusses some important Java classes for working with sampled static visual content. Finally, it considers how to design and implement a sampled static visual content system. It is important to remember throughout this discussion that this chapter is concerned with how the content is **represented**. Sampled static visual content can be **displayed/presented** on both vector and raster output devices.

5.1 A 'Quick Start'

Many people interested in computing are impatient to 'get started.' So, before considering the design and implementation of a complete sampled static visual content system, it is worth

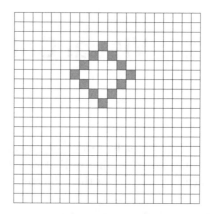

Figure 5.1   A Raster Representation

developing a simple app that will provide some instant gratification. For simplicity this app will use the badly designed visual content system illustrated in Figure 4.15 on page 89. Subsequent apps will use the well-designed system in Figure 4.21 on page 93 (i.e., the system that is used throughout the remainder of this book).

In Java, sampled static visual content is encapsulated by the abstract `Image` class. The easiest way to create an `Image` object is to read the sampled static visual content from a file. While there are several ways to do this, the most straightforward uses the `read()` method in the `ImageIO` class (which can be passed an `InputStream` object, `File` object, or a `URL` object).

There are several ways to render sampled static visual content in Java. The easiest is with the `drawImage()` method in the `Graphics` class. This method has four parameters: the `Image` to render, the coordinates at which to render the upper-left corner of the image, and an `ImageObserver` that can be used to track the reading process (which is not needed when the image is a 'resource' since the image will always be read completely).

This makes it very easy to create a concrete extension of a `JComponent` class, called `ImageCanvas`, that can render static sampled content. This class has the following overall structure:

```java
import java.awt.*;
import javax.swing.*;

public class ImageCanvas extends JComponent
{
    private Image        image;

    public ImageCanvas(Image image)
    {
        this.image = image;
    }
}
```

The paint() method uses the drawImage() method in the Graphics class to perform the rendering.

```
public void paint(Graphics g)
{
    Graphics2D         g2;

    // Cast the rendering engine appropriately
    g2 = (Graphics2D)g;

    // Render the image
    g2.drawImage(image,   // The Image to render
                0,        // The horizontal coordinate
                0,        // The vertical coordinate
                null);    // An ImageObserver
}
```

This class can be used in a simple ImageCanvasApp that has the following structure:

```
import java.awt.Image;
import java.io.*;
import javax.imageio.*;
import javax.swing.*;

import app.*;
import io.*;

public class    ImageCanvasApp
        extends AbstractMultimediaApp
{
    public ImageCanvasApp()
    {
        super();
    }
}
```

The init() method in the ImageCanvasApp class first gets the file name from parameter/argument "0" (see Section 3.2.1).

```
public void init()
{
    Image                   image;
    InputStream             is;
    ResourceFinder          finder;
    String                  name;

    // Get the file name
    name    = rootPaneContainer.getParameter("0");
    if (name == null) name = "scribble.png";
```

The init() method in the ImageCanvasApp class then uses a ResourceFinder (see Section 3.2.2 on page 63) to locate the 'file' containing the sampled static visual content and the ImageIO class to read it into an Image object.

```
    // Construct a ResourceFinder
    finder = ResourceFinder.createInstance(this);

    // Read the image
    image   = null;
    try
    {
        is = finder.findInputStream(name);
        if (is != null)
        {
            image = ImageIO.read(is);
            is.close();
        }
    }
    catch (IOException io)
    {
        // image will be null
    }
```

Finally, the init() method in the ImageCanvasApp class creates an ImageCanvas, and adds the ImageCanvas to the content pane of the MultimediaRootPaneContainer.

```
    ImageCanvas              canvas;
    JPanel                   contentPane;

    // Create the component that will render the image
    canvas      = new ImageCanvas(image);
    canvas.setBounds(0,
                     0,
                     image.getWidth(null),
                     image.getHeight(null));

    // Add the ImageCanvas to the main window
    contentPane = (JPanel)rootPaneContainer.getContentPane();
    contentPane.add(canvas);
}
```

With this as an introduction, it is now possible to turn to a more complete discussion of sampled static visual content.

5.2 Encapsulating Sampled Static Visual Content

The most important child of the abstract `Image` class is the `BufferedImage` class. Unlike a `VolatileImage`, a `BufferedImage` will not lose its content,[1] and, unlike some other specializations of `Image`, the image data in a `BufferedImage` can be manipulated.

A `BufferedImage` consists of a `ColorModel` and a `Raster`. A `ColorModel` contains methods for translating a pixel value (i.e., the value contained in a particular grid cell) into color components, the details of which depend on the `ColorSpace` being used (e.g., RGB). A `Raster` contains the image data (i.e., the pixel values). A `WriteableRaster` is, loosely speaking, a `Raster` that can be modified.

A good way to see how these classes interact is to consider a method that copies a source `BufferedImage` into an empty destination `BufferedImage`.

```
private void copy(BufferedImage src, BufferedImage dst)
{
    ColorModel      dstColorModel, srcColorModel;
    int             dstRGB, height, srcRGB, width;
    int[]           dstColor, srcColor;
    Raster          srcRaster;

    width           = src.getWidth();
    height          = src.getHeight();
```

---

[1]The `VolatileImage` class manages hardware-accelerated offscreen images that can be lost at any time.

```
srcColorModel    = src.getColorModel();
srcRaster        = src.getRaster();
srcColor         = new int[4];

dstColorModel = dst.getColorModel();

for (int x=0; x<width; x++)
{
    for (int y=0; y<height; y++)
    {
        srcRGB = src.getRGB(x, y);
        srcColorModel.getComponents(srcRGB,srcColor,0);

        dstRGB = dstColorModel.getDataElement(srcColor,0);
        dst.setRGB(x, y, dstRGB);
    }
}
}
```

This method loops over all of the columns (from 0 to `width-1`) and rows (from 0 to `height-1`) in the grid. For each pixel, the `getRGB()` method returns the red, green, blue, and α values as a single `int` (each value occupying 2 bytes of the 8-byte `int`). The `getComponents()` method is then used to extract the components (into the empty array). The process is then reversed to set the pixel in the destination.

___

An Aside: Bit Masks

In the 'early' days of computing, when memory was at a premium, it was very common to pack multiple values into a single `int`. For example, a 16-bit representation of an `int` would be used to store 16 different boolean values. The different bits were set and retrieved using bitwise logical operators.

Though this is less common today, there are still situations in which this technique is both used and useful. One example is packing red, green, blue and α values into a single `int`. Since each channel often takes on values in the interval $[0, 255]$ each channel can be represented by 1 byte, and a 4-byte `int` can represent an entire color.

The individual channels can be retrieved from such an `int` by performing the bitwise 'and' operator with the *masks* AMASK = 0xFF000000, RMASK = 0x00FF0000, GMASK = 0x0000FF00, and BMASK = 0x000000FF. So, for example, given an `int` named `color`, the different channels can be retrieved as follows:

```
int    alpha, red, green, blue;

blue  = (color & BMASK);
green = (color & GMASK) >> 8;
```

```
red   = (color & GMASK) >> 16;
alpha = (color & GMASK) >> 24;
```

Note that the bit-shift operator is used to move each of the individual bytes into bits 0–7 (so that they will be in the interval $[0, 255]$ when treated as 8-byte int values).

Similarly, the channels can be set using the bitwise 'or' operator and shifting bits to the left. For example, assuming that alpha, red, green, and blue are all in the interval $[0, 255]$, they can be packed into the int named color as follows:

```
int   alpha, red, green, blue;

color = (alpha << 24) | (red << 16) |
        (green <<  8) | blue;
```

There are two aspects of the `Image` and `BufferedImage` class that provide a great deal of flexibility but are somewhat inconvenient. First, `BufferedImage` objects can vary in the number of channels (i.e., whether there is an α channel or not), the ordering of the channels (e.g., RGB vs. BGR), and the number of bytes/bits used for each channel. Second, though the `read()` method in the `ImageIO` class actually returns a `BufferedImage` object, not all images in Java are `BufferedImage` objects. Fortunately, it is fairly easy to 'render' any image into a `BufferedImage` of a particular type.

The first step in the process is to create an empty `BufferedImage` of the appropriate size and type (in this case, either RGB or αRGB).

```
int             type;
if (channels == 3) type = BufferedImage.TYPE_INT_RGB;
else               type = BufferedImage.TYPE_INT_ARGB;
```

The second step is to get a rendering engine (i.e., a `Graphics` object) that can be used to render into this `BufferedImage`.

```
BufferedImage      bi;
bi = null;
bi = new BufferedImage(image.getWidth(null),
                       image.getHeight(null),
                       type);
```

The final step in the process is to render the generic `Image` into the `BufferedImage` as follows:

```
Graphics2D            g2;
g2 = bi.createGraphics();
g2.drawImage(image, null, null);
```

While this process is straightforward, it would be both tedious and repetitive to include this code in every class that needs to work with an Image. Instead, it would be better to have a system that can

F5.1 Create a BufferedImage from an Image.

F5.2 Create a BufferedImage from a file containing an Image of any kind.

F5.3 Create either RGB or αRGB images.

Though there are many possible ways to design such a system, the factory-method pattern is clearly ideal. In other words, a good way to proceed is to include this functionality in an ImageFactory class (in the visual.statik.sampled package).

The createBufferedImage() method in the ImageFactory class includes the code discussed above.

```
public BufferedImage createBufferedImage(Image image,
                                         int    channels)
{
    int               type;
    if (channels == 3) type = BufferedImage.TYPE_INT_RGB;
    else               type = BufferedImage.TYPE_INT_ARGB;
    BufferedImage     bi;
    bi = null;
    bi = new BufferedImage(image.getWidth(null),
                           image.getHeight(null),
                           type);
    Graphics2D        g2;
    g2 = bi.createGraphics();
    g2.drawImage(image, null, null);
    return bi;
}
```

This class also has a method that creates a buffered image from the contents of a 'file.'

```
public BufferedImage createBufferedImage(String name,
                                         int channels)
{
```

```
BufferedImage    image, result;
InputStream      is;
int              imageType;


image = null;
is    = finder.findInputStream(name);

if (is != null)
{
    try
    {
        image    = ImageIO.read(is);
        is.close();
    }
    catch (IOException io)
    {
        image    = null;
    }
}

// Modify the type, if necessary
result = image;
if (image != null)
{
    imageType = image.getType();
    if (((channels == 3) &&
        (imageType != BufferedImage.TYPE_INT_RGB)) ||
        ((channels == 4) &&
        (imageType != BufferedImage.TYPE_INT_ARGB))    )
    {
        result = createBufferedImage(image, channels);
    }
}

return result;
}
```

This method first reads in a BufferedImage and then checks to determine whether it is the appropriate type. (The ResourceFinder named finder is created in the constructor.) If not, it uses the createBufferedImage() method to create a new BufferedImage.

5.3   Operating on Sampled Static Visual Content

Sampled static visual content can be operated on in a variety of different ways. Some of these operations can be performed 'in place,' and others require a destination (i.e., another raster that will contain the result). For the sake of simplicity, this book distinguishes between the source and the destination, even for operations that can be performed 'in place.'

In Java, single-input/single-output operations are typically performed by objects that implement the `BufferedImageOp` interface using the `public void BufferedImage filter(BufferedImage src, BufferedImage dst)` method. By convention, if this method is passed an existing `dst`, its pixels are 'filled in' by the operation. If `dst` is `null`, a new image is created and returned.

To illustrate, consider an `IdentityOp` class that implements the `BufferedImageOp` in the most trivial way, by creating a copy of the source image (using the `copy()` method discussed above). The first method in the interface, the `createCompatibleDestImage()` method, creates an empty destination image that is compatible with the source model. To do so, it must both create a 'copy' of the `ColorModel` and create a raster with the same dimensions. This is implemented as follows:

```
public BufferedImage createCompatibleDestImage(
                                    BufferedImage src,
                                    ColorModel    dstCM)
{
    BufferedImage      dst;
    int                height, width;
    WritableRaster     raster;


    if (dstCM == null) dstCM = src.getColorModel();

    height = src.getHeight();
    width  = src.getWidth();
    raster = dstCM.createCompatibleWritableRaster(width,
                                        height);

    dst = new BufferedImage(dstCM, raster,
                    dstCM.isAlphaPremultiplied(),
                    null);

    return dst;
}
```

The second method in the interface, the `filter(BufferedImage src, BufferedImage dst)` method, performs the single-input/single-output operation. For the `IdentityOp` it needs to copy the pixels (as in the earlier fragment).

```
public BufferedImage filter(BufferedImage src,
                            BufferedImage dst)
{
    // Construct the destination image if one isn't provided
    if (dst == null)
    {
        dst = createCompatibleDestImage(src,
                                        src.getColorModel());
    }

    // Copy the source to the destination
    copy(src, dst);

    // Return the destination (in case it is new)
    return dst;
}
```

The other three methods in the BufferedImageOp interface are the getBounds2D() method that returns a rectangle that contains the destination image, the getPoint2D() method that returns the point in the destination image that corresponds to a given point in the source image, and the getRenderingHints() method that returns the java.awt.RenderingHints object that should be used when rendering the destination image. For the IdentifyOp class, they are implemented as follows:

```
public Rectangle2D getBounds2D(BufferedImage src)
{
    Raster        raster;

    raster = src.getRaster();

    return raster.getBounds();
}

public Point2D getPoint2D(Point2D srcPt, Point2D dstPt)
{
    if (dstPt == null) dstPt = (Point2D)srcPt.clone();
    dstPt.setLocation(srcPt);

    return dstPt;
}

public RenderingHints getRenderingHints()
```

```
    {
        return null;
    }
```

Of course, the `IdentityOp` is not at all interesting in and of itself. However, it does provide some of the functionality required by other operations. For example, consider a `GrayExceptOp` class that converts a color image to a gray scale image, while preserving one particular color. This class needs an attribute to store the color that is being preserved/highlighted.

```java
import java.awt.*;
import java.awt.geom.*;
import java.awt.image.*;

import math.*;

public class GrayExceptOp extends IdentityOp
{
    private int[]              highlightColor;

}
```

Now some care is needed. The phrase "a particular color" probably does not mean one RGB combination. Instead, it probably means all of the colors that are close to one RGB combination. So, this class needs an `areSimilar()` method that can be used to determine if two 3-vectors are close enough to each other to be classified as similar. This method will determine whether two colors are close enough to each other using the rectilinear (or Manhattan) metric, though many other metrics could also be used.[2]

An Aside: Metrics

The distance between two numbers (i.e., scalars) is traditionally defined as the absolute value of the difference between them. Unfortunately, a color is not represented by a single number, it is represented by a vector with three elements. When dealing with vectors, there is no 'traditional' definition of distance. That is, there are many reasonable distances (or *metrics*).

---

[2]Colors are sometimes compared using spherical coordinates rather than Euclidean coordinates. Using this approach, colors are said to be similar if they are on the same ray and the distance between them is the distance between them along the ray.

A metric is a function, d, that satisfies the following properties for any two n-dimensional vectors of real numbers, a and b:

$$d(a, b) \geq 0$$

$$d(a, b) = 0 \text{ iff } a = b$$

$$d(a, b) = d(b, a)$$

and satisfies the following property for any three n-dimensional vectors of real numbers, a, b, and c:

$$d(a, b) \leq d(a, c) + d(c, b) \text{ (triangle inequality)}$$

Most people are familiar with the Euclidean metric, which is the square root of the sum of the squares of the component differences. Letting R_i, G_i, and B_i denote the red, green, and blue component of color i, respectively, the Euclidean distance between two colors, d_E, can be written as

$$d_E = \sqrt{(R_1 - R_2)^2 + (G_1 - G_2)^2 + (B_1 - B_2)^2}.$$

The rectilinear (or Manhattan) distance, on the other hand, is the sum of the absolute values of the component differences. That is,

$$d_M = |R_1 - R_2| + |G_1 - G_2| + |B_1 - B_2|.$$

Interestingly, even though this is a seemingly simple task, there are two ways to proceed.

 The most obvious design includes the algorithm for calculating the rectilinear distance in the `areSimilar()` method. Though this would obviously work, it is inflexible. That is, the only way to change the metric is to modify the `areSimilar()` method.

 A better design uses the strategy pattern. In this case, this involves the creation of a `Metric` interface and a `RectilinearMetric` class. The `GrayExceptOp` method then has a `Metric` attribute that the `areSimilar()` method uses. The advantage of this design is that, in the future, someone can create an alternative `Metric` and use it in the `GrayExceptOp` without making any changes to that class.

The `Metric` interface is defined as follows:

```
package math;

public interface Metric
{
    public abstract double distance(double[] x, double[] y);
}
```

Then, as an example, a `RectilinearMetric` class is implemented as follows:

```
package math;

public class       RectilinearMetric
       implements Metric
{
    public double distance(double[] x, double[] y)
    {
        double  result;
        int     n;

        result = 0.0;
        n      = Math.min(x.length, y.length);

        for (int i=0; i<n; i++)
        {
            result += Math.abs(x[i]-y[i]);
        }

        return result;
    }
}
```

With this design in mind, two explicit value constructors are included in the `GrayExceptOp` class, one that is passed a color and a `Metric` and another that is just passed a color.

```
    public GrayExceptOp(int r, int g, int b)
    {
        this(r, g, b, new RectilinearMetric());
    }

    public GrayExceptOp(int r, int g, int b, Metric metric)
    {
        highlightColor      = new int[3];
        highlightColor[0] = r;
        highlightColor[1] = g;
        highlightColor[2] = b;

        this.metric = metric;
    }
```

The `areSimilar()` method is now implemented as follows:

```
private boolean areSimilar(int[] a, int[] b)
{
    boolean         result;
    double          distance;

    for (int i=0; i<3; i++)
    {
        x[i] = a[i];
        y[i] = b[i];
    }

    result   = false;
    distance = metric.distance(x, y);

    if (distance <= TOLERANCE) result = true;

    return result;
}
```

There are two details to note about this implementation. First, because the `Metric` interface uses arrays of `double` values, this method must copy the `int` color arrays into `double` arrays. (Though Java will automatically widen an `int` to a `double`, it will not automatically widen an `int[]` to a `double[]`.) Second, this implementation ignores the α channel since it is irrelevant to the task at hand.

Finally, the `filter()` method must be implemented. This method must get a pixel from the source and determine whether it is close to the color being preserved. If it is, it must copy the pixel. If it isn't, it must create a gray value that has the same luminance as the pixel in the origin.

Given the way colors are being modeled, creating the appropriate gray color is relatively easy. Since it must have the same luminance, and the perceived luminance is based on the total amount of ρ, β, and γ signals transmitted to the brain, the sum of the three components must be the same. Letting c denote the value 'in color' and g denote the value 'in gray' (aka black and white, respectively), the following constraint must be satisfied:

$$R_g + G_g + B_g = R_c + G_c + B_c. \tag{5.1}$$

In addition, all grays satisfy the following:

$$R_g = G_g = B_g. \tag{5.2}$$

Combining (5.1) and (5.2) it is easy to see that

$$R_g = G_g = B_g = (R_c + G_c + B_c)/3. \tag{5.3}$$

That is, the red, green, and blue component of the destination pixel must equal the mean of the red, green, and blue components, respectively, of the source pixel. This is implemented as follows:

```java
public BufferedImage filter(BufferedImage src,
                            BufferedImage dest)
{
    ColorModel      destColorModel, srcColorModel;
    int             grayRGB, highlightRGB, srcRGB, srcHeight, srcWidth;
    int[]           gray, srcColor;
    Raster          srcRaster;

    srcWidth      = src.getWidth();
    srcHeight     = src.getHeight();
    srcColorModel = src.getColorModel();
    srcRaster     = src.getRaster();
    srcColor      = new int[4];
    gray          = new int[4];

    if (dest == null) dest = createCompatibleDestImage(src, srcColorModel);

    destColorModel = dest.getColorModel();
    highlightRGB   = destColorModel.getDataElement(highlightColor, 0);

    for (int x=0; x<srcWidth; x++)
    {
        for (int y=0; y<srcHeight; y++)
        {
            srcRGB = src.getRGB(x, y);
            srcColorModel.getComponents(srcRGB, srcColor, 0);

            if (areSimilar(srcColor, highlightColor))
            {
                dest.setRGB(x, y, highlightRGB);
            }
            else
            {
                gray[0]=(srcColor[0]+srcColor[1]+srcColor[2])/3;
                gray[1]=gray[0];
                gray[2]=gray[0];
                grayRGB=destColorModel.getDataElement(gray,0);
                dest.setRGB(x, y, grayRGB);
            }
        }
    }
    return dest;
}
```

It is now time to consider some more interesting operations.

$$-1\ 0\ +1$$

$$\begin{matrix} -1 \\ 0 \\ +1 \end{matrix}$$

Figure 5.2   A 3 × 3 Convolution Kernel

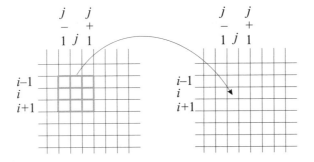

Figure 5.3   Obtaining One Pixel in the Destination Image

5.3.1   Convolutions

In its most general usage, a convolution is a product of two functions. As it is being used in this book:

....

Definition 5.3 A *convolution* is a way of calculating the color of a pixel in a destination image from that same pixel and its neighbors in a source image.

....

The way in which the neighboring pixels in the source are used to calculate the color of the pixel in the destination is specified using a kernel. A kernel contains weights that are applied to the source pixels to obtain the destination pixels. Since the source and destination pixels can be thought of as a grid, it makes sense to think of the kernel as a grid as well. The structure of a 3 × 3 convolution kernel is illustrated in Figure 5.2.

The size of the kernel determines the size of the neighborhood that is used when determining the value if a destination pixel. Figure 5.3 illustrates part of a source image on the left and part of a destination image on the right, with a 3 × 3 convolution kernel centered on a particular pixel in the source.

The color in the destination pixel is calculated using the weights in the kernel and the colors in the appropriate part of the source. Letting $s_{i,j}$ denote the value in source pixel (i,j), $k_{r,c}$ denote the value in element (r,c) of the kernel, and $d_{i,j}$ denote the value in destination pixel (i,j), a 3 × 3 spatial convolution can be defined as follows:

$$d_{i,j} = \sum_{r=-1}^{1} \sum_{c=-1}^{1} s_{i+r,j+c} k_{r,c}. \tag{5.4}$$

1	1	1	1
1	0	1	1
1	0	1	1
1	1	1	1

Figure 5.4 The Source Image

.5	.5	0
0	0	0
0	0	0

Figure 5.5 The Kernel

.5 1	.5 1	0 1	1
0 1	0 0	0 1	1
0 1	0 0	0 1	1
1	1	1	1

Figure 5.6 Getting Started

Thus, for a 3×3 kernel, nine abstract multiplications and additions[3] must be performed to determine each pixel in the destination.

The easiest way to understand how convolutions work is to use a 'gray scale' raster representation in which 0 denotes black, 1 denotes white, and numbers in between represent different gray values. Now, suppose the 4×4 source image has two black pixels as illustrated in Figure 5.4 and that the kernel shown in Figure 5.5 is applied.

To calculate the value of the pixel in the second row and column of the destination image, center the kernel on the corresponding row and column in the source image as shown in Figure 5.6. Then multiply each kernel value by the corresponding pixel value and add all of the results. This yields $.5 \cdot 1 + .5 \cdot 1 + 0 \cdot 1 + 0 \cdot 1 + 0 \cdot 0 + 0 \cdot 1 + 0 \cdot 1 + 0 \cdot 0 + 0 \cdot 1 = 1$, which becomes the pixel value in the destination. This is illustrated in Figure 5.7 on the next page.

To calculate the value of the pixel in the second row and third column of the destination image, center the kernel on the corresponding row and column in the source image and perform the nine multiplications and additions as illustrated in Figure 5.8 on the following page.

The calculation of the value of the pixel in the third row and second column is illustrated in Figure 5.9 on the next page and the calculation of the value of the pixel in the third row and third column is illustrated in Figure 5.10 on the following page.

[3]The term "abstract multiplications and additions" is used because the value in each pixel may not be a scalar, it may be a vector (for example, containing the red, green, and blue channels).

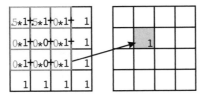

Figure 5.7   The First Pixel

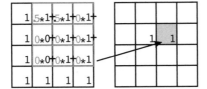

Figure 5.8   The Second Pixel

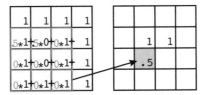

Figure 5.9   The Third Pixel

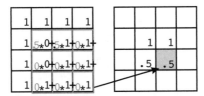

Figure 5.10   The Fourth Pixel

Notice that one cannot use this approach for the edge pixels in the destination since the convolution kernel would 'hang off' the source image. So, one must use some other approach. One common approach is to make the edge pixels a predefined color, another is to copy the source pixels (often called a "no op"). Using the latter approach yields the final destination image shown in Figure 5.11 on the next page.

For multichannel color models (e.g., RGB) the same basic approach is used but each pixel is processed channel by channel. Thus, for the RGB color model, each pixel in the destination image requires 27 multiplications and 27 additions when using a 3×3 kernel.

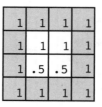

Figure 5.11 The Result

One boring but understandable kernel is the identity kernel:

0	0	0
0	1	0
0	0	0

It should be clear that this kernel copies the source image into the destination.

At this point it is natural to wonder why anyone would possibly want to do this. However, it turns out that, with the proper choice of kernel, convolutions can be very useful. One interesting example is the blurring kernel, which can be used, for example, to provide a depth cue.

As discussed in Chapter 4, visual content appears blurry when the lens does not focus the rays of light entering the pupil properly and a single 'point' is sensed by multiple photoreceptors on the retina. Hence, to blur sampled visual content, each pixel in the source image must be 'spread' over multiple pixels in the destination image. This can be accomplished with a kernel like the following:

1/9	1/9	1/9
1/9	1/9	1/9
1/9	1/9	1/9

After applying the blurring kernel, each pixel in the destination image will be the arithmetic mean of the corresponding pixel in the source image and its immediate neighbors. Again, the impact of this can be illustrated using a gray scale image. In the example below, the source image contains a small diagonal black line. Applying the blurring kernel results in a destination image with a gray line that has been 'spread' (or blurred) into a square, as shown in Figure 5.12.

Figure 5.12 Blurring

The blurring kernel is an example of a *symmetric* kernel, because the terms above the main diagonal are a reflection of the terms below the main diagonal. It is also an example of a *low-pass* kernel because it attenuates large values.

Another interesting example of a symmetric kernel is the edge-detection kernel. For example:

0	-1	0
-1	4	-1
0	-1	0

In this case, if a source pixel is identical to its vertical and horizontal neighbors, then the resulting destination pixel will be black. To see this, suppose the value of the source pixel (and its neighbors) is given by x. Then, the value of the corresponding destination pixel is $-x + -x + 4x + -x + -x = 0$. On the other hand, if the source pixel is brighter than its vertical and horizontal neighbors, the resulting destination pixel will be bright. Hence, this filter will tend to highlight pixels that are brighter than their neighbors (i.e., edges) and blacken those that are similar to their neighbors.[4]

If one 'adds' an 'edge-detected image' to the source, one gets an image that has sharper edges than the original (without changing the off-edge pixels since adding black to a pixel does not change it). Rather than trying to 'add' images, one can add the edge-detection kernel to the identity kernel (element by element) and achieve the same effect. The resulting sharpening kernel is

0	-1	0
-1	5	-1
0	-1	0

The sharpening kernel is symmetric, but it is an example of a *high-pass* kernel. That is, it tends to emphasize discrepancies. It is also an example of a kernel in which the elements sum to a value larger than 1. As a result, the destination image will be brighter than the source.

In Java, convolutions are encapsulated by the `ConvolveOp` class (which implements the `BufferedImageOp` interface, and spatial convolution kernels are encapsulated by the `Kernel` class). Since multimedia programs are likely to use large numbers of these objects and use them frequently, the system must

★2 **F5.4** Create different `BufferedImageOp` objects.

N5.5 Conserve the amount of memory used by kernels.

Again, the factory-method pattern can help.

At a high level of abstraction, the question arises of whether to create a `ConvolutionFactory` or a `BufferedImageOpFactory`. Since the user of an object that implements the `BufferedImageOp` interface does not need to know the actual class of the object,

---

[4]Formally, the edge-detection kernel is the negative of the 2-dimensional Laplacian. That is, it is the sum of the second-order partial derivatives in the horizontal and vertical directions.

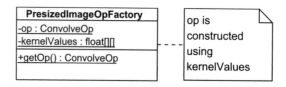

Figure 5.13   An Inflexible Factory for Creating `BufferedImageOp` Objects

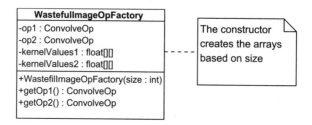

Figure 5.14   A Wasteful Factory for Creating `BufferedImageOp` Objects

there is no reason for him or her to have to know what kind of factory to use. Hence, it is better to create a `BufferedImageOpFactory`.

 One design for such a system is illustrated in Figure 5.13. This design satisfies Requirement N5.5 on the page before by making the arrays containing the kernel values static (i.e., belong to the class). The limitation of this design is that all of the kernels have to be pre-sized.

 A better design is illustrated in Figure 5.14. In this design, the constructor is passed the size and uses it to construct appropriately sized arrays to hold the kernel values. The principal shortcoming of this design is that Requirement N5.5 on the page before is not satisfied. In particular, note that one factory must be constructed for each size and each must allocate memory for all of the kernel values, even those that are never used. In addition, this design may be difficult to understand in some cases. While all `ConvolveOp` objects are size-dependent, this is not true of all objects that implement the `BufferedImageOp`. Hence, if methods that construct other types of `BufferedImageOp` objects need to be added, the size will play no role and will be quite confusing.

 A good design is illustrated in Figure 5.15 on the following page. This design keeps a pool of `BufferedImageOp` objects of each type, organized by size. The factory methods first check the pools to see whether an appropriate object has already been created. If so, it is returned; if not, an object is created, added to the pool, and returned. This helps satisfy Requirement N5.5 on the page before but, in and of itself, it is not enough. In particular, note that someone could construct multiple `BufferedImageOpFactory` objects. To ensure that that doesn't happen, this design also makes use of the singleton pattern.

 This design is partially implemented in the following class that includes methods for creating blurring operations and edge-detection operations. It has a method that gets the values for each kernel. The details of these methods are not important. The methods that are important

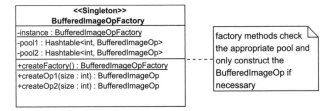

Figure 5.15 A Good `BufferedImageOpFactory`

are those that use the kernel values to create `ConvolveOp` objects. The method that creates the blurring op is implemented as follows:

```
public ConvolveOp createBlurOp(int size)
{
    ConvolveOp      op;
    float           denom;
    float[]         kernelValues;
    Integer         key;

    key = new Integer(size);
    op  = blurOps.get(key);
    if (op == null)
    {
        kernelValues = getBlurValues(size);

        op = new ConvolveOp(new Kernel(size,size,kernelValues),
                            ConvolveOp.EDGE_NO_OP,
                            null);

        blurOps.put(key, op);
    }

    return op;
}
```

The method that creates the edge detection op is implemented as follows:

```
public ConvolveOp createEdgeDetectionOp(int size)
{
    ConvolveOp      op;
    float           denom;
    float[]         kernelValues;
```

```
int            center;
Integer        key;

key = new Integer(size);
op  = edgeOps.get(key);
if (op == null)
{
    kernelValues = getEdgeValues(size);

    op = new ConvolveOp(new Kernel(size,size,kernelValues),
                        ConvolveOp.EDGE_NO_OP,
                        null);

    edgeOps.put(key, op);
}

return op;
}
```

Unfortunately, this implementation is very repetitive and, as a result, difficult to maintain. That is, the `createBlurOp()` and `createEdgeDetectionOp()` methods are very similar. They vary only in the object pool that is used and the method that is used to get the values in the convolution kernel. If one were to add factory methods to create more convolution operations, they would all be very similar.

This shortcoming (i.e., the repetitiveness of the factory methods) can be overcome by using the command pattern. This would allow one to pass the method used to get the kernel values (along with the pool) to a 'generic' `createOp()` method. While this would work, it seems overly complicated and would result in a large number of classes.

This shortcoming can also be overcome using an enumerated type. Specifically, one can implement a 'generic' `createOp()` method that is passed an element of the `Convolutions` enumeration that can be used both to get the appropriate object pool and the appropriate kernel values. This is illustrated in the following fragment:

```
private ConvolveOp createOp(Convolutions type, int size)
{
    ConvolveOp                         op;
    Hashtable<Integer, ConvolveOp>     pool;
    Integer                            key;

    key  = new Integer(size);
    pool = convolutionPools.get(type);
    op   = pool.get(key);
```

```
      if (op == null)
      {
          op = new ConvolveOp(new Kernel(size,size,
                                      type.getKernelValues(size)),
                                      ConvolveOp.EDGE_NO_OP,
                                      null);
          pool.put(key, op);
      }

      return op;
   }
```

The most obvious way to implement this enumerated type is to have a `getKernelValues()` method that uses a `switch` statement to determine the return values based on the enumerated value (e.g., BLUR, EDGE). This is illustrated in the following fragment (that omits some private methods):

```
package visual.statik.sampled;

enum UnmaintainableConvolutions
{
   BLUR,
   EDGE;

   float[] getKernelValues(int size)
   {
      switch (this)
      {
         case BLUR:      return getBlurValues(size);
         case EDGE:      return getEdgeValues(size);

         default:        return getIdentityValues(size);
      }
   }
}
```

The problem with this implementation is that it is difficult to maintain. In particular, every time a new convolution is added (e.g., EMBOSS or SHARPEN) a `case` must be added to the `switch` statement in the `getKernelValues()` method, and there is no way to force this to happen. That is, one can add an enumerated value and forget to add the corresponding `case`, and this problem will not be caught by the compiler.

The implementation that follows gets around this using *constant specific methods*. That is, the `getKernelValues()` method in this implementation is abstract, and each value in the enumeration includes an implementation in the declaration.

```java
package visual.statik.sampled;

enum Convolutions
{
    BLUR {float[] getKernelValues(int size)
          {
              return getBlurValues(size);
          }
         },
    EDGE {float[] getKernelValues(int size)
          {
              return getEdgeValues(size);
          }
         },
    EMBOSS {float[] getKernelValues(int size)
          {
              return getEmbossValues(size);
          }
         },
    IDENTITY {float[] getKernelValues(int size)
          {
              return getIdentityValues(size);
          }
         },
    SHARPEN {float[] getKernelValues(int size)
          {
              return getSharpenValues(size);
          }
         };


    abstract float[] getKernelValues(int size);
}
```

The concrete methods can then be added easily. For example, the `getBlurValues()` method is implemented as follows:

```
private static float[] getBlurValues(int size)
{
    float       denom;
    float[]     result;

    denom  = (float)(size*size);
    result = new float[size*size];

    for (int row=0; row<size; row++)
        for (int col=0; col<size; col++)
            result[indexFor(row,col,size)] = 1.0f/denom;

    return result;
}
```

Similarly, the `getEdgeValues()` method is implemented as follows:

```
private static float[] getEdgeValues(int size)
{
    float[]     result;
    int         center;

    center = size/2;
    result = new float[size*size];

    result[indexFor(center-1, center  , size)] = -1.0f;
    result[indexFor(center  , center-1, size)] = -1.0f;
    result[indexFor(center  , center  , size)] =  4.0f;
    result[indexFor(center  , center+1, size)] = -1.0f;
    result[indexFor(center+1, center  , size)] = -1.0f;

    return result;
}
```

Both of these methods use the following private method that converts a 2-dimensional index (i.e., row and column) into a 1-dimensional index.

```
private static int indexFor(int row, int col, int size)
{
    return row*size + col;
}
```

With this enumerated type, the remainder of the `BufferedImageOpFactory` can be implemented. First, consider the structure around the `createOp()` method. This involves the declaration and construction of a `Hashtable` of `Hashtable` objects to hold the different object pools (keyed on the `Convolution` and the size, respectively).

```java
package visual.statik.sampled;

import java.awt.*;
import java.awt.color.*;
import java.awt.geom.*;
import java.awt.image.*;
import java.util.*;

public class BufferedImageOpFactory
{
    private ConvolveOp createOp(Convolutions type, int size)
    {
        ConvolveOp                      op;
        Hashtable<Integer, ConvolveOp>  pool;
        Integer                         key;

        key  = new Integer(size);
        pool = convolutionPools.get(type);
        op   = pool.get(key);

        if (op == null)
        {
            op = new ConvolveOp(new Kernel(size,size,
                                     type.getKernelValues(size)),
                                ConvolveOp.EDGE_NO_OP,
                                null);
            pool.put(key, op);
        }

        return op;
    }
}
```

Next consider the visible methods that can be used to construct the `ConvolveOp` objects. Obviously, they simply call the `createOp()` method, passing the appropriate parameters. For example, the `createBlurOp()` method is implemented as follows:

```
public ConvolveOp createBlurOp(int size)
{
    return createOp(Convolutions.BLUR, size);
}
```

and the `createEdgeDetectionOp()` method is implemented as follows:

```
public ConvolveOp createEdgeDetectionOp(int size)
{
    return createOp(Convolutions.EDGE, size);
}
```

Some detailed design decisions used in this implementation warrant further discussion. First, notice that the factory methods in this class are not implemented as shown in Figure 5.15 on page 133. That is, their return type is `ConvolveOp`, not `BufferedImageOp`. Since `ConvolveOp` implements `BufferedImageOp`, any caller that wants to treat the returned object as a `BufferedImageOp` can. Using `ConvolveOp` as the return type gives callers the opportunity to be more type-specific if they so desire. Second, notice that `Hashtable` objects are used for the pools, even though the keys are integers. This makes sense since the pools are likely to be sparse.

5.3.2 Affine Transformations

The discussion of the rendering process in Section 4.5.1 on page 84 notes that it is often possible to transform the coordinate space used by the rendering engine. In many situations, one doesn't want to transform the coordinate space; instead one wants to transform the content itself. The most important and common transforms for sampled content are scaling and rotation.[5]

In Java, affine transforms are encapsulated in the `AffineTransform` class. They can be applied to images using the `AffineTransformOp` class, which implements the `BufferedImageOp` interface.

For example, to scale an image by a factor of two in both dimensions, one must first create a scaling instance of the `AffineTransform` class, and then use this object to create an `AffineTransformOp`. This is illustrated in the following example:

```
AffineTransform     at;
AffineTransformOp   op;

at = AffineTransform.getScaleInstance(xScale, yScale);
```

_____

[5]Sampled content is not generally translated because it is generally easier, and more efficient, to render the content at the translated location.

```
op = new AffineTransformOp(
                    at,
                    AffineTransformOp.TYPE_BILINEAR);
```

While the scaling of sample content is straightforward, it is also crude since the only way to accomplish an increase in scale is to duplicate pixels.

Rotations are much more complicated conceptually, but are easy to implement in Java. For example, suppose one wants to rotate a `BufferedImage` around its midpoint by the angle `theta`. The first step is to get the midpoint of the image and create an `AffineTransform` object.

```
AffineTransform    rotate;

rotate = AffineTransform.getRotateInstance(
                    theta,
                    width/2.0,
                    height/2.0);
```

The next step is to create a `RenderingHints` object that determines how to interpolate color values.

```
RenderingHints             hints;

// Value can be BILINEAR or NEAREST_NEIGHBOR
hints = new RenderingHints(
        RenderingHints.KEY_INTERPOLATION,
        RenderingHints.VALUE_INTERPOLATION_BILINEAR
                    );
```

The third step is to create an `AffineTransformOp` object.

```
AffineTransformOp          op;

op = new AffineTransformOp(rotate, hints);
```

The final step is to apply the `AffineTransformOp` by calling the `filter()` method.

It is important to note that the rotated image may be much larger than the original. Consider, for example, a 45° rotation of a square image. The rotated image will have a width and height that is equal to the length of the diagonal in the original image. This is illustrated

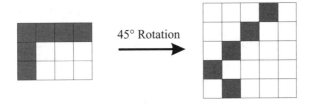

Figure 5.16   A 45° Rotation of Sampled Static Visual Content

in Figure 5.16. In this example, the original image is 3×3 and the resulting image (i.e., after a rotation of 45°) is 5×5.

5.3.3   Lookups

A natural way to modify an image is to change the color values of the pixels. This can be easily accomplished using a lookup table that contains a list of all of the color component values in an image and what these values should be changed to. Not surprisingly, lookup tables can not be applied to images that use an indexed color model.

A *component-independent lookup table* is a single array with as many elements as there are component values (e.g., 256 entries for the component values 0 through 255). The element at index i contains the destination value for source components with a value of i. So, for example, an entry of 156 in element 2 indicates that values of 2 (in the red, green, and blue) components should be changed to 156. A *component-by-component lookup table* contains one array for each color component (e.g., three arrays of length 256 for a 24-bit RGB system). So, for example, an entry of 0 in element 255 of the red array means that any red values of 255 should be replaced with 0.

The following example uses a lookup table to produce the "photo negative" of an image. That is, it subtracts each value in the source from 255, making large values small and small values large.

```
LookupTable              lookupTable;
short[]                  lookup;

lookup = new short[256];

for (int i=0; i<lookup.length; i++)
{
    lookup[i] = (short)(255 - i);
}

lookupTable = new ShortLookupTable(0, lookup);
negativeOp  = new LookupOp(lookupTable, null);
```

If the source is in shades of gray (commonly called 'black and white'), dark colors in the source will correspond to light colors in the destination, and vice versa.

Another interesting example of a lookup is a 'night vision' filter. To create this classic green effect, one need only remove all of the red and blue from an image, as follows:

```
LookupTable              lookupTable;
short[]                  leave, remove;
short[][]                lookupMatrix;


leave  = new short[256];
remove = new short[256];

for (int i=0; i < leave.length; i++) {

    leave[i]  = (short)(i);
    remove[i] = (short)(0);
}

lookupMatrix    = new short[3][];

lookupMatrix[0] = remove;
lookupMatrix[1] = leave;
lookupMatrix[2] = remove;


lookupTable    = new ShortLookupTable(0, lookupMatrix);
nightVisionOp = new LookupOp(lookupTable, null);
```

Columns 0 and 2 of the `lookupMartix`, which correspond to the red and blue values, contains nothing but 0s. Column 1, which corresponds to the green values, has the value equal to the index (i.e., element 0 has value 0, element 1 has value 1, etc.).

5.3.4 Rescaling

The `RescaleOp` class applies a linear function to the source pixels when creating the destination pixels. When constructing a `RescaleOp`, one passes in the scale factor to use (i.e., the multiplicative parameter), the offset to use (i.e., the additive parameter), and the rendering hints to use (or `null` for none). For example, one can brighten an image by scaling it up and darken it by scaling it down, as follows:

```
brightenOp = new RescaleOp(1.5f, 0.0f, null);
darkenOp = new RescaleOp(0.5f, 0.0f, null);
metalOp = new RescaleOp(1.0f, 128.0f, null);
```

The `metalOp` in the above fragment adds a value of 128 to each pixel. Since the color components of resulting pixels are 'capped,' this makes the image appear to be metallic.

5.3.5 Color Space Conversion

A `ColorModel` consists of a `ColorSpace` (e.g., GRAY, RGB, sRGB, CIEXYZ) and a color depth (e.g., 24-bit). The `ColorConvertOp` class can be used to convert from one color space to another.

The following fragment can be used to make a black-and-white version of a `BufferedImage`:

```
public ColorConvertOp createGrayOp()
{
    if (grayOp == null)
    {
        ColorConvertOp        op;
        ColorSpace            cs;

        cs = ColorSpace.getInstance(ColorSpace.CS_GRAY);
        op = new ColorConvertOp(cs, null);
        grayOp = op;
    }
    return grayOp;
}
```

5.3.6 Cropping/Cutting

The extraction of a rectangular sub-image from a `BufferedImage` is referred to as cropping or cutting. This can be accomplished using the `getSubImage()` method in the `BufferedImage` class.

5.4 Design of a Sampled Static Visual Content System

Given the obvious importance of this kind of static visual content, the visual content system must

F5.6 Support the addition of sampled static visual content.

F5.7 Support the removal of sampled static visual content.

F5.8 Support z-ordering of sampled static visual content.

F5.9 Support the transformation of sampled static visual content.

F5.10 Support the rendering of sampled static visual content.

While `Image` objects have most of the information they need for rendering, they do not 'stand alone.' Most importantly, they do not contain location information and/or information about other ways they might be transformed. The system designed in Section 4.6 on page 88 does not satisfy these requirements because `Image` objects do not implement the `SimpleContent` interface. Hence, in order to use sampled static visual content in the visual content system, this functionality must be added. The natural location for the classes/interfaces/etc. that provide this functionality is the `statik.sampled` package.

 One way to add this functionality to the `BufferedImage` class is with specialization. While this is not impossible, it will likely lead to code duplication when, for example, described static visual content is added to the system. Indeed, the `AbstractTransformableContent` class (in the `visual.statik` package) was created to avoid precisely this kind of duplication.

 Another way to add this functionality is to use the decorator pattern. Using this approach, one would decorate `Image` objects with another class that provides the additional functionality. While this would be better, it would probably lead to confusion because the `Image` interface includes methods like `getGraphics()` and `getScaledInstance()` that are not relevant for most apps.

 Alternatively, one can create a class that delegates to a `BufferedImage` object but doesn't implement the `Image` interface. This involves the creation of a specialization of the `statik.TransformableContent` interface that contains the additional requirements of sampled content and a class that extends the `AbstractTransformableContent` that implements this interface, in part by delegating to a `BufferedImage` object. Since this avoids the potential confusion of using the decorator pattern, it seems like the better alternative. Also, this is a fairly risk-free decision since the methods in the `Image` interface that are being omitted now can always be added later.

The `statik.sampled.TransformableContent` interface needs two additional methods, one to satisfy Requirement F5.9 and one to help satisfy Requirement F5.10.

```
package visual.statik.sampled;

import java.awt.*;
import java.awt.image.*;

public interface TransformableContent
```

```
            extends    visual.statik.TransformableContent
{
    public abstract void setBufferedImageOp(BufferedImageOp op);

    public abstract void setComposite(Composite c);
}
```

The `statik.sampled.Content` class can be implemented in two different ways.

The most obvious implementation of this class would have a `BufferedImage` attribute that would be transformed whenever the `render()` method or `getBounds()` method was called (using the `AffineTransform` returned by the `getAffineTransform()` class). The problem with this approach is that transformations are relatively time-consuming. Hence, they should only be performed when necessary.

To avoid this problem, one can keep both the original `BufferedImage` and the transformed `BufferedImage` as attributes. In addition, one can have two `Rectangle2D` objects as attributes that contain the bounds of the original and transformed `BufferedImage` objects.[6] This is illustrated in Figure 5.17 on the next page. This design leads to an implementation with the following overall structure:

```
package visual.statik.sampled;

import java.awt.*;
import java.awt.geom.*;
import java.awt.image.*;

public class Content
            extends    visual.statik.AbstractTransformableContent
            implements TransformableContent

{
    private boolean            refiltered;
    private BufferedImageOp    imageOp;
    private Composite          composite;
    private BufferedImage      originalImage, transformedImage;
    private Rectangle2D.Double originalBounds,transformedBounds;

    private static final double       DEFAULT_X       = 0.0;
    private static final double       DEFAULT_Y       = 0.0;

    public Content()
    {
```

----

[6]One can, in fact, store multiple transformed versions if necessary. See, for example, Exercise 10 on page 284.

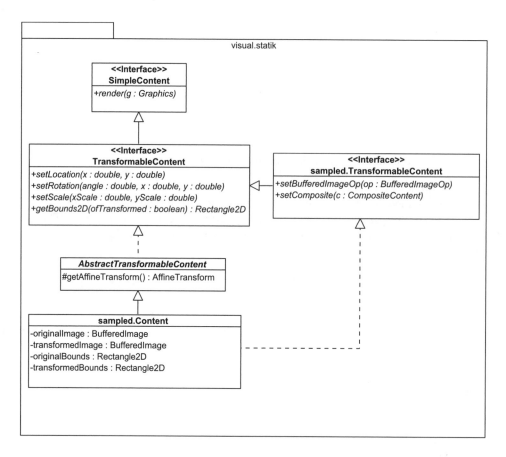

Figure 5.17   Encapsulating Sampled Static Visual Content

```
        this(null, DEFAULT_X, DEFAULT_Y);
    }

    public Content(BufferedImage  image,
                              double x, double y)
    {
        this(image, x, y, true);
    }
}
```

One subtle issue arises when implementing this design, however. As mentioned earlier, it is much less time-consuming to render a BufferedImage at a particular location than it is to translate it to that location. Hence, one would rather not have to translate the BufferedImage object. Unfortunately, if the BufferedImage has been rotated, it must be explicitly translated. Thus it is important to distinguish between sampled transformable content objects that can and can't be rotated.

To that end, this class includes a `boolean` attribute named `rotatable` and overrides the 'setter' methods so that they distinguish between the two cases.

```
public void setBufferedImageOp(BufferedImageOp op)
{
   imageOp    = op;
   refiltered = true;
}

public void setComposite(Composite c)
{
   composite = c;;
}

public void setLocation(double x, double y)
{
   if (!rotatable)
   {
      this.x = x;
      this.y = y;

      transformedBounds.x = this.x;
      transformedBounds.y = this.y;
   }
   else
   {
      super.setLocation(x, y);
   }
}

public void setRotation(double angle, double x, double y)
{
   if (rotatable) super.setRotation(angle, x, y);
}
```

The creation of the transformed content is implemented in the obvious way.

```
private void createTransformedContent(BufferedImageOp op)
{
   BufferedImage   tempImage;
   Rectangle2D     temp;

   try
   {
```

```
            // Apply the filter
            tempImage = originalImage;
            if (imageOp != null)
            {
                tempImage = imageOp.filter(originalImage, null);
            }

            // Create the transformed version
            transformedImage = op.filter(tempImage, null);

            temp = op.getBounds2D(originalImage);

            transformedBounds.x      = temp.getX();
            transformedBounds.y      = temp.getY();
            transformedBounds.width  = temp.getWidth();
            transformedBounds.height = temp.getHeight();

            if (!rotatable)
            {
                transformedBounds.x += x;
                transformedBounds.y += y;
            }

            setTransformationRequired(false);
        }
        catch (RasterFormatException rfe)
        {
            // Unable to transform
            transformedImage = null;
        }
    }
```

as is the render() method,

```
    public void render(Graphics g)
    {
        Composite      oldComposite;
        Graphics2D     g2;

        g2 = (Graphics2D)g;


        if (originalImage != null)
        {
            oldComposite = g2.getComposite();
```

```
            if (composite != null) g2.setComposite(composite);


            // Transform the Image (if necessary)
            if (isTransformationRequired())
            {
                createTransformedContent();
            }

            // Render the image
            if (!rotatable)
                g2.drawImage(transformedImage,(int)x,(int)y,null);
            else
                g2.drawImage(transformedImage,0,0,null);


            g2.setComposite(oldComposite);
        }
    }
```

and the getBounds2D() method.

```
    public Rectangle2D getBounds2D(boolean transformed)
    {
        if   (transformed) return transformedBounds;
        else               return originalBounds;
    }
```

For convenience, it is also useful to implement a factory (that uses the ImageFactory discussed in Section 5.2 on page 115) that can be used to create Content objects. This class has the following overall structure:

```
package visual.statik.sampled;

import java.awt.*;
import java.awt.image.*;
import java.io.*;
import java.util.Arrays;

import io.ResourceFinder;

public class ContentFactory
{
```

```
    private ImageFactory              imageFactory;

    private static final int      DEFAULT_CHANNELS = 3;
    private static final boolean  ROTATABLE        = true;

    public ContentFactory()
    {
       imageFactory = new ImageFactory();
    }

    public ContentFactory(ResourceFinder finder)
    {
       imageFactory = new ImageFactory(finder);
    }
}
```

It has the following method for creating `Content` from an `Image`,

```
    public Content createContent(Image   image,
                                 int     channels,
                                 boolean rotatable)
    {
       BufferedImage        bi;

       bi = imageFactory.createBufferedImage(image, channels);
       return createContent(bi, rotatable);
    }
```

as well as several overloaded methods that handle default values of the different parameters.
It has the following method for creating `Content` from a named resource,

```
    public Content createContent(String name,
                                 int channels,
                                 boolean rotatable)
    {
       BufferedImage          bi;

       bi = imageFactory.createBufferedImage(name, channels);
       return createContent(bi, rotatable);
    }
```

as well as several overloaded methods that handle default values of the different parameters.

EXERCISES ···

1. Consider the following raster representation of a black-and-white source (in which 0 represents black and 1 represents white):

0	0	0	0
0	1	1	0
0	0	0	0
0	0	0	0

and the following 3 × 3 kernel:

0	1	0
0	0	0
0	0	0

What black-and-white destination will result from applying a convolution with the above kernel to the above source (when no operation is applied along the edges)?

2. (*Library Research*) Define the term "sepia tone."

3. Using your answer to Exercise 3 above, create a sepia-tone filter.

4. Modify your sepia-tone filter so that it is a general tone filter. That is, modify it so it will work with any base color (often called the pigment).

5. Create an oil painting filter that makes a piece of static visual content appear to be an oil painting. (Hint: For each pixel in the source, find the most frequent similar color in the neighborhood of that pixel.)

6. Create a water drop filter that makes it appear like drops of water were placed at random on the source.

7. Write a simple image-processing app that displays a piece of static visual content and has the following buttons (that make use of the obvious filters): "Blur," "Brighten," "Darken," "Edge," "Gray," "Negative," "NightVision," and "Sharpen." It should also have an "Undo" button that reverts to the original piece of static visual content.

8. Create a `BufferedImageBinaryOp` interface that contains the requirements of dual-source/single-destination operations performed on `BufferedImage` objects. Should this interface extend `BufferedImageOp`? Why or why not?

9. Create a concrete `DifferenceOp` class that implements the `BufferedImageBinaryOp` interface in the previous question. The destination image 'returned' by the `filter()` method must contain all of the pixels that are different in the two source images. This class must have an explicit value constructor that is passed a tolerance and a `Metric` that will be used by the `filter()` method. It must also have a default constructor that assumes a tolerance of 0.

10. Describe several applications in which the `DifferenceOp` in the previous question might be useful.

11. Write a simple slideshow app that displays an ordered collection of static visual content. It should have "<" and ">" buttons that display the previous/next element in the collection. It should read the names of the files containing the different pieces of static visual content from a file (that is passed to the app as a command-line or applet parameter).

12. The campus Office of Resource Management has taken digital photographs of the front wall of all of the classrooms on campus that show just the front wall and the whiteboard/blackboard. They have asked you to develop a GUI component that renders such an image. You must NOT use the classes in this book. Instead, you must complete the `renderBackground()` method in the following `FrontWall` class:

```java
import java.awt.*;
import java.awt.geom.*;
import javax.swing.*;


/**
 * A GUI component that displays the front wall of a classroom
 */
public class FrontWall extends JPanel
{
    protected double              imageHeight, imageWidth;
    protected double              wallHeight, wallWidth;
    protected Image               image;

    /**
     * Default Constructor
     */
    public FrontWall()
    {
        super();
        ImageIcon      icon;

        // Load the background image
        icon      = new ImageIcon("frontwall.gif");
        image     = icon.getImage();

        // Get the width and height of the background image
        imageHeight = (double)image.getHeight(null);
        imageWidth  = (double)image.getWidth(null);
    }

    /**
     * Render this component
```

```
 *
 * @param g    The rendering engine to use
 */
public void paint(Graphics g)
{
    super.paint(g);
    Dimension          d;
    Graphics2D         g2;

    g2 = (Graphics2D)g;

    // Determine the size of this component
    d = getSize();
    wallWidth  = (double)d.width;
    wallHeight = (double)d.height;

    renderBackground(g2);
}


/**
 * Render the background image on this component.  When rendered,
 * the image must fill this component (that is, it must be
 * wallWidth x wallHeight pixels), even if it changes its aspect
 * ratio.
 *
 * @param g2          The rendering engine to use
 */
protected void renderBackground(Graphics2D g2)
{



    // YOUR CODE HERE!



}
}
```

REFERENCES AND FURTHER READING

Burger, W., and M. Burge. 2007. *Digital image processing: An algorithmic introduction using Java.* New York: Springer.

Gonzales, R., and R. Woods. 2007. *Digital image processing.* Upper Saddle River, NJ: Prentice Hall.

Kay, D. C., and J. R. Levine. 1995. *Graphics file formats.* New York: Windcrest.

Terrazas, A., J. Ostuni, and M. Barlow. 2002. *Java media APIs.* Indianapolis, IN: SAMS.

Described Static Visual Content

6

The description of static visual content involves, at a minimum, the description of *geometric shapes* and the way in which they should be rendered. Two common examples of described static visual content are *scalable graphics* and *outline fonts*.

Descriptions of static visual content are often called *vector representations*; however, this term can be somewhat confusing. In particular, it is important to remember that the internal representation of the content is completely independent of how it is presented on an output device. Described static visual content can be presented/displayed on both vector and raster output devices.

Simple geometric shapes are often categorized based on their dimensionality. While this concept can be formalized, an intuitive notion is sufficient for the purposes of this book. Loosely, a shape is said to be 0-dimensional if it has no 'extent' (i.e., can't be measured) on the real line, 1-dimensional if it has 'extent' on the real line but not in the plane, and 2-dimensional if it has 'extent' on the plane. (This book does not consider 3-dimensional shapes.) Some common simple geometric shapes are listed in Table 6.1.

Descriptions of the way in which a shape should be rendered vary with the type of the shape. For example, a description of how a line should be rendered would include the color and line type, while the description of how a rectangle should be rendered would also include a fill color and pattern.

This chapter begins with a small taste of what is to follow. It then discusses some important Java classes for working with described static visual content. Finally, it considers the design and implementation of a described static visual content system.

6.1 A 'Quick Start'

In Java, the requirements of geometric shapes are specified in the **Shape** interface. This interface is implemented by a variety of different classes, including the **Rectangle** class used below.

Shape objects are rendered with the **draw()** method in the **Graphics2D** class. This can be illustrated with a specialization of the **JComponent** class that creates a **Rectangle** with random attributes and renders it. The structure of this class is as follows:

0-Dimensional	1-Dimensional	2-Dimensional
Point	Line	Rectangle
	Curve	Polygon
		Ellipse

Table 6.1 Some Common (Simple) Geometric Shapes

```
import java.awt.*;
import java.awt.geom.*;
import java.util.Random;
import javax.swing.*;

public class RandomRectangleCanvas extends JComponent
{
    private Random       generator;

    public RandomRectangleCanvas()
    {
        super();
        generator = new Random(System.currentTimeMillis());
    }
}
```

This class includes a default constructor that instantiates a random number generator that will be used to generate the rectangle.

This class must also include a paint() method that first gets the height and width of the renderable area of this JComponent; then randomly generates values for a Rectangle object's x, y, width, and height; then instantiates a Rectangle object; and finally renders the Rectangle object. This can be implemented as follows:

```
    public void paint(Graphics g)
    {
        Graphics2D      g2;
        int             height, maxHeight, maxWidth, width, x, y;
        Rectangle       rectangle;


        g2 = (Graphics2D)g;

        maxHeight = getHeight();
        maxWidth  = getWidth();

        x      = generator.nextInt(maxWidth  - 1);
        y      = generator.nextInt(maxHeight - 1);
        width  = generator.nextInt(maxWidth  - x - 1);
        height = generator.nextInt(maxHeight - y - 1);

        rectangle = new Rectangle(x, y, width, height);
```

```
        g2.draw(rectangle);
    }
```

With this as an overview, it is possible to turn to a more detailed discussion of described static visual content. As this discussion proceeds, it is important to remember that, as with Chapter 5, this chapter is concerned with how the content is **represented**. Described static visual content can be **displayed/presented** on both vector and raster output devices.

6.2 Encapsulating Simple Geometric Shapes

In Java, points are encapsulated in the `Point2D` class, lines are encapsulated in the `Line2D` class, curves are encapsulated in the `CubicCurve2D` and `QuadCurve2D` classes, rectangles and rounded rectangles are encapsulated in the `Rectangle2D` and `RoundRectangle2D` classes, respectively, and ellipses are encapsulated in the `Ellipse2D` class. Java actually has two versions of each of these geometric shapes, one that uses `float` values for the coordinates and one that uses `double` values. They are nested inside of the abstract classes listed above.

6.2.1 0-Dimensional Shapes

A point is defined by its coordinates. On the plane, which is the concern of this book, a point has two coordinates, usually called the x-coordinate (i.e., horizontal coordinate) and y-coordinate (i.e., vertical coordinate). In Java, one normally specifies these coordinates when constructing a `Point2D` object. For example:

```
// Construct a point
point = new Point2D.Double(20.0, 30.0);
```

To clarify, this example constructs an instance of the class `Point2D.Double`—it's x and y values are both `double` values.

6.2.2 1-Dimensional Shapes

Lines can be defined in a variety of different ways. Most people are familiar with the *explicit form*, also known as the slope-intercept form, which defines a line as the set of pairs, (x, y) that satisfy:

$$y = Ax + B \tag{6.1}$$

for given values of the slope, A, and the vertical intercept, B.

This approach has three big shortcomings for computing applications. First, it does not enable us to represent vertical lines. Second, one is generally interested in line segments, not lines. Third, though familiar, it is not very intuitive. Hence, it is much more common to use a *parametric form*.

In a parametric form, the values of x and y that are on the line segment are written as a function of a parameter, u, that takes on values in the interval $[0, 1]$. This book defines the *parametric form of a line segment* in terms of the coefficients $a = (a_x, a_y)$ and $b = (b_x, b_y)$ as

$$
\begin{aligned}
x(u) &= u^0 a_x + u^1 b_x = a_x + u b_x & (6.2) \\
y(u) &= u^0 a_y + u^1 b_y = a_y + u b_y. & (6.3)
\end{aligned}
$$

In Java, a line segment is defined in terms of its two end points, p and q. To ensure that $(x(0), y(0))$ equals p, one needs to set $a_x = p_x$ and $a_y = p_y$. In addition, to ensure that $(x(1), y(1))$ equals q, one needs to set $b_x = q_x - p_x$ and $b_y = q_y - p_y$. To see that this works, observe that

$$
\begin{aligned}
x(u) &= p_x + u(q_x - p_x) & (6.4) \\
y(u) &= p_y + u(q_y - p_y) & (6.5)
\end{aligned}
$$

and, hence, that

$$
\begin{aligned}
x(0) &= p_x & (6.6) \\
y(0) &= p_y & (6.7) \\
x(1) &= p_x + (q_x - p_x) = q_x & (6.8) \\
y(1) &= p_y + (q_y - p_y) = q_y. & (6.9)
\end{aligned}
$$

Conveniently, Java's `Line2D` class does this calculation. Hence, to specify a line segment in Java, one need only provide the two end points (either as `Point2D` objects or pairs of coordinates). For example:

```
// Construct a line
line = new Line2D.Double(0.0, 0.0, 50.0, 75.0);
```

This example constructs an instance of the class `Line2D.Double`—the x and y values of the two end points are both `double` values.

Before continuing, it is useful to observe that, collecting terms, (6.4) and (6.5) can be rewritten as follows:

$$
\begin{aligned}
x(u) &= p_x + u q_x - u p_x = (1 - u)p_x + u q_x & (6.10) \\
y(u) &= p_y + u q_y - u p_y = (1 - u)p_y + u q_y & (6.11)
\end{aligned}
$$

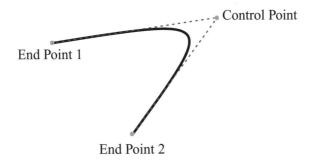

Figure 6.1   A Quadratic Curve

That is, $x(u)$ is a weighted combination[1] of p_x and p_y, and $y(u)$ is a weighted combination of q_x and q_y (with weights $(1 - u)$ and u).

Curves, too, can be defined in a variety of different ways. In computing applications parametric approaches are, by far, the most common. This book considers the most common curves used in computer graphics, Bézier curves.

A *quadratic Bézier curve segment* is defined in terms of the two end points, p and q, and one *control point*, r, as follows:

$$x(u) = (1 - u)^2 p_x + 2(1 - u)u r_x + u^2 q_x \tag{6.12}$$

$$y(u) = (1 - u)^2 p_y + 2(1 - u)u r_y + u^2 q_y \tag{6.13}$$

for $u \in [0, 1]$. (Note the similarities to equations [6.10] and [6.11].) The slope of the curve at each end point is the slope of the line segment connecting that end point and the control point. This is illustrated in Figure 6.1.

Quadratic Bézier curve segments are encapsulated in the Java class `QuadCurve2D`. To construct a quadratic curve segment in Java, one need only provide the two end points and a control point (either as `Point2D` objects or pairs of coordinates). For example:

```
// Construct a quadratic curve
quadraticCurve = new QuadCurve2D.Double(
                     120.0, 120.0,  // End 1
                     300.0, 180.0,  // Control
                     130.0, 190.0); // End 2
```

---

[1]More formally, it is a *convex combination*. The notion of convex and nonconvex shapes will be considered informally later. The informal definitions can be formalized in terms of convex combinations.

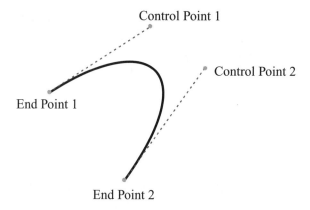

Figure 6.2   A Cubic Curve

Finally, a *cubic Bézier curve segment* is defined in terms of the two end points, p and q, and two control points, r and s, as follows:

$$x(u) = (1-u)^3 p_x + 3(1-u)^2 u r_x + 2(1-u)^2 u s_x + u^3 q_x \tag{6.14}$$
$$y(u) = (1-u)^3 p_y + 3(1-u)^2 u r_y + 2(1-u)^2 u s_y + u^3 q_y \tag{6.15}$$

for $u \in [0,1]$. (Again, note the similarities to equations (6.10) and (6.11).) The slope of the curve at each end point is the slope of the line segment connecting that end point and its associated control point. This is illustrated in Figure 6.2.

Cubic Bézier curve segments are encapsulated in the Java class `CubicCurve2D`. To construct such a curve one need only provide the two end points and two control points in the proper order. For example:

```
// Construct a cubic curve
cubicCurve = new CubicCurve2D.Double(320.0, 320.0,  // End 1
                                     300.0, 180.0,  // Control 1
                                     330.0, 370.0,  // End 2
                                     360.0, 390.0); // Control 2
```

6.2.3   2-Dimensional Shapes

The first 2-dimensional shape to consider is the *rectangle*, which can loosely be defined as a four-sided shape with four right angles in which the sides are parallel to the coordinate axes.[2] By now you should not be surprised to learn that rectangles can be defined in several different ways. Probably the most natural way is to define the rectangle in terms of its four

---

[2]Note that this is a fairly restrictive definition of a rectangle. It is, however, the one that is commonly used in computer graphics.

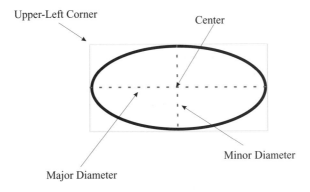

Figure 6.3 An Ellipse

corners. However, if you give it a little thought, you will quickly realize that this approach includes redundant information. That is, the two top points will have the same y-coordinate, the two bottom points will have the same y-coordinate, the two left points will have the same x-coordinate, and the two right points will have the same x-coordinate.

Hence, instead, it is common to define a rectangle in terms of one corner and its width and height. In Java, rectangles are encapsulated in the `Rectangle2D` class, and the upper-left corner is used. For example:

```
// Construct a rectangle
rectangle = new Rectangle2D.Double(10.0, 20.0, // Upper Left
                                   30.0,       // Width
                                   60.0);      // Height
```

This example constructs an instance of the class `Rectangle2D.Double`. The upper-left corner, width, and height are all `double` values.

Ellipses are defined in a similar way, though this is probably different than the approach you are used to. When you studied geometry, you probably represented an ellipse using its center, and its major and minor diameters (or major and minor axes). In Java, an ellipse is defined in terms of the upper-left corner, width, and height of the rectangle that contains it. This is illustrated in Figure 6.3. Of course, the width is the same as the major diameter and the height is the same as the minor diameter. In addition, the center can be determined easily by offsetting the upper-left corner by half the width and half the height. Hence, the two approaches are clearly equivalent.

An arc can also be represented in a number of different ways. In Java, it is represented as a part of an ellipse, with the portion defined by a starting angle and an angular extent. This is illustrated in Figure 6.4 on the following page. In Java, these angles are measured in degrees, with 0 being to the right of the center point. So, the example in Figure 6.4 has a starting

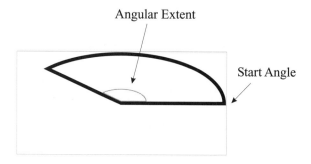

Figure 6.4 An Arc

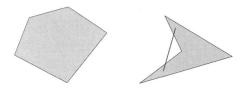

Figure 6.5 A Convex and Nonconvex Shape

angle of $0°$ and an angular extent of $135°$. One can construct such an arc (with a containing rectangle that has its upper-left corner at $[10, 200]$) as follows:

```
// Construct an arc
arc = new Arc2D.Double(10.0, 200.0, // Upper Left
                       150.0,       // Width
                       100.0,       // Height
                       0.0,         // Starting Angle
                       135.0,       // Angular Extent
                       Arc2D.PIE);  // Type
```

Two-dimensional shapes are either *closed* (i.e., they have a well-defined interior and exterior) or open. Closed two-dimensional shapes (i.e., shapes that have positive area) such as polygons can either be convex or nonconvex. Loosely speaking, a shape is convex if a line segment drawn between any two points in the shape lies entirely inside the shape.[3] This is illustrated in Figure 6.5. In general, it is much easier to operate on convex shapes than nonconvex shapes. Hence, it is quite common to build static described visual content from convex shapes (e.g., triangles).

---

[3]That is, if the convex combinations of the two points are all in the shape.

Two Glyphs   One Glyph
              (a ligature)

Figure 6.6 'f' and 'i' as Two Glyphs and as a Ligature

6.3 Encapsulating Glyphs and Fonts

Some of the most common described content, the descriptions of the shapes of characters, is also the most complicated. Such shapes are called "glyphs."

Definition 6.1 A *glyph* is a shape that represents one or more characters (in a character set).

Most of the time, a glyph represents a single character. However, for aesthetic reasons, multiple characters are sometimes represented by a single glyph called a ligature. This is illustrated in Figure 6.6.

Glyphs (with common characteristics) are grouped together into something called a "font." More formally:

Definition 6.2 A *font* is a set of glyphs.

Fonts are said to have a *face* or *family* (e.g., Garamond, Times New Roman) and a *style* (e.g., italic, bold).

6.3.1 Glyphs as Shapes

Even at first glance, it should be apparent that glyphs are fairly complicated shapes. It turns out that they are even more complicated than you might think. Font designers tend to be very concerned about aesthetics and this can complicate the definition of glyphs considerably.

Each glyph has a *width*, a *left-side bearing* (LSB), and a *right-side bearing* (RSB). The advance is simply the sum of the three. The width is always positive, but the bearings can be either positive or negative. This is illustrated in Figure 6.7 on the next page.

The use of different bearings for different glyphs is called kerning. It is used for aesthetic reasons as illustrated in Figure 6.8 on the following page. In the bottom example, the 'W' has a right-side bearing of 0 and the 'A' has a left-side bearing of 0. Even so, most people think that there is too much white space between the two letters. On the other hand, in the top example, either the 'W' has a negative right-side bearing or the 'A' has a negative left-side bearing or both (the specifics don't matter here). In this case, the 'W' and 'A' actually share the same space. That is, if you draw two rectangles, each just containing their corresponding letters, they will overlap. Most people find this approach more pleasing.

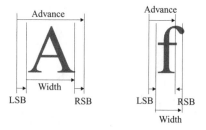

Figure 6.7 Positive and Negative Right-Side Bearings

Figure 6.8 The Same Word With and Without Kerning

In Java, the rendering engine (i.e., a `Graphics2D` object) keeps information about fonts in a `FontRenderContext` object. Given a `FontRenderContext` a `Font` object can create a `GlyphVector` that has several `getOutline()` methods, each of which returns a `Shape`. One version of this method is passed two parameters, the x and y coordinates (called the *registration point*) for the resulting `Shape`. This process is illustrated in the following `paintGlyphs()` method:

```
protected void paintGlyphs(Graphics2D g2, String text)
{
    FontRenderContext      frc;
    GlyphVector            glyphs;
    Shape                  shape;

    frc = g2.getFontRenderContext();

    glyphs = font.createGlyphVector(frc, text);
    shape = glyphs.getOutline(0.0f, 100.0f);

    g2.setColor(Color.BLACK);
    g2.draw(shape);
}
```

6.3.2 Measuring Glyphs and Fonts

A variety of measurements are used in typesetting, including the *ascent*, *descent*, and *leading* (pronounced led-ing), all of which are illustrated in Figure 6.9 on the next page.

The leading gets its name from the way movable type used to be set. A person known as a typesetter would put a small piece of lead between two lines of type in order to separate

Figure 6.9 Font Metrics

them. The ascent refers to the amount of vertical space required by the tallest character. The descent, on the other hand, refers to the (maximum) amount of space below the baseline that is used by letters like 'y' and 'j.' The *height* of a font is simply the sum of the three.

Given a `FontRenderContext`, a `Font` can provide a `LineMetrics` object that can be used to get information about the font's metrics. Assuming one has a `Graphics2D` object named `g2` and a `String` object named `text`, the first step in the process is to create the `GlyphVector` as before.

```
FontRenderContext        frc;
GlyphVector              glyphs;

frc     = g2.getFontRenderContext();
glyphs  = font.createGlyphVector(frc, text);
```

The second step in the process is to get the `LineMetrics` object.

```
LineMetrics              lm;

lm      = font.getLineMetrics(text, frc);
```

The final step in the process is to get the metrics themselves.

```
float                    ascent, descent, height, leading;

// Get the various metrics
ascent  = lm.getAscent();
descent = lm.getDescent();
height  = lm.getHeight();
leading = lm.getLeading();
```

A `GlyphVector` can also provide a `Rectangle2D` object that contains the bounding box that encloses its glyphs.

```
          // Get the bounding box
          bounds = glyphs.getVisualBounds();
```

This can be used, for example, to center the text. To do so, one needs to get the bounds of the visual component, calculate the coordinates that will center the text, and get the Shape translated to the centering point (which is the baseline-left point). This can be accomplished as follows:

```
          Dimension                 d;
          float                     x, y;

          d = getSize();

          // Center the text
          x = (float)(d.width/2.  - bounds.getWidth()/2. );
          y = (float)(d.height/2. + bounds.getHeight()/2.);

          // Get the outline when centered
          shape = glyphs.getOutline(x,y);
```

Note that in the horizontal direction, the translation is negative because the leftmost point is being determined; however, in the vertical direction, the translation is positive because the baseline is being determined (and the vertical coordinates are larger at the bottom than the top). Note also that d.width/2.-bounds.getWidth()/2. is equivalent to (d.width-bounds.getWidth())/2., and d.height/2.+bounds.getHeight()/2. is equivalent to (d.height+bounds.getHeight())/2..

6.3.3   Convenience Methods

It is sometimes inconvenient to create the Shape objects and render them in distinct steps. Hence, the Graphics2D class has several convenience methods, including

```
     drawGlyphVector(GlyphVector, float, float)
     drawString(String, float, float)
```

There is also a convenience method that can be used to render text with *attributes*:

```
     drawString(AttributedCharacterIterator, float, float)
```

Again, assuming one has a Graphics2D object named g2 and a String object named text, one can increase the size of each char[4] in text as follows:

---

[4]It is worth noting that Unicode has a special character called the *replacement charac-ter* (specifically '\uFFFC') and that the AttributedString class supports it (using the attribute

```
AttributedString          as;

as = new AttributedString(text);
for (int i=0; i < text.length(); i++)
{
    as.addAttribute(TextAttribute.FONT,
                    new Font("Serif", Font.PLAIN, (i+10)),
                    i, i+1);
}
```

and then render the `AttributedString` as follows:

```
g2.setColor(Color.BLACK);
g2.drawString(as.getIterator(), 0, 100);
```

6.4 **Encapsulating Complicated Geometric Shapes**

A common way to describe complicated geometric shapes is with a sequence of "move to," "line to," "quadratic-curve to," and/or "cubic-curve to" segments. In Java, the `Path2D` object provides this functionality.[5] For example, the following fragment constructs a complicated shape from a sequence of "move to" and "line to" operations:

```
bodyShape = new Path2D.Float();
bodyShape.moveTo( 20, 50);
bodyShape.lineTo( 20, 70);
bodyShape.lineTo( 20, 90);
bodyShape.lineTo( 10, 90);
bodyShape.lineTo( 10,100);
bodyShape.lineTo( 80,100);
bodyShape.lineTo( 80, 90);
bodyShape.lineTo( 40, 90);
bodyShape.lineTo( 40, 70);
bodyShape.lineTo( 40, 50);
bodyShape.closePath();
```

`TextAttribute.CHAR_REPLACEMENT`). An occurrence of a replacement character can be replaced with either an `ImageGraphicAttribute` or a `ShapeGraphicAttribute`.

[5]In earlier versions of Java, this functionality was provided by the `GeneralPath` class.

In addition to providing moveTo(), lineTo(), quadTo(), and curveTo() methods, it can append() any object that implements the Shape interface.

All objects that implement the Shape interface have a getPathIterator() method that returns a PathIterator object that can be used to 'loop through' a sequence of segments using the iterator pattern. This functionality is used in the discussion of dynamic visual content (see Section 9.3.2 on page 275).

6.5 Operating on Multiple Shapes

There are many different ways to conceptualize operations on multiple shapes.

....

Definition 6.3 *Constructive area geometry* (CAG) is the process of performing set-theoretic operations (e.g., union, intersection, difference, symmetric difference) on two-dimensional shapes.

....

In Java, constructive area geometry functionality is provided by the **Area** class, which can be used to decorate (in the sense of the decorator pattern) any object that implements the Shape interface. That is, **Area** objects implement the Shape interface and can be created from objects that implement the Shape interface. This is demonstrated in the following code fragment from a paint() method:

```
        e = new Area(ellipse);
        r = new Area(rectangle);

        if      (op.equalsIgnoreCase("Union"))
                        e.add(r);
        else if (op.equalsIgnoreCase("Intersection"))
                        e.intersect(r);
        else if (op.equalsIgnoreCase("Difference"))
                        e.subtract(r);
        else
                        e.exclusiveOr(r);

        g2.setPaint(GOLD);
        g2.fill(e);
        g2.setPaint(PURPLE);
        g2.draw(e);
```

This fragment first creates two **Area** objects, one from an Ellipse2D object and one from a Rectangle2d object. These two Shape objects are shown in Figure 6.10. It then applies either the add(), intersect(), subtract(), or exclusiveOr() method based on the value of the String variable named op. Finally, it fills and strokes the resulting **Area** (which is, of course, a Shape). The results of each of these operations is shown in Figure 6.11.

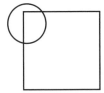

Figure 6.10   Two Shape Objects

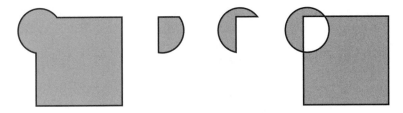

Figure 6.11   Results of the `add()`, `intersect()`, `subtract()`, and `exclusiveOr()` Operations

6.6   Operating on Individual Shapes

The discussion of the rendering process in Section 4.5.1 on page 84 noted that it is often possible to transform the coordinate space used by the rendering engine. In many situations, one doesn't want to transform the coordinate space; instead one wants to transform the content itself. Again, the most common transforms are translation, scaling, rotation, and reflection. In Java, transforms are implemented in the `AffineTransform` class.

Translation is an equal horizontal and/or vertical displacement of every point in the object being drawn. That is, a constant horizontal and/or vertical displacement is added to the coordinates of every point in the object. An example of translating a square is shown in Figure 6.12. In Java, the static method `AffineTransform.getTranslateInstance(double, double)` creates a translation transform.

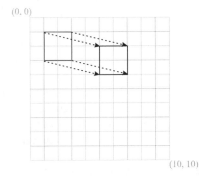

Figure 6.12   A Translation

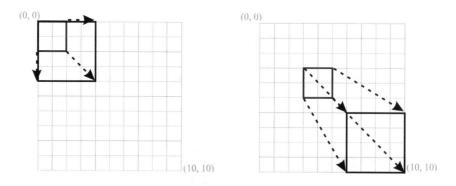

Figure 6.13 Two Scalings

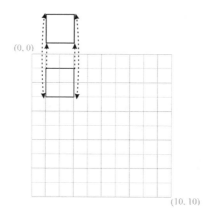

Figure 6.14 A Reflection

To scale an object, the coordinates of each point are multiplied by the same factor. The horizontal factor and the vertical factor need not be the same, but the same factor is applied to every point. Two examples of 'equal' scaling (i.e., scalings that preserve the aspect ratio) are shown in Figure 6.13. Note that, in the one example, the lower left-hand corner of the rectangle is at (0, 0) and, hence, doesn't change when it is multiplied by the scaling factor of 2. In the other example, all of the points change when they are scaled (again, by a factor of 2). In Java, the static method `AffineTransform.getScaleInstance(double, double)` creates a scaling transform.

Objects can also be reflected about a line (the most common lines being the x-axis and y-axis). Reflection around the y-axis changes the sign of the x-coordinate of every point in the object being drawn. Reflection around the x-axis changes the sign of the y-coordinate of every point in the object being drawn. An example of reflection around the x-axis is shown in Figure 6.14.

There is no static method in Java for creating reflection transforms. Hence, two such `AffineTransform` objects, one that reflects around the x-axis and another that reflects around the y-axis, are defined below. Unfortunately, a detailed discussion of reflection requires an understanding of linear algebra that is beyond the scope of this book. Hence, they are presented without explanation.

```
AffineTransform       aroundX, aroundY;

aroundX = new AffineTransform( 1.0, 0.0, 0.0,-1.0, 0.0, 0.0);
aroundY = new AffineTransform(-1.0, 0.0, 0.0, 1.0, 0.0, 0.0);
```

Rotation is probably the most complicated transform. An example of rotating a square around a particular point is shown in Figure 6.15. In Java, the static method `AffineTransform.getRotateInstance(double)` creates a rotational transform for rotating around the point $(0, 0)$. Note that the rotation angle is measured in radians.

It is important to remember that a **Shape** can be rotated around any arbitrary point. The point need not be in the **Shape**, or even near it. As an example, the following fragment creates a shape from some text, and then rotates it and translates it to create the effect illustrated in Figure 6.16.

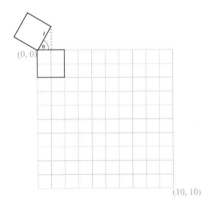

Figure 6.15 Rotation Around the Origin

Figure 6.16 Iteratively Rotating a Complicated Shape

```
    protected void paintGlyphs(Graphics2D g2, String text)
    {
        AffineTransform        at, trans;
        AlphaComposite         alpha;
        Dimension              d;
        float                  angle, x, y;
        FontRenderContext      frc;
        GlyphVector            glyphs;
        int                    i;
        Shape                  shape, transformedShape;

        d = getSize();

        frc = g2.getFontRenderContext();
        glyphs = font.createGlyphVector(frc, text);
        shape = glyphs.getOutline(0.0f, 100.0f);
        g2.setColor(Color.BLACK);

        for (i=0; i < 6; i++)
        {
            angle = (float)(Math.PI/6.0 * i);
            x = (float)(d.width/2.0);
            y = (float)(d.height/2.0);
            at = AffineTransform.getRotateInstance(angle,x,y);
            trans = AffineTransform.getTranslateInstance(x,y);
            at.concatenate(trans);

            transformedShape = at.createTransformedShape(shape);

            g2.fill(transformedShape);
        }
    }
```

6.7   Rendering Described Content

There are two unique steps in the process of rendering described visual content: stroking and filling. They are illustrated in Figure 6.17 on the next page.

....

Definition 6.4 *Stroking* is the rendering of the border (i.e., outline) of the described content.

....

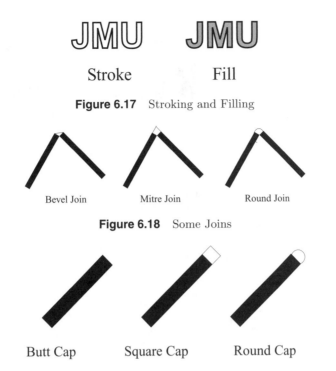

Stroke   Fill

Figure 6.17 Stroking and Filling

Bevel Join   Mitre Join   Round Join

Figure 6.18 Some Joins

Butt Cap   Square Cap   Round Cap

Figure 6.19 Caps

There are various properties that determine the way in which the stroking is performed. The simplest are the *line width* and *dash* attributes.[6]

The join determines what is rendered when two segments of the outline share a common end point and the outline has a width of more than one pixel. Joins are illustrated in Figure 6.18 in which the solid black rectangles represent two linear segments of an outline that share a common end point. Since the segments have thickness, there are several possible ways to render the common end point. As illustrated, the three most common are the *bevel join*, the *mitre join*, and the *round join*.

The *cap* determines what is rendered at the other end points when the outline has a width of more than one pixel. The three most common are the *butt cap*, the *square cap*, and the *round cap* illustrated in Figure 6.19. When a butt cap is used, the outline ends at these end points. When a square cap or round cap is used, the outline extends past these end points. The difference between a square cap and round cap is the shape of the cap.

Another step in the process is filling, which can be defined as follows:

....

Definition 6.5 *Filling* is the rendering of the interior of the content.

....

Filling most commonly involves a solid color, a gradient color, or sampled visual content, as illustrated in Figure 6.20.

---

[6]Some rendering engines use the notion of a brush to describe the properties of the stroke. The `Graphics2D` class does not provide this kind of functionality.

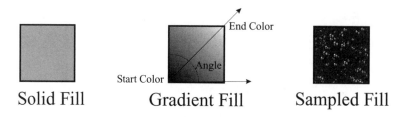

Figure 6.20   Fill Techniques

In Java, the process of stroking is encapsulated in the `Stroke` interface. In addition, there is a `BasicStroke` class that defines the important attributes used in the stroking process. Filling, on the other hand, is done with objects that implement the `Paint` interface. This includes objects in the `Color`, `GradientPaint`, and `TexturePaint` classes.

The following example creates a rectangle, fills it with gold, and strokes it with a 5-pixel-wide solid purple line (using a butt cap and a mitered join):

```
// The first rectangle
rectangle = new Rectangle2D.Double( 10.0,  20.0,
                                    100.0,
                                    150.0);

// Fill in JMU Gold
g2.setPaint(new Color(0xC2, 0xA1, 0x4D));
g2.fill(rectangle);


// Stroke in JMU purple
stroke = new BasicStroke(5.0f,
                         BasicStroke.CAP_BUTT,
                         BasicStroke.JOIN_MITER);
g2.setStroke(stroke);
g2.setColor(new Color(0x45, 0x00, 0x84));
g2.draw(rectangle);
```

The next example creates a different rectangle, fills it with a `GradientPaint` object that fades from cyan to white, and strokes it with a 10-pixel-wide solid black line (using a butt cap and a rounded join).

```
// The second rectangle
rectangle = new Rectangle2D.Double( 200.0, 200.0,
                                    100.0,
                                    150.0);
```

```
// Fill using a gradient
gradient=new GradientPaint(200.0f, 275.0f, Color.CYAN,
                           300.0f, 275.0f, Color.WHITE);
g2.setPaint(gradient);
g2.fill(rectangle);

// Stroke in black
stroke = new BasicStroke(10.0f,
                         BasicStroke.CAP_BUTT,
                         BasicStroke.JOIN_ROUND);
g2.setStroke(stroke);
g2.setColor(Color.BLACK);
g2.draw(rectangle);
```

The final example creates a third rectangle, fills it with a yellow that is 50% transparent, and does not stroke it.

```
// The third rectangle
rectangle = new Rectangle2D.Double( 50.0, 50.0,
                                    200.0,
                                    250.0);

// Use alpha blending to achieve a transparency effect
composite = AlphaComposite.getInstance(
                         AlphaComposite.SRC_OVER,
                         0.5f);
g2.setComposite(composite);

// Fill in gray
g2.setPaint(Color.YELLOW);
g2.fill(rectangle);

// Don't stroke
```

6.8 Design of a Described Static Visual Content System

Given the obvious importance of described static visual content, the visual content system must

F6.1 Support the addition of described static visual content.

F6.2 Support the removal of described static visual content.

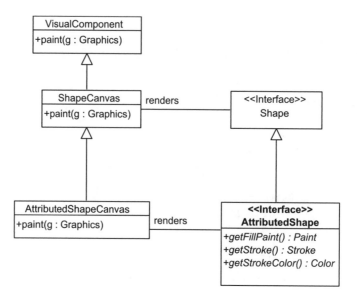

Figure 6.21   A Design Using an AttributedShape Interface

F6.3 Support the *z*-ordering of described static visual content.

F6.4 Support the transformation of described static visual content.

F6.5 Support the rendering of described static visual content.

As was the case with sampled static visual content, the Java classes that encapsulate described static visual content do not contain all of the information required for rendering and, hence, do not/cannot implement the `SimpleContent` interface. Most importantly, they do not contain information related to stroking and filling. Hence, in order to use described static visual content in the visual content system, this functionality must be added. A natural place for the relevant class/interfaces/etc. is the `statik.described` package.

   One way to overcome this shortcoming is to extend the `Shape` interface and create an `AttributedShape` interface as illustrated in Figure 6.21. One advantage of this approach is that any GUI component that is capable of drawing a `Shape` is capable of drawing a `RenderableShape`.

   An alternative approach, illustrated in Figure 6.22 on the next page, is to use the decorator pattern rather than specialization. In this case, a `DecoratedShape` object is constructed from a `Shape` object, adding the necessary additional functionality (i.e., the attributes).

The problem with both of these designs is that, while `AttributedShape` and `DecoratedShape` both implement the `Shape` interface, logic is still needed to render them correctly. That is, the `JComponent` that does the rendering must get the `Paint`, fill the `Shape`, get the `Stroke` and `Color`, and draw the `Shape`. Hence, the specialization of the `JComponent` class must both manage `Shape` objects and render them. Thus, it is not cohesive.

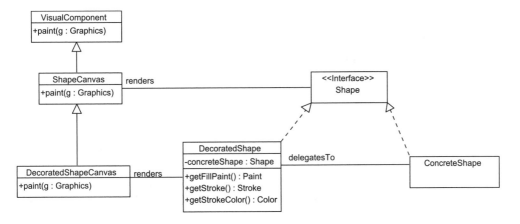

Figure 6.22 A Design Using the Decorator Pattern

As with sampled content, it seems better to have a class that is responsible for maintaining its state and rendering itself. This can be accomplished by adding a `Content` class to the `visual.statik.described` package that extends the `AbstractTransformableContent` in the `visual.statik` package. Also, as with sampled content (see the discussion on page 145), it makes sense to keep both the original `Shape` and the transformed `Shape` as attributes and to keep two `Rectangle2D` objects as attributes that contain the bounds of the original and transformed `Shape` objects. This is illustrated in Figure 6.23 on the next page.

The first thing to do is create a specialization of the `statik.TransformableContent` interface that contains the additional requirements of described content as follows:

```java
package visual.statik.described;

import java.awt.*;
import java.awt.geom.*;

public interface TransformableContent
       extends   visual.statik.TransformableContent
{
    public abstract void setColor(Color color);

    public abstract void setPaint(Paint paint);

    public abstract void setStroke(Stroke stroke);
}
```

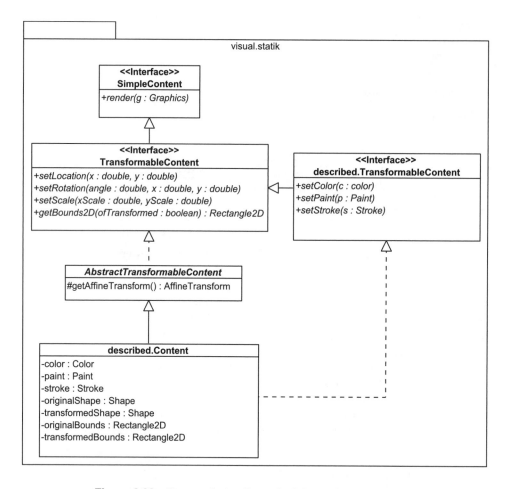

Figure 6.23   Encapsulating Described Static Visual Content

The next thing to do is create a `statik.described.Content` class with the following overall structure:

```
package visual.statik.described;

import java.awt.*;
import java.awt.geom.*;

public class Content
            extends visual.statik.AbstractTransformableContent
            implements TransformableContent
{
    private Color               color;
    private Paint               paint;
```

```java
    private Rectangle2D.Double    originalBounds;
    private Rectangle2D.Double    transformedBounds;
    private Shape                 originalShape;
    private Shape                 transformedShape;
    private Stroke                stroke;

    private final Stroke          DEFAULT_STROKE =
                                    new BasicStroke();

    private final AffineTransform IDENTITY =
                                    new AffineTransform();

    public Content()
    {
       this(null, null, null, null);
    }

    public Content(Shape  shape,  Color color, Paint paint,
                   Stroke stroke)
    {
       super();

       setColor(color);
       setPaint(paint);
       setStroke(stroke);

       setShape(shape);
    }
    private void getBoundsFor(Rectangle2D.Double r, Shape s)
    {
       Rectangle2D        temp;

       if (s != null)
       {
          temp = s.getBounds2D();

          if (temp != null)
          {
             r.x      = temp.getX();
             r.y      = temp.getY();
             r.width  = temp.getWidth();
             r.height = temp.getHeight();
          }
       }
    }
}
```

This class can then add include the following 'getters':

```
public Color getColor()
{
   return color;
}

public Paint getPaint()
{
   return paint;
}
public Stroke getStroke()
{
   return stroke;
}
```

and the following 'setters':

```
public void setColor(Color color)
{
   this.color = color;
}

public void setPaint(Paint paint)
{
   this.paint = paint;
}
```

The creation of the transformed content can be implemented in the obvious way.

```
private void createTransformedContent(AffineTransform at)
{
   transformedShape = at.createTransformedShape(
                                    originalShape);
   setTransformationRequired(false);

   getBoundsFor(transformedBounds, transformedShape);
}
```

The same is true of the getBounds2D() method.

```
public Rectangle2D getBounds2D(boolean transformed)
{
    if   (transformed) return transformedBounds;
    else                    return originalBounds;
}
```

The render() method must set the Paint, fill the Shape, set the Color, and draw the Shape as follows:

```
public void render(Graphics g)
{
    Color        oldColor;
    Graphics2D   g2;
    Paint        oldPaint;
    Stroke       oldStroke;

    g2 = (Graphics2D)g;

    // Transform the Shape (if necessary)
    if (isTransformationRequired())
    {
        createTransformedContent();
    }

    if (transformedShape != null)
    {
        // Save the state
        oldColor      = g2.getColor();
        oldPaint      = g2.getPaint();
        oldStroke     = g2.getStroke();


        // Fill the Shape (if appropriate)
        if (paint != null)
        {
            g2.setPaint(paint);
            g2.fill(transformedShape);
        }

        // Stroke the Shape if appropriate
        if (color != null)
        {
            if (stroke != null) g2.setStroke(stroke);
```

```
            g2.setColor(color);
            g2.draw(transformedShape);
        }

        // Restore the state
        g2.setColor(oldColor);
        g2.setPaint(oldPaint);
        g2.setStroke(oldStroke);
    }
}
```

EXERCISES

1. What is a convex shape?

2. Illustrate a mitered join.

3. Provide an example of a ligature.

4. Write a public paint method that is passed a `Graphics` object, returns nothing, and draws a red rectangle centered in a solid black background.

5. Why doesn't the `Area` class include an `inclusiveOr()` method in addition to its `exclusiveOr()` method?

6. Given two `Area` objects, `a` and `b`, what is the result of:

```
        a.intersect(b);
        a.subtract(b);
```

7. Given the following definition of the `RectangleCanvas` class:

```
public class RectangleCanvas extends JPanel
{
    private AffineTransform       at, rotate, scale;
    private Rectangle2D.Double    r;

    public RectangleCanvas()
    {
        r = new Rectangle2D.Double(50.0, 50.0, 100.0, 100.0);

        rotate = AffineTransform.getRotateInstance(0.75, 100.0, 100.0);
        scale  = AffineTransform.getScaleInstance(3.0, 2.0);
        at     = new AffineTransform();
    }
```

```
    public void paint(Graphics g)
    {
      Graphics2D     g2;
      Shape          s;

      g2 = (Graphics2D)g;
      at.setToIdentity();
      at.preConcatenate(rotate);
      at.preConcatenate(scale);

      s = at.createTransformedShape(r);
      g2.draw(s);
      }
  }
```

what will be rendered the first time a `RectangleCanvas` is 'painted?' What will be rendered the second time it is 'painted?'

8. Modify the `RectangleCanvas class` above so that it contains a second rectangle with parameters (50, 50, 100, 100). The original rectangle must be rendered first in opaque red and the 'new' rectangle must be rendered second in 50% transparent blue. The background must be opaque white.

9. Write a simple line-drawing app that displays different line segments in a randomly selected color. Each time the user clicks at two different points, the app should draw a line between those points.

10. Modify the line-drawing app from Exercise 9 above so that each time the user clicks at three different points, the app draws a quadratic curve between the first and last point, using the second point as the control point.

11. The campus Office of Information Technology heard about the `FrontWall` class you developed for Exercise 12 on page 152 and want you to extend it so that it also shows the 'movie/projector' screen either raised, partially lowered, or completely lowered. Again, you must NOT use the classes in this book. Instead, you must complete the `renderScreen()` method in the following `FrontWallWithScreen` class:

```
import java.awt.*;
import java.awt.geom.*;
import javax.swing.*;

/**
 * A GUI component that displays the front wall of a classroom
 * with a "movie" screen (that can be partially lowered)
 */
```

```
public class FrontWallWithScreen extends FrontWall
{
    protected double              amountLowered;
    protected Rectangle2D.Double  screen;

    /**
     * Default Constructor
     */
    public FrontWallWithScreen()
    {
        super();
        screen = new Rectangle2D.Double();
    }

    /**
     * Render this component
     *
     * @param g    The rendering engine to use
     */
    public void paint(Graphics g)
    {
        Graphics2D      g2;

        super.paint(g);
        g2 = (Graphics2D)g;
        renderScreen(g2);
    }

    /**
     * Set how low the movie screen is (i.e., what percentage of the
     * height of the front wall is covered by the movie screen)
     *
     * @param amountLowered    The percentage lowered (in [0, 1])
     */
    public void setAmountLowered(double amount)
    {
        if ((amount >= 0.0) && (amount <= 1.0)) amountLowered = amount;
    }

    /**
     * Change the amount that the screen is lowered
     *
     * @param change     The amount of the change
     */
    public void changeAmountLowered(double change)
    {
        setAmountLowered(amountLowered + change);
```

```
    }

    /**
     * Render the "movie/projector" screen on the front wall.
     *
     * The "movie" screen must be half as wide as the front wall and
     * must occupy the middle half of the wall (i.e., the left-most
     * quarter of the wall and the right-most quarter of the wall must
     * never be covered by the screen).
     *
     * The screen must be fully raised when amountLowered is 0.0,
     * partially lowered when amountLowered is between 0.0 and 1.0
     * (e.g., when amountLowered is .28 it must be 28 percent lowered),
     * and fully lowered when amountLowered is 1.0.
     *
     * @param g2        The rendering engine to use
     */
    protected void renderScreen(Graphics2D g2)
    {

        // YOUR CODE HERE!

    }
```

REFERENCES AND FURTHER READING ···

Ammeraal, L., and K. Zhang. 2007. *Computer graphics for Java programmers.* Hoboken, NJ: John Wiley and Sons.

Angel, A. 2006. *Interactive computer graphics.* Boston: Pearson.

Farin, G., and D. Hansford. 2005. *Practical linear algebra: A geometry toolbox.* Wellesley, MA: A. K. Peters.

Laszlo, M. 2002. *Object oriented programming featuring graphical applications in Java.* Reading, MA: Addison-Wesley Publishing.

A Static Visual Content System

7

Suppose one must render a comic book character and that the character's head must be one `BufferedImage` and its body must be a different `BufferedImage`. Given the current system, one could create two `sampled.Content` objects and put them in one `Visualization`, but the character could not be treated as a coherent whole.

Similarly, suppose one must create an illustration of a house using described content and that the door and roof must be different colors. Again, given the current system, one could create a `described.Content` object for each part of the house and add them all to a single `Visualization`, but the house could not be treated as a coherent whole.

In other words, as the system is currently designed (and implemented), a `sampled.Content` object has only one `BufferedImage` object and a `described.Content` object has only one `Shape`, `Color`, `Paint`, and `Stroke` object. As the two examples above illustrate, this is insufficient in many situations. Hence, to be really useful, the system must

F7.1 Support visual content that has multiple component parts.

That is, the system must support `sampled.Content` objects that have multiple `BufferedImage` objects as components (e.g., a head and a body). In addition, the system must support `described.Content` objects that have multiple `Shape` objects as components (e.g., a door and a roof), each with its own `Color`, `Paint`, and `Stroke`.

This chapter considers how to add this functionality. It begins by considering different high-level (i.e., ignoring the distinction between sampled and described content) designs that satisfy this requirement. It next considers how to satisfy this requirement while incorporating different content types. Finally, it considers some examples of things that can be done with the improved system.

7.1 Design Alternatives Ignoring Content Types

Since the system is already fairly complicated, it makes sense to initially consider design alternatives at a high level of abstraction. Specifically, it makes sense to ignore the fact that the system must support both sampled and described content. That is, to get started, it is simpler to ignore the differences between `statik.sampled.Content` and `statik.described.Content` objects and consider only `statik.Content` objects. Then, after a good high-level design is in place, the details needed to support the differences between `statik.sampled.Content` and `statik.described.Content` can be added. (In fact, since they aren't necessary, at this level of abstraction, package names will be omitted completely.)

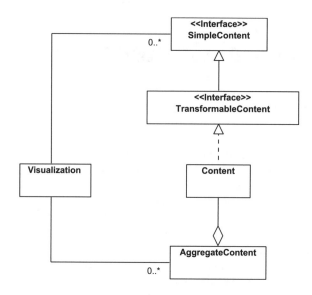

Figure 7.1   A Design That Uses Aggregation

The most obvious way to satisfy Requirement F7.1 is to create an **AggregateContent** class that contains multiple **Content** objects. To do so, one must add functionality to the **Visualization** class so that it can contain **AggregateContent** objects, and the **VisualizationView** class so that it can render **AggregateContent** objects. This design is illustrated in Figure 7.1. The biggest shortcoming of this design is that both the **Visualization** and **VisualizationView** classes must now distinguish between **Content** objects and **TransformableContent** objects. As a result, the **Visualization** class becomes more complicated and repetitive because it must now manage two different collections. Also as a result, the **VisualizationView** class becomes less cohesive because it must contain logic that retrieves the **Content** objects in the **AggregateContent** and renders them (in the appropriate order).

A better way to satisfy Requirement F7.1 is to use the composite pattern. This involves the creation of a **CompositeContent** class that consists of **TransformableContent** objects and implements the **TransformableContent** interface. This design is illustrated in Figure 7.2 on the next page. When a **CompositeContent** object's **render()** method is called, it simply delegates to all of its components' **render()** methods. When a **Composite** object's **getBounds2D()** method is called, it calls each of its components' **getBounds2D()** methods and constructs the smallest rectangle that contains them all.

In this context, the composite pattern allows both the **Visualization** and **VisualizationView** classes to treat **SimpleContent** objects and **CompositeContent** objects in exactly the same way. The obvious advantage of this design is that it does not require any changes to the **Visualization** class. Since a **Visualization** object has a collection of **SimpleContent** objects and **CompositeContent** implements the **SimpleContent** interface, one can add **CompositeContent** objects to a **Visualization**.

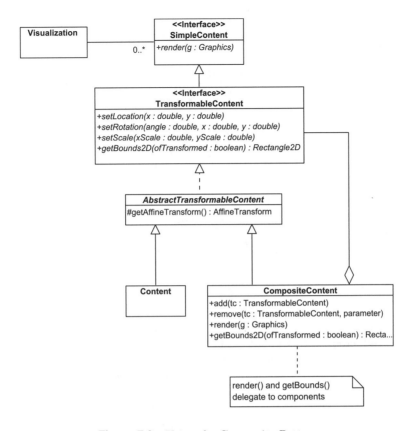

Figure 7.2   Using the Composite Pattern

The less obvious advantage of this design is that it enables the creation of content that is very complicated. In particular, observe that a `CompositeContent` object is composed of `TransformableContent` objects, and is itself a `TransformableContent` object. Hence, a `CompositeContent` can contain both 'leaf' `TransformableContent` objects (e.g., `Content` objects) and other `CompositeContent` objects. Hence, one can create a character in a game that has a head and a body, and the head and the body can both be `CompositeContent` objects if necessary.

7.2 Design Alternatives Incorporating Content Types

It is now time to consider ways to make use of the composite pattern while distinguishing between different types of static visual content. In other words, it is time to consider ways to add the `statik.sampled.Content` and `statik.described.Content` classes to the design illustrated in Figure 7.2.

The most obvious way to proceed is, in essence, to make three 'copies' of the design illustrated in Figure 7.2; one for `statik.sampled.Content`, one for `statik.described.Content`, and one for either/both. This is illustrated in Figure 7.3 on the following page.

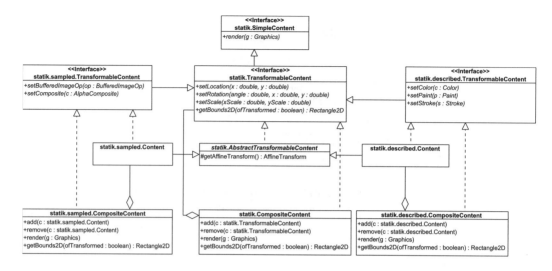

Figure 7.3 A Design with Code Duplication

The shortcoming of this design is that the `statik.sampled.CompositeContent`, `statik.described.CompositeContent`, and `statik.CompositeContent` classes all must have `add()`, `remove()`, `render()`, and `getBounds2D()` methods that contain (virtually) identical code. The `add()` and `remove()` methods will manage collections in identical ways, varying only in the type of object in the collection. The `getBounds2D()` methods will iterate over a collection, getting the bounds of the objects in the collection and constructing the smallest rectangle that contains them all. Again, the only thing that will vary is the type of object in the collection. Finally, the `render()` methods will all iterate over a collection, delegating to the `render()` methods of the objects in the collection. Once again, the only thing that will vary is the type of object in the collection.

 One way to eliminate this code duplication is to eliminate the type-specific `CompositeContent` classes. That is, to have a `statik.CompositeContent` class that can contain any kind of `statik.TransformableContent` object, including both `statik.sampled.Content` and `statik.described.Content` objects. This is illustrated in Figure 7.4 on the next page. The shortcoming of this design is that it allows only operations that make sense for all `statik.Content` objects. In other words, it doesn't allow operations that are either specific to `statik.sampled.Content` or `statik.described.Content` objects to be applied to `statik.CompositeContent` objects. For example, it does not allow the application of a `BufferedImageOp` to a `statik.CompositeContent` because the composite might include described content for which the `BufferedImageOp` does not make sense. So, even if the `statik.CompositeContent` object contains nothing but `statik.sampled.Content` objects, you cannot apply a `BufferedImageOp` to it.

 Another way to eliminate the code duplication is to add an abstract parent of the `statik.sampled.CompositeContent` and `statik.described.CompositeContent` classes. This is illustrated in Figure 7.5 on page 192. This design allows for operations that are specific to `statik.sampled.Content` and `statik.described.Content` because there are distinct

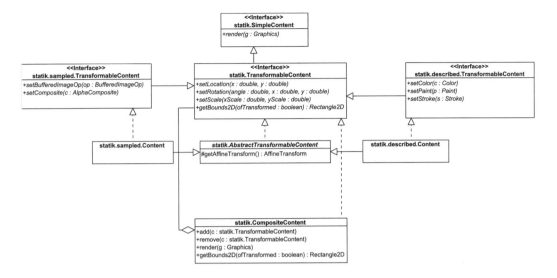

Figure 7.4 A Design That Excludes Some Operations

`statik.sampled.CompositeContent` and `statik.described.CompositeContent` classes. It eliminates code duplication by moving the common code to the abstract parent (i.e., the `statik.AbstractCompositeContent` class). Hence, in many respects, it is a good design.

This design does, however, have one minor inconvenience. Since the `statik.AbstractCompositeContent` class contains `statik.TransformableContent` objects, so do the `statik.sampled.CompositeContent` and `statik.described.CompositeContent` classes. That is, since the abstract parent manages the collection, the collection must contain `statik.TransformableContent` objects rather than the more specific `statik.sampled.Content` and `statik.described.Content` objects. This means that the `statik.sampled.CompositeContent` and `statik.described.CompositeContent` classes are not immediately type-safe.

The easy way to make the `statik.sampled.CompositeContent` and `statik.described` `.CompositeContent` classes type-safe is to add typed `add()` and `remove()` methods to them. These methods need do nothing more than delegate to the methods with the same names in the `statik.AbstractCompositeContent` class. However, this is likely to lead to mistakes in the future since any modifications made to the `statik.AbstractCompositeContent` class will also have to be made to the child classes.

This shortcoming can be eliminated using generics. In particular, one can include a parameterized parent class that contains either sampled content, described content, or both. Then, one can include typed specializations that need only bind the parameterized type. This design is illustrated in Figure 7.6 on the next page.

While this design still has the `statik.sampled.CompositeContent` and `statik.described.CompositeContent` classes, they don't need to have type-safe methods for managing the collection. Instead, they achieve type-safety by binding a particular class (`statik.sampled.TransformableContent` and `statik.described.TransformableContent`, respectively) to the parameterized type. They then include whatever functionality is spe-

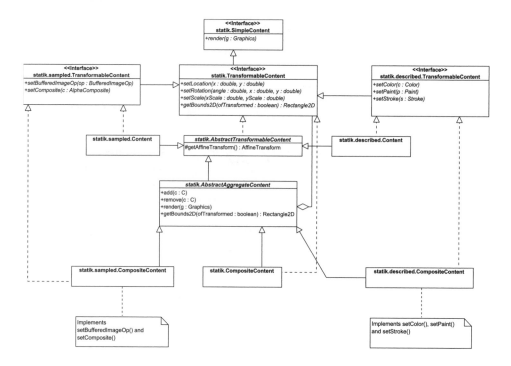

Figure 7.5 A Design with a Minor Inconvenience

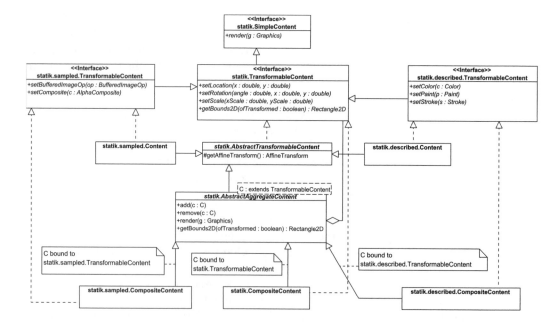

Figure 7.6 The Complete Design

cific to their specific type of content. So, the `statik.sampled.CompositeContent` class has `setBufferedImageOp()` and `setComposite()` methods, and the `statik.described` `.CompositeContent` class has `setColor()`, `setPaint()`, and `setStroke()` methods.

The details of implementing this design can now be considered.

7.2.1   The `visual.statik` Package

The first step is to create an `AbstractAggregateContent` class that uses the parameterized type `<C extends TransformableContent>`. Then, C can be bound to either `statik.sampled.TransformableContent`, `statik.described.TransformableContent`, or `statik.TransformableContent`. This enables the creation of one specialization of `AbstractAggregateContent` that can contain only sampled content, another specialization of `AbstractAggregateContent` that can contain only described content, and a third specialization of `AbstractAggregateContent` that can contain both.

The overall structure for this implementation is relatively straightforward. The `AbstractAggregateContent` class can use the functionality of the `Abstract-TransformableContent`, which has code for maintaining state information (e.g., the details of the transformations). It adds methods for managing a collection of (specializations of) the `TransformableContent` class.

```
package visual.statik;

import java.awt.*;
import java.awt.geom.*;
import java.util.*;

public abstract class
              AbstractAggregateContent<C extends TransformableContent>
       extends  AbstractTransformableContent
{
    // A LinkedList is used to order the components.
    // Since we don't expect many components to be removed
    // this doesn't raise efficiency concerns.
    //
    // Alternatively, we could have a z-order.
    protected LinkedList<C>        components;

    public AbstractAggregateContent()
    {
        super();
        components = new LinkedList<C>();
    }
}
```

The management of the `TransformableContent` objects can be handled with `add()`, `remove()`, and `iterator()` methods as follows:

```
public void add(C component)
{
    components.add(component);
}
public Iterator<C> iterator()
{
    return components.iterator();
}

public void remove(C component)
{
    components.remove(component);
}
```

Calls to the `render()` method are delegated to the `TransformableContent` objects, after the `TransformableContent` objects are transformed, as appropriate.

```
public void render(Graphics g)
{
    Iterator<C>   i;
    C             component;

    i = components.iterator();
    while (i.hasNext())
    {
        component = i.next();

        component.setLocation(x, y);
        component.setRotation(angle, xRotation, yRotation);
        component.setScale(xScale, yScale);

        component.render(g);
    }
}
```

Note that one could, alternatively, transform the component `TransformableContent` objects each time the composite object is transformed. However, for the reasons given in the discussion of the `AbstractTransformableContent` class (see Section 4.6.3 on page 103), this is not a good idea.

To simplify the exposition, this implementation does not store bounds, it calculates them when needed using the `getBounds2D()` method in the `TransformableContent` objects. (Alternatively, this class could calculate the bounds whenever they change.)

```java
public Rectangle2D getBounds2D(boolean ofTransformed)
{
    double                  maxX, maxY, minX, minY, rx, ry;
    Iterator<C>             i;
    Rectangle2D             bounds;
    TransformableContent    component;

    maxX = Double.NEGATIVE_INFINITY;
    maxY = Double.NEGATIVE_INFINITY;
    minX = Double.POSITIVE_INFINITY;
    minY = Double.POSITIVE_INFINITY;

    i = components.iterator();
    while (i.hasNext())
    {
        component = i.next();
        bounds    = component.getBounds2D(ofTransformed);

        if (bounds != null)
        {
            rx = bounds.getX();
            ry = bounds.getY();
            if (rx < minX) minX = rx;
            if (ry < minY) minY = ry;

            rx = bounds.getX() + bounds.getWidth();
            ry = bounds.getY() + bounds.getHeight();
            if (rx > maxX) maxX = rx;
            if (ry > maxY) maxY = ry;
        }
    }
    // Note: We could, instead, use an object pool
    return new Rectangle2D.Double(minX, minY, maxX-minX, maxY-minY);
}
```

The `render()` and `getBounds2D()` methods make it clear why the parameterized type C must be restricted to be an extension of `TransformableContent`. In particular, since the `setLocation()`, `setRotation()`, `setScale()`, `render()`, and `getBounds2D()` messages are sent to objects of type C, one must ensure that objects of type C have these methods.

Finally, the `statik.AbstractAggregateContent` class can be used to create a `statik.CompositeContent` class that can contain both sampled and described content. Indeed, all that is required is to bind the parameterized type to the statik.TransformableContent class as follows.

```
package visual.statik;

public class       CompositeContent
       extends      AbstractAggregateContent<TransformableContent>
       implements TransformableContent
{
    public CompositeContent()
    {
        super();
    }
}
```

A default constructor is included as a matter of style.

7.2.2   The visual.statik.sampled **Package**

The CompositeContent class in the sampled package must extend the Abstract-AggregateContent class, binding the parameterized type to the TransformableContent class in the sampled package.

```
package visual.statik.sampled;

import java.awt.Composite;
import java.awt.image.BufferedImageOp;
import java.util.Iterator;

import visual.statik.AbstractAggregateContent;

public class       CompositeContent
       extends      AbstractAggregateContent<TransformableContent>
       implements TransformableContent
{
    public CompositeContent()
    {
        super();
    }
}
```

Now, the TransformableContent interface in the sampled package must be implemented. The implementation of the setBufferedImageOp method simply delegates to the method with the same name in each component.

```
public void setBufferedImageOp(BufferedImageOp op)
{
   Iterator<TransformableContent>  i;

   i = iterator();
   while (i.hasNext())
   {
      i.next().setBufferedImageOp(op);
   }
}
```

Similarly, the implementation of the setComposite method also delegates to each component.

```
public void setComposite(Composite c)
{
   Iterator<TransformableContent>  i;

   i = iterator();
   while (i.hasNext())
   {
      i.next().setComposite(c);
   }
}
```

One troubling aspect of this design is that these two methods contain almost identical blocks of code. Unfortunately, eliminating this code duplication would complicate the design considerably (e.g., using the command pattern).

7.2.3 The visual.statik.described **Package**

The CompositeContent class in the described package also extends the Abstract-AggregateContent class. However, this class binds C to TransformableContent in the described package.

```
package visual.statik.described;

import java.awt.*;
import java.util.Iterator;

import visual.statik.AbstractAggregateContent;
```

```
public class       CompositeContent
       extends      AbstractAggregateContent<TransformableContent>
       implements TransformableContent
{
    public CompositeContent()
    {
        super();
    }
}
```

In keeping with the composite pattern, this class implements the `TransformableContent` interface in the `described` package. Hence, it implements the `setColor()` method,

```
public void setColor(Color color)
{
    Iterator<TransformableContent>  i;

    i = iterator();
    while (i.hasNext())
    {
        i.next().setColor(color);
    }
}
```

the `setPaint()` method,

```
public void setPaint(Paint paint)
{
    Iterator<TransformableContent>  i;

    i = iterator();
    while (i.hasNext())
    {
        i.next().setPaint(paint);
    }
}
```

and the `setStroke()` method.

```
public void setStroke(Stroke stroke)
{
```

Figure 7.7 Buzzy

```
    Iterator<TransformableContent>  i;

    i = iterator();
    while (i.hasNext())
    {
        i.next().setStroke(stroke);
    }
}
```

7.3 Some Examples

In principle, if one has talent, this design can be used to create amazingly complicated and interesting static visual content. That's a big "if."

7.3.1 An Example of described.CompositeContent

As an example where the "if" is not satisfied, consider the specialization of described .CompositeContent (called Buzzy) shown in Figure 7.7.

The overall structure of the class is simple; it extends the described.CompositeContent class and has no attributes.

```
import java.awt.*;
import java.awt.geom.*;
import javax.swing.*;

import visual.statik.described.*;

public class BoringBuzzy extends CompositeContent
{
}
```

All of the work is done in the constructor. First, several local variables are declared and the necessary `Color` and `Stroke` objects are constructed.

```
    public BoringBuzzy()
    {
        super();
        Arc2D.Float          helmetShape, visorShape;
        BasicStroke          stroke;
        Color                black, gold, gray, purple;
        CompositeContent     head;
        Content              body, hair, helmet, visor;
        Path2D.Float         bodyShape;
        QuadCurve2D.Float    hairShape;

        black  = Color.BLACK;
        gold   = new Color(0xc2,0xa1,0x4d);
        gray   = new Color(0xaa,0xaa,0xaa);
        purple = new Color(0x45,0x00,0x84);

        stroke = new BasicStroke();
    }
```

Next, the body `Shape` is constructed, the body `described.Content` is constructed, and the body is added.

```
        bodyShape = new Path2D.Float();
        bodyShape.moveTo( 20, 50);
        bodyShape.lineTo( 20, 70);
        bodyShape.lineTo( 20, 90);
        bodyShape.lineTo( 10, 90);
        bodyShape.lineTo( 10,100);
        bodyShape.lineTo( 80,100);
        bodyShape.lineTo( 80, 90);
        bodyShape.lineTo( 40, 90);
        bodyShape.lineTo( 40, 70);
        bodyShape.lineTo( 40, 50);
        bodyShape.closePath();
        body = new Content(bodyShape, black, purple, stroke);
        add(body);
```

Next, the head is constructed (which is, itself, a `described.CompositeContent` object) and added.

Figure 7.8 Buzzy with a Fancy Helmet

```
head = new CompositeContent();
add(head);
```

After that, the `described.Content` objects that make up the head are created. This process begins with the hair,

```
hairShape = new QuadCurve2D.Float(10,2,40,10,30,25);
hair = new Content(hairShape, purple, null, stroke);
head.add(hair);
```

continues with the helmet,

```
helmetShape = new Arc2D.Float(2,20,70,40,2,360,Arc2D.OPEN);
helmet=new Content(helmetShape, black, gold, stroke);
head.add(helmet);
```

and, finally, the visor.

```
visorShape = new Arc2D.Float(40,25,35,30,315,90,Arc2D.PIE);
visor=new Content(visorShape, black, gray, stroke);
head.add(visor);
```

7.3.2 An Example of Mixed `CompositeContent`

This example adds a logo to Buzzy's helmet. What makes this example interesting is that the logo is sampled content, as shown in Figure 7.8.

This class extends `statik.CompositeContent` as follows:

```
import java.awt.*;
import java.awt.geom.*;
import javax.swing.*;

public class FancyBuzzy extends visual.statik.CompositeContent
{
}
```

Now, of course, all of the class names must be fully qualified.

```
Resource Finder                           finder;
visual.statik.CompositeContent            head;
visual.statik.described.Content           body, hair, helmet, visor;
visual.statik.sampled.Content             screw;
visual.statik.sampled.ContentFactory      factory;
```

Not much else changes, except that the logo must be constructed,

```
finder = ResourceFinder.createInstance(this);
factory = new visual.statik.sampled.ContentFactory(finder);
screw = factory.createContent("/visual/statik/screw.png", 4);
```

and the head must now be a `statik.CompositeContent` object.

```
head = new visual.statik.CompositeContent();
head.add(hair);
head.add(helmet);
head.add(screw);
head.add(visor);

add(head);
```

7.3.3   An Example of a Visualization

The next example is a `Visualization` that contains a `ComponentContent` object and a `Content` object. Specifically, it will contain Buzzy in the foreground and a forest in the background. This is shown in Figure 7.9 on the next page.

Figure 7.9 Buzzy in the Woods

A natural place to start is with the woods, which is sampled content. In order to make the woods appear to be in the distance, one can take advantage of what we know about depth cues and blur the image slightly.

```
factory   = new ContentFactory(finder);
opFactory = BufferedImageOpFactory.createFactory();

woods   = factory.createContent("woods.png",
                                3);
woods.setLocation(0,0);
woods.setBufferedImageOp(opFactory.createBlurOp(3));
```

Next, Buzzy is constructed and positioned appropriately.

```
buzzy   = new FancyBuzzy();
buzzy.setLocation(200, 318);
```

After that, the `Visualization` is constructed, the two pieces of content are added in the appropriate order,

```
visualization = new Visualization();
view          = visualization.getView();

view.setBounds(0,0,471,418);
view.setSize(471,418);
```

Figure 7.10   Picture-in-a-Picture

```
visualization.add(woods);
visualization.add(buzzy);
```

and the `VisualizationView` is added to the content pane of the `ApplicationWindow`.

```
// The content pane
contentPane = (JPanel)rootPaneContainer.getContentPane();
contentPane.add(view);
```

7.3.4   An Example of Multiple Visualizations

The final example uses two `Visualization` objects, each with its own view. This is, in essence, a simple example of 'picture-in-a-picture.' The big 'picture' is Buzzy in the woods, and the small 'picture' is a house with a white picket fence. This is shown in Figure 7.10.

The overall structure is straightforward.

```
import java.awt.*;
import java.awt.geom.*;
import javax.swing.*;

import app.*;
import visual.*;
```

```
import visual.statik.sampled.*;

public class    StaticPIPApp
       extends AbstractMultimediaApp
{
    public void init()
    {
        BufferedImageOpFactory          opFactory;
        Content                         woods, house;
        ContentFactory                  factory;
        FancyBuzzy                      buzzy;
        JPanel                          contentPane;
        Visualization                   model1, model2;
        VisualizationRenderer           renderer1, renderer2;
        VisualizationView               view1, view2;

        factory   = new ContentFactory(ResourceFinder.createInstance(this);
        opFactory = BufferedImageOpFactory.createFactory();
    }
}
```

The first `Visualization` is created exactly as above, except that a `ScaledView` is used (in case there is a need to switch between the main and subsidiary 'pictures').

```
woods   = factory.createContent("woods.png",
                                    3);
woods.setLocation(0,0);
woods.setBufferedImageOp(opFactory.createBlurOp(3));

buzzy   = new FancyBuzzy();
buzzy.setLocation(200, 318);

model1 = new Visualization();
model1.add(woods);
model1.add(buzzy);

view1     = model1.getView();
renderer1 = view1.getRenderer();
view1.setRenderer(new ScaledVisualizationRenderer(renderer1,
                                                471.0,
                                                418.0));
view1.setBounds(0,0,471,418);
view1.setSize(471,418);
```

The second `Visualization` contains a single piece of sampled content.

```
house = factory.createContent("house.png",
                                3);
house.setLocation(0,0);

model2 = new Visualization();
model2.add(house);

view2    = model2.getView();
renderer2 = view2.getRenderer();
view2.setRenderer(new ScaledVisualizationRenderer(renderer2,
                                           525.0,
                                           375.0));

view2.setBounds(50,50,160,120);
view2.setSize(160,120);
```

Finally, the content pane needs to be told to display both `Visualization` objects.

```
// The content pane
contentPane = (JPanel)rootPaneContainer.getContentPane();
contentPane.add(view2);
contentPane.add(view1);
```

EXERCISES

1. Why does the design in Figure 7.2 on page 189 include an `AbstractTransformable-Content` class rather than just include the `getAffineTransform()` method in the `TransformableContent` interface?

2. The design in Figure 7.3 on page 190 clearly leads to code duplication. What problems are caused by this kind of code duplication?

3. Explain why it is a good idea to create a `CompositeContent` object for Buzzy's `head` that consists of his `hair`, `helmet`, and `visor`.

4. Why does the order in which Buzzy's `hair`, `helmet`, and `visor` are added to his `head` matter? What would happen if, for example, the `visor` was added first?

5. Design and implement a filter that creates a binoculars effect (i.e., the destination image is black except for two side-by-side circles that contain the source image). In other words, the destination image should be the source image as viewed through a pair of binoculars (with no magnification).

6. Combine the night vision filter in Section 5.3.3 with the binoculars above to create a night vision binoculars filter.

7. The architects working with the university heard about your `FrontWallWithScreen` class from Exercise 11 on page 183 and want to be able to use it to visualize the classrooms with the lights on and off, but they do not want to take new photographs of all of the classrooms (all of the originals were taken with the lights on). Again, you must NOT use the classes in this book. Instead, you must complete the `renderBackground()` method in the following `FrontWallWithScreenAndLights` class (which overrides the version in the `FrontWall` class).

```java
import java.awt.*;
import java.awt.geom.*;
import javax.swing.*;

/**
 * A GUI component that displays the front wall of a classroom.
 * The way in which this component is rendered depends on whether
 * lightsOn is true or false (simulating the lights in the room
 * being on or off).
 */
public class FrontWallWithScreenAndLights extends FrontWallWithScreen
{
    protected boolean                 lightsOn = true;

    /**
     * Default Constructor
     */
    public FrontWallWithScreenAndLights()
    {
        super();
        setBackground(new Color(102,102,102)); // Dark grey
    }

    /**
     * Render this component
     *
     * @param g    The rendering engine to use
     */
    public void paint(Graphics g)
    {
        Graphics2D      g2;

        super.paint(g);
        g2 = (Graphics2D)g;
        renderBackground(g2);
        renderScreen(g2);
    }
```

```java
/**
 * Turn the lights off
 */
public void turnLightsOff()
{
   lightsOn = false;
   repaint();
}

/**
 * Turn the lights on
 */
public void turnLightsOn()
{
   lightsOn = true;
   repaint();
}

/**
 * Render the background image on this component.
 *
 * The way in which the image is composed with the background
 * depends on the value of the lightsOn attribute.  When lightsOn
 * is true the image must be rendered "as is", whereas when
 * lightsOn is false it must appear to be "darker".
 *
 * @param g2        The rendering engine to use
 */
protected void renderBackground(Graphics2D g2)
{

    // YOUR CODE HERE!

}
}
```

REFERENCES AND FURTHER READING

Freeman, E., E. Freeman, B. Bates, and K. Sierra. 2004. *Head first design patterns*. Sebastopol, CA: O'Reilly.

Sampled Dynamic Visual Content

8

Strictly speaking, dynamic visual content is any visual content that changes over time. This book is concerned, in particular, with visual content that changes over time in a way that causes the perception of *apparent motion*. In other words, this book is interested in visual content that changes over time in such a way as to trick the brain into thinking that something is moving. Note that many people use the term "animation" to describe the group of techniques that make visual content appear to move. It comes from the root "animate," which means "to give life or motion." Unfortunately, different people use the term "animation" in different ways. To avoid any ambiguity that might arise, this book uses the term "dynamic visual content" instead.

As discussed in Section 5 on page 111, the sampling of **static** visual content involves sampling from all possible colors and sampling from all points in space. The sampling of **dynamic** visual content, on the other hand, involves sampling from all possible points in time. That is, as illustrated in Figure 8.1, the sampling of dynamic visual content involves the 'recording' of the visual content at a discrete set of points in time. Each such sample is often called a *frame*, a reference to the individual images in a film. The number of frames per unit of time (i.e., the sampling rate) is referred to as the *frame rate*.

In sampled **static** visual content each pixel is treated as atomic (i.e., a coherent whole that can't be divided into smaller parts). In sampled **dynamic** visual content each frame is atomic. Of course, at a lower level of abstraction, each frame actually consists of static visual content, and that content can either be sampled or described. However, at the current (higher) level of abstraction, the nature of each frame is of no consequence.

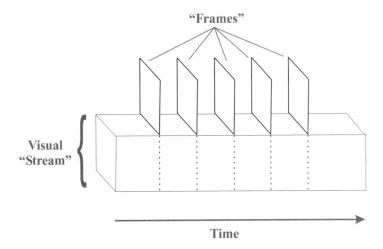

Figure 8.1 Sampling from a Visual Stream

As before, this chapter begins with a small taste of what is to come. It then delves into the details (including the encapsulation of sampled dynamic visual content and operations on this content) and, ultimately, considers the design and implementation of a sampled dynamic visual content system.

8.1   A 'Quick Start'

At some point in your life, you may have been bored in class and decided to keep yourself occupied by creating a flip book. First, you drew a sequence of stick figures in slightly different positions on the corners of the pages of your textbook. Then you flipped through the pages, making the stick figure appear to move. Finally, you flipped through the pages in the other order, making the stick figure appear to move backward.

The goal of this chapter is to create a system that behaves like a flip book for `SimpleContent` objects. That is, the system must:

F8.1 Render a sequence of `SimpleContent` objects over time.

To satisfy this requirement the system must have an object that manages the collection of `SimpleContent` objects, a process that controls the rendering of the objects in the sequence, and a GUI component that presents the `SimpleContent` objects. Fortunately, the visual content system developed thus far already contains almost everything required. The only missing component is an 'enhanced' `Visualization` object to manage the collection of `SimpleContent` objects.

One way to provide the additional functionality is to actually add code to the `Visualization` class. The shortcoming of this approach is that it makes this class more complicated and more difficult to understand for those who have no interest in dynamic content. In other words, why should someone who has no interest in dynamic content have to understand these aspects of the `Visualization` class in order to use it?

Another way to provide the additional functionality is to use the decorator pattern. As you should know from earlier chapters, the decorator pattern makes the most sense when one wants to add functionality to individual objects, rather than to the class. In the current context, this seems highly unlikely—it is hard to imagine a situation in which, at runtime, one would want to add these kinds of capabilities to a `Visualization` object. In general, the app will know in advance whether it will need to manage and present dynamic content. Hence, while the decorator pattern could be used, it is less than ideal.

A third way to provide the additional functionality is to create a specialization of the `Visualization` class that includes the attributes and methods needed to manage and present dynamic content. Given the discussion above, this seems like the best approach.

This decision means that the system will include a class that extends the `Visualization` class. In keeping with the film analogy introduced above, this specialization of the `Visualization` class is called the `Screen` class.

The next thing to consider is the control of the rendering process. Not surprisingly, there are several different ways to proceed.

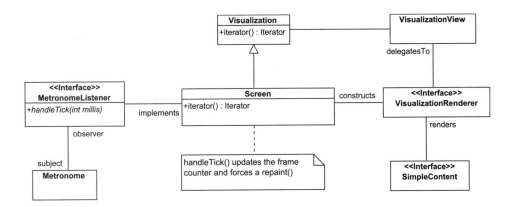

Figure 8.2   A Simple System for Rendering Sampled Dynamic Content

One obvious, but inappropriate, approach is to have the `Screen` class iterate through the collection of `SimpleContent` objects sending each a `render()` message in turn. The shortcoming with this approach is that it does not provide control over the amount of time each `SimpleContent` object is visible. In other words, one `SimpleContent` object will render itself 'as fast as it can' (i.e., taking as much time as is required) and then the next `SimpleContent` object will render itself. So, there is no way to control the frame rate and there is no way to ensure that the frame rate is constant over time.

A better approach is to use a `Metronome` object (see Section 2.5 on page 30) to control the timing and have a `Screen` object play the role of `MetronomeListener`. With this design, each time the `metronome` 'ticks', the `Screen` object gets the next `SimpleContent` object to render, and informs the `VisualizationView` to render it. This design is illustrated in Figure 8.2.

The `Screen` class must manage the individual frames and control and respond to the `Metronome`. Hence, it has the following overall structure:

```
package visual.dynamic.sampled;

import java.awt.*;
import java.awt.event.*;
import javax.swing.*;
import java.util.*;

import collectionframework.*;
import event.*;
import visual.*;
import visual.statik.SimpleContent;

public class Screen extends    Visualization
                    implements MetronomeListener
{
```

```java
    private   boolean                      repeating;
    private   int                          frameDelay, frameNumber;
    private   Iterator<SimpleContent>      frames;
    protected Metronome                    metronome;
    protected SimpleContent                currentFrame;

    public static final int                DEFAULT_FRAME_DELAY = 42;

    public Screen()
    {
       this(new Metronome(DEFAULT_FRAME_DELAY));
    }

    public Screen(int frameRate)
    {
       this(new Metronome((int)(1000.0 / frameRate)));
    }

    public Screen(Metronome metronome)
    {
       super();
       this.metronome = metronome;
       metronome.addListener(this);
       setRepeating(false);
    }

    public void start()
    {
       reset();
       if (frames != null) metronome.start();
    }

    public void stop()
    {
       metronome.stop();
    }
}
```

To make this class more flexible, it has two constructors. The default constructor constructs the Metronome while the explicit value constructor is passed the Metronome. The default constructor will be used most frequently. The explicit value constructor provides the ability to, for example, have several Screen objects use the same Metronome (to synchronize them).

The `Screen` class has a `setRepeating()` method that can be used to control whether the frames should repeat/loop after the last frame is rendered.

```
public void setRepeating(boolean repeating)
{
    this.repeating = repeating;
}
```

Not surprisingly, it has a 'getter' that can be used to obtain the current frame number.

```
public int getFrameNumber()
{
    return frameNumber;
}
```

Each time the `Metronome` 'ticks' it sends a `handleTick()` message to the `Screen` object. So, this method must first initiate the rendering process (by calling the inherited `repaint()` method).

```
public void handleTick(int time)
{
    if (frames != null)
    {
        // See if we're done
        if (frameNumber < 0)
        {
            if   (repeating) reset();
            else             stop();
        }

        // Start the rendering process (i.e., request that the
        // paint() method be called)
        repaint();

        // Advance the frame
        advanceFrame();
    }
}
```

It must then increase the frame index (for the next tick) and make the next frame 'active' (so that it will be rendered).

```
    private void advanceFrame()
    {
        if ((frames != null) && (frames.hasNext()))
        {
            currentFrame = frames.next();
            frameNumber++;
        }
        else
        {
            currentFrame = null;
            frameNumber  = -1;
        }
    }
```

The Screen class modifies the behavior of its parent Visualization class in one important way. Its iterator() method does not contain all of the frames, it only contains the current frame. This is accomplished with the help of the NullIterator class.

An Aside: 0- and 1-Element Iterators

Though it isn't immediately obvious to beginning programmers, everyone who has worked with arrays extensively has learned the value of 0-length and 1-length arrays. For example, it is very convenient to be able to write a total() method that can handle an array with n elements, an array with one element, or an array with zero elements. The same is true of iterators.

Hence, it is often convenient to have an Iterator that can contain zero or one element, and can be set and reset easily. This can be accomplished with a NullIterator class that has the following structure:

```
package collectionframework;

import java.util.*;

public class      NullIterator<E>
        implements Enumeration<E>, Iterator<E>
{
    private boolean    done;
    private E          element;

    public NullIterator()
    {
        clear();
    }
```

```
        public NullIterator(E element)
        {
            setElement(element);
        }

        public void clear()
        {
            done      = true;
        }
        public void reset()
        {
            done = false;
        }

        public void setElement(E element)
        {
            this.element = element;
            reset();
        }
    }
}
```

Note that this class implements both the `Iterator` interface and the `Enumeration` interface so that it can be used with either the 'old' collection framework or the 'new' collection framework. To realize the `Iterator` interface it implements the following methods:

```
    public boolean hasNext()
    {
        return !done;
    }

    public E next() throws NoSuchElementException
    {
        if (done) throw(new NoSuchElementException());

        done = true;
        return element;
    }

    public void remove() throws UnsupportedOperationException
    {
        throw(new UnsupportedOperationException());
    }
```

To realize the `Enumeration` interface it implements the following methods:

```
    public boolean hasMoreElements()
    {
       return hasNext();
    }

    public E nextElement() throws NoSuchElementException
    {
       return next();
    }
```

The Screen class contains an attribute of the NullIterator class as follows:

```
    protected NullIterator<SimpleContent> currentFrameIterator;
```

This attribute is initialized in the constructor,

```
    currentFrameIterator = new NullIterator<SimpleContent>();
```

and is used in the iterator() method.

```
    public Iterator<SimpleContent> iterator()
    {
       currentFrameIterator.setElement(currentFrame);
       if (frameNumber < 0) currentFrameIterator.clear();

       return currentFrameIterator;
    }

    public Iterator<SimpleContent> iterator(boolean all)
    {
       Iterator<SimpleContent>        result;

       if  (all) result = super.iterator();
       else       result = iterator();

       return result;
    }
```

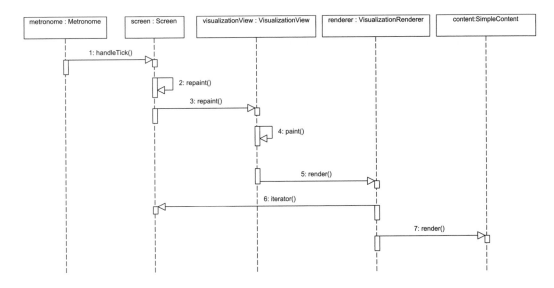

Figure 8.3   The Process of Rendering Sampled Dynamic Content

Recall that the `repaint()` method in the `Visualization` class just calls the `repaint()` method in each of its associated `VisualizationView` objects, which, in turn, calls the `render()` method of its `VisualizationRenderer`. Each frame, which is a `SimpleContent` object, is then sent a `render()` message. This sequence is illustrated in Figure 8.3.

With this as an overview, the time has come to consider a more detailed discussion of sampled dynamic visual content.

8.2 Encapsulating Sampled Dynamic Content

The `Screen` class (actually, the parent `Visualization` class) encapsulates sampled dynamic content as an ordered collection of `SimpleContent` objects. The specific collection is not very important, though it does have an impact on the functionality of the system. For example, one could use a queue for this purpose, but that would make it impossible to move both backward and forward in time. So, it makes sense to use a collection that can return either an associated `Iterator` or an associated `ListIterator` (that supports bidirectional traversal). The `CopyOnWriteArrayList` provides thread-safety and the objects in this class can return both types of iterators.

Though an individual frame can be any kind of `SimpleContent`, most commonly the individual frames contain sampled static visual content. In such situations each frame is often contained in a file, and these files may or may not have similar file names. In order to facilitate the reading of these files, it makes sense to add methods to the `ResourceFinder` class. For flexibility, this implementation assumes that the names of the frames are contained in a text file, one file per line. This text file can be read with the following `loadResourceNames()` method:

```
public String[] loadResourceNames(String listName)
```

```
{
    ArrayList<String>        buffer;
    BufferedReader           in;
    InputStream              is;
    String                   line;
    String[]                 names;

    names = null;
    is    = findInputStream(listName);

    if (is != null)
    {
        try
        {
            in     = new BufferedReader(new InputStreamReader(is));
            buffer = new ArrayList<String>();

            while ((line=in.readLine()) != null)
            {
                buffer.add(line);
            }
            names = new String[buffer.size()];
            buffer.toArray(names);
        }
        catch (IOException ioe)
        {
            // Can't read the list
        }
    }
    return names;
}
```

One can then iteratively call either the findInputStream() method or the findURL() method in the ResourceFinder class to read the individual frames.

An Aside: File Filters

If you are sure that the frames are in the file system, then you can use an object that implements the FilenamFilter interface to obtain the list of files. Such classes must have a boolean accept(File dir, String name) method that returns false if the given name should be 'filtered out' (i.e., excluded). For example, consider the following ImageSequenceFilter class:

```
package visual.dynamic.sampled;
```

```
import java.io.*;

public class ImageSequenceFilter implements FilenameFilter
{
    private String        prefix;

    public ImageSequenceFilter(String prefix)
    {
        this.prefix = prefix;
    }

    public boolean accept(File dir, String name)
    {
        return name.startsWith(prefix);
    }
}
```

The `accept()` method in this class simply returns `true` if the name of the file begins with a given prefix.

8.3   Rendering Individual Frames

Given that each individual frame is, most likely, a `sampled.Content` object that knows how to render itself, one would think that there is no reason to discuss the rendering of individual frames any further. However, it turns out that, when rendered in quick succession, the frames have a tendency to "flicker." This is because it takes a small, but noticeable, amount of time to do the pre-rendering, rendering, and post-rendering.

One way to get around this problem is to use a *double buffering* scheme in which the rendering engine does not write directly to the 'screen' (i.e., video memory). Instead, the rendering engine writes to a *background image* or *screen buffer* and then this buffer is transfered to the screen in its entirety (very quickly).[1]

Double buffering is best provided by the `VisualizationView` class as this will make it available to be used with all kinds of content. The natural place to begin is by adding the attributes required to maintain the state information.

```
    // Attributes used for double-buffering
    protected boolean            useDoubleBuffering;
    protected Graphics2D         bg;
```

---

[1]In Java, all Swing components support double buffering. However, the approach used is not suitable for the purposes of this book because it does not offer fine-grained control of when the buffering takes place. Hence, the system developed here uses its own implementation of double buffering and deactivates the default double buffering.

```
protected Image              offscreenImage;
protected int                height, width;
```

Note that this group of additional attributes includes a `Graphics2D` object that is used for the off-screen rendering. This rendering engine is obtained from the off-screen `Image` object. The off-screen `Image` object and `Graphics2D` rendering engine are created in the private `createOffScreenBuffer()` method. This method creates a new off-screen `Image` (and associated rendering engine) if the size of the `VisualizationView` has changed.

```
private Graphics2D createOffscreenBuffer()
{
    Dimension                    d;

    d = getSize();
    if ((d.height != height) || (d.width != width))
    {
        height = d.height;
        width  = d.width;

        offscreenImage = createImage(width, height);
        bg = (Graphics2D)offscreenImage.getGraphics();
        bg.setClip(0,0,width,height);
    }

    return bg;
}
```

The `paint()` method, which is called whenever the `VisualizationView` object needs to render itself, calls the `preRendering()`, `render()`, and `postRendering()` methods with the appropriate rendering engine (depending on whether double buffering is or isn't being used).

```
public void paint(Graphics g)
{
    Graphics2D        bg;

    if (useDoubleBuffering) bg = createOffscreenBuffer();
    else                    bg = (Graphics2D)g;

    if (bg != null)
    {
        // Perform necessary operations before rendering
```

```
      preRendering(bg);

      // Render the visual content
      render(bg);

      // Perform necessary operations after rendering
      postRendering(bg);

      if (useDoubleBuffering)
      {
         // Put the offscreen image on the screen
         g.drawImage(offscreenImage, 0, 0, null);

         // Reset the clipping area
         bg.setClip(0,0,width,height);
      }
   }
}
```

If double buffering is being used, those methods render into the off-screen image, which is then copied to the screen (i.e., video memory).[2]

8.4 Operating on Multiple Frames

Recall from Section 5.3.1 on page 127 that when working with sampled static visual content it is important to be able to perform operations that involve multiple pixels. When working with sampled dynamic visual content it is important to be able to perform operations that involve multiple frames. To understand why it is important to first understand the term "straight cut":

....

Definition 8.1 A *straight cut* involves rendering frame $n + 1$, in its entirety, immediately after frame n.

....

As it has been implemented thus far, the Screen class always uses straight cuts.

An alternative way to render a sequence of frames is to use a *transition*. When using a transition, an operation is performed on either frame n or $n + 1$ before frame $n + 1$ is rendered. This section discusses three different kinds of transitions: *fades*, *dissolves*, and *wipes*. They are implemented using the pre-rendering and post-rendering capabilities that are included in the VisualizationView class.

---

[2]The performance of double buffering can be improved using *hardware acceleration*. In Java, this can be accomplished, among other ways, using the VolatileImage class. These topics are beyond the scope of this book.

8.4.1 Fades

There are two very common fades.

....

Definition 8.2 A *fade from black* is a progressive brightening and a *fade to black* is a progressive darkening.

....

The fade from black is a specific example of a *fade-in* (or *fade-up*) and the fade to black is a specific example of a *fade-out* (or *fade-to*).

The easy way to fade to or from black is to compose the frame with a black rectangle. To use this approach one needs to be able to set all of the destination pixels (in the Porter–Duff sense) to black. This can be accomplished by stroking and filling a `Rectangle` that is as big as the current clipping rectangle.

```
protected void setDestinationPixels(Graphics g)
{
    Graphics2D      g2;
    Rectangle       r;

    g2 = (Graphics2D)g;

    r = g2.getClipBounds();

    g2.setComposite(AlphaComposite.Src);
    g2.setColor(g2.getBackground());
    g2.fill(r);
    g2.draw(r);
}
```

The pre-rendering method needs to save the existing `Composite` and make the `Composite` an `AlphaComposite` with a value of α based on the current frame number and the duration of the `Fade`. For example, for a fade from black with a duration of four frames, the α value will go from 0.25 to 0.50 to 0.75 to 1.00. This will make the initial composite rendering very dark. Subsequent composite renderings will be less dark until the final frame is rendered completely opaque.

```
        g2 = (Graphics2D)g;
        originalComposite = g2.getComposite();

        alpha = ((float)(frame - first + 1))/(float)duration;
        if (direction == FADE_OUT) alpha = 1.0f - alpha;

        if      (alpha > 1.0f) alpha = 1.0f;
```

```
        else if (alpha < 0.0f) alpha = 0.0f;

        setDestinationPixels(g2);

        ac  = AlphaComposite.getInstance(AlphaComposite.SRC_OVER,
                                          alpha);
        g2.setComposite(ac);
```

To reset the state, the post-rendering method needs to restore the original `Composite`.

```
        g2 = (Graphics2D)g;
        if (originalComposite != null) g2.setComposite(originalComposite);
```

8.4.2 Dissolves

A dissolve is normally described as two fades. That is, frame n fades out while frame $n + 1$ fades in. Commonly, a dissolve simply involves a fade-in without an intermediate solid background. So, a `Dissolve` class need only specialize the **Fade** class and override the `setDestinationPixels()` method so that it does nothing.

```java
package visual.dynamic.sampled;

import java.awt.*;

public class Dissolve extends Fade
{
    public Dissolve(int first, int duration)
    {
        super(FADE_IN, first, duration);
    }

    protected void setDestinationPixels(Graphics g)
    {
        // Use the last frame
    }
}
```

In this way, one frame will seem to dissolve into the other until the final frame of the transition (which will be completely opaque).

8.4.3   Wipes

There are transitions that are completely unrelated to fades. One of the most common is called a "wipe."

Definition 8.3 In a *wipe*, a frame (or frames) is clipped to a series of (one or more) geometric shapes.

There are many different kinds of wipes, including the circle wipe, the fly-on wipe, the line wipe, the quivering wipe (made famous in "Wayne's World" from *Saturday Night Live*), the rectangle wipe, the star wipe (made famous in an episode of *The Simpsons*), the venetian blind wipe, and the zoom wipe. This section implements two: the rectangle wipe and the line wipe. Others can be implemented in a similar fashion.

In a *rectangle wipe* a rectangular 'hole' appears in the center of frame n and subsequent frames are clipped to this rectangular 'hole,' which gets progressively larger. This kind of transition is implemented in the `RectangleWipe` class. It has a private method that calculates the size of the rectangular 'hole' based on the frame number and the duration.

```
    protected Rectangle2D calculateClip(float width,
                                        float height,
                                        int   frame)
{
    float               h, w, x, y;
    Rectangle2D         clip;

    w = scale*frame*width;
    h = scale*frame*height;
    x = width/2.0f   - w/2.0f;
    y = height/2.0f - h/2.0f;

    clip = new Rectangle2D.Float(x, y, w, h);

    return clip;
}
```

The rest of the functionality is handled during the pre-rendering and post-rendering phases.

The `preRendering()` method saves the existing clipping **Shape** and sets the new clipping rectangle.

```
        g2 = (Graphics2D)g;
        originalClip = g2.getClip();

        bounds = g2.getClipBounds();
```

```
height = (float)(bounds.getHeight());
width  = (float)(bounds.getWidth());


clip = calculateClip(width, height, frame-first+1);
g2.setClip(clip);
```

The postRendering() method, on the other hand, restores the original clipping Shape.

```
g2 = (Graphics2D)g;

if (originalClip != null) g2.setClip(originalClip);
```

A *line wipe* is similar to a rectangle wipe except that the 'hole' starts at the left, right, top, or bottom and moves 'across' the screen to the other edge. This can be viewed as a rectangle wipe in which the hole is as wide (or high) as the content and grows vertically (or horizontally) over time. Hence, one can think of the LineWipe class as a specialization of the RectangleWipe class. The only real difference between the two is in the calculateClip method.

```
protected Rectangle2D calculateClip(float width,
                                    float height,
                                    int frame)
{
    float            h, w, x, y;
    Rectangle2D      clip;

    w = width;
    h = height;
    x = 0.0f;
    y = 0.0f;

    if       (direction == RIGHT)
    {
        w = scale*frame*width;
        h = height;
        x = 0.0f;
        y = 0.0f;
    }
    else if (direction == LEFT)
    {
        w = scale*frame*width;
        h = height;
        x = width - w;
```

```
            y = 0.0f;
        }
        else if (direction == UP)
        {
            w = width;
            h = scale*frame*height;
            x = 0.0f;
            y = height - h;
        }
        else
        {
            w = width;
            h = scale*frame*height;
            x = 0.0f;
            y = 0.0f;
        }

        clip = new Rectangle2D.Float(x, y, w, h);

        return clip;
    }
```

8.5 Operating on Individual Frames

Of course, a variety of operations can be performed on the individual frames when they are created/produced (many such operations were considered in the chapters on static visual content). However, it is important to note that one can also perform operations on individual frames while they are being presented in a dynamic setting. This section considers one such operation—superimposition.

Definition 8.4 A *superimposition* is visual content that is to be added to an existing frame while it is being rendered.

It is very common to superimpose 'text' on frames. For example, films superimpose credits, sporting events superimpose statistics, television shows superimpose closed captioning, etc. It is also very common to superimpose 'graphics'/'images' on frames. For example, television shows superimpose network logos, football games superimpose first-down lines, etc.

Since the superimposed content can be either described or sampled it is useful to have an AbstractSuperimposition class. This class is principally responsible for handling position information. The constructor is passed the first frame, the duration, and a description of the position.

```
    public AbstractSuperimposition(int first,
                                   int duration,
```

```
                                int position)
{
    super(first, duration);

    this.position = SwingConstants.SOUTH_EAST;
    if ((position == SwingConstants.NORTH)       ||
        (position == SwingConstants.NORTH_EAST) ||
        (position == SwingConstants.EAST)        ||
        (position == SwingConstants.SOUTH_EAST) ||
        (position == SwingConstants.SOUTH)       ||
        (position == SwingConstants.SOUTH_WEST) ||
        (position == SwingConstants.WEST)        ||
        (position == SwingConstants.NORTH_WEST) ||
        (position == SwingConstants.CENTER     )    )
    {
        this.position = position;
    }
}
```

The `calculateRegistrationPoint()` method uses the position and the size of the content to determine the horizontal and vertical coordinates as follows:

```
protected Point2D calculateRegistrationPoint(double frameWidth,
                                             double frameHeight,
                                             double siWidth,
                                             double siHeight)
{
    double        left, top;

    top  = 0.0;
    left = 0.0;
    if      (position == SwingConstants.NORTH)
    {
        top  = siHeight;
        left = frameWidth/2.0 - siWidth/2.0;
    }
    else if  (position == SwingConstants.NORTH_EAST)
    {
        top  = siHeight;
        left = frameWidth - siWidth - 1;
    }
    else if  (position == SwingConstants.EAST)
    {
        top  = frameHeight/2.0 - siHeight/2.0;
```

```
         left = frameWidth - siWidth - 1;
      }
      else if  (position == SwingConstants.SOUTH_EAST)
      {
         top  = frameHeight - siHeight - 1;
         left = frameWidth - siWidth - 1;
      }
      else if  (position == SwingConstants.SOUTH)
      {
         top  = frameHeight - siHeight - 1;
         left = frameWidth/2.0 - siWidth/2.0;
      }
      else if  (position == SwingConstants.SOUTH_WEST)
      {
         top  = frameHeight - siHeight - 1;
         left = 0.0;
      }
      else if  (position == SwingConstants.WEST)
      {
         top  = frameHeight/2.0 - siHeight/2.0;
         left = 0.0;
      }
      else if  (position == SwingConstants.NORTH_WEST)
      {
         top  = siHeight;
         left = 0.0;
      }
      else if  (position == SwingConstants.CENTER)
      {
         top  = frameHeight/2.0 - siHeight/2.0;
         left = frameWidth/2.0 - siWidth/2.0;
      }

      return new Point2D.Double(left, top);
   }
```

With this, it is relatively easy to create the concrete children. What follows, for example, is a concrete TransformableContentSuperimposition that can be used to superimpose any TransformableContent object on the frames. The constructor of this class must be passed the TransformableContent object.

```
   public TransformableContentSuperimposition(
                     TransformableContent content,
                     int first, int duration,
                     int position)
```

```
    {
        super(first, duration, position);

        this.content = content;
    }
```

During the pre-rendering phase, nothing is done. During the post-rendering phase, the TransformableContent object is rendered at the appropriate position.

```
            g2 = (Graphics2D)g;

            // Transform the TransformableContent so that
            // it is positioned properly
            frameBounds   = g2.getClipBounds();
            frameWidth    = (double)frameBounds.width;
            frameHeight   = (double)frameBounds.height;

            contentBounds = content.getBounds2D(false);
            contentWidth  = contentBounds.getWidth();
            contentHeight = contentBounds.getHeight();


            rp = calculateRegistrationPoint(frameWidth,
                                            frameHeight,
                                            contentWidth,
                                            contentHeight);

            content.setLocation(rp.getX(), rp.getY());
            content.render(g);
```

8.6 Design of a Sampled Dynamic Visual Content System

The system must now satisfy the following additional requirements:

F8.2 Support transitions (other than straight cuts) between frames of sampled dynamic content.

F8.3 Support the superimposition of static visual content on one or more frames of sampled dynamic content.

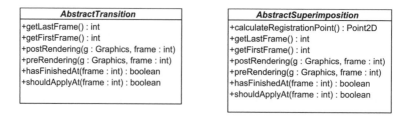

Figure 8.4 A Design of Transitions and Superimpositions with Duplication

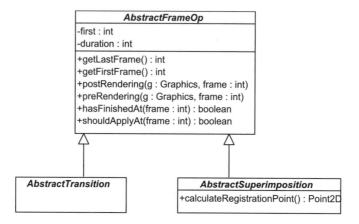

Figure 8.5 An Inflexible Design of Transitions and Superimpositions

Given the flexibility of the existing design, these two requirements can be satisfied fairly easily.

 The most obvious design involves an `AbstractTransition` class, an `AbstractSuperimposition` class, and a variety of different concrete specializations. This design is illustrated in Figure 8.4. While this design is easy to understand, it leads to an enormous amount of code duplication. In particular, except for the `calculateRegistrationPoint()` method, these two abstract classes have all of the same methods.

 The obvious way to eliminate this code duplication is to create an (abstract) parent that contains the methods that are common to the `AbstractTransition` and `AbstractSuperimposition` classes. This design is illustrated in Figure 8.5. The shortcoming of this design is that it does not lend itself to the addition of transition/superimposition classes that do not extend the `AbstractTransition` or `AbstractSuperimposition` classes.

 This flexibility can be provided by including a `FrameOp` interface that is implemented by the `AbstractFrameOp` class but can also be implemented by other transitions and/or superimpositions if necessary. This design is illustrated in Figure 8.6 on the following page. This is a pretty good design, but it can be improved. In particular, observe that at the level of the interface it does not distinguish between transitions and superimpositions. Since the two do not provide identical functionality, this might lead to type safety problems in the future.

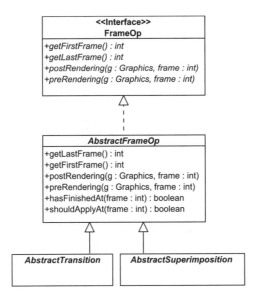

Figure 8.6 A Design of Transitions and Superimpositions That Lacks Type Safety

 The best design provides type safety by adding a `Transition` interface and a `Superimposition` interface. This design is illustrated in Figure 8.7 on the next page. While this design appears to be a little complicated at first glance, most programmers need only concern themselves with the `AbstractTransition` class and/or the `AbstractSuperimposition` class.

The `FrameOp` interface includes the two methods that are responsible for the operations that must be performed during the pre-rendering and post-rendering phases, as well as accessor methods for obtaining the first and last frame.

```
package visual.dynamic.sampled;

import java.awt.Graphics;

public interface FrameOp
{
    public abstract int getFirstFrame();

    public abstract int getLastFrame();

    public abstract void postRendering(Graphics g, int frame);

    public abstract void preRendering(Graphics g, int frame);
}
```

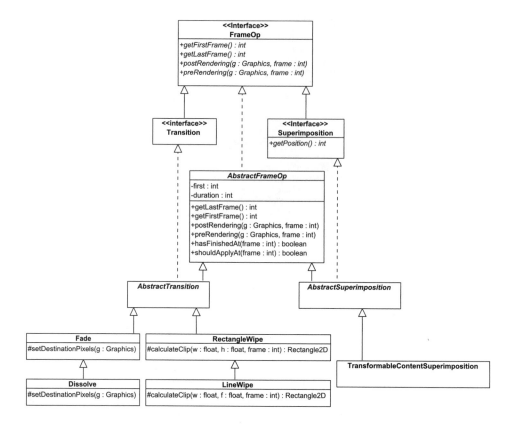

Figure 8.7 The Best Design of Transitions and Superimpositions

A Superimposition, in addition, must be able to provide information on its position. This leads to the following interface:

```
package visual.dynamic.sampled;

import java.awt.*;

public interface Superimposition extends FrameOp
{
    public abstract int getPosition();
}
```

The Transition interface extends the FrameOp interface but adds no additional requirements. It is included to provide semantic information.

Now, since all FrameOp objects have a first frame and a duration, it makes sense to add an AbstractFrameOp class that includes these attributes:

```
package visual.dynamic.sampled;

import java.awt.Graphics;

public abstract class        AbstractFrameOp
                implements FrameOp
{
    protected int               duration, first;

    public AbstractFrameOp(int first, int duration)
    {
        this.first    = first;
        this.duration = 0;
        if (duration > 0) this.duration = duration;
    }
}
```

In addition, this class includes convenience methods for obtaining and working with these
attributes. Most importantly, this includes methods for determining whether this FrameOp
should be applied and whether this FrameOp has finished.

```
    public int getFirstFrame()
    {
        return first;
    }

    public int getLastFrame()
    {
        return first+duration;
    }

    protected boolean hasFinishedAt(int frame)
    {
        return (frame >= (first+duration-1));
    }

    protected boolean shouldApplyAt(int frame)
    {
        return ((frame >= first) && (frame <= (first+duration-1)));
    }
```

The Screen class, introduced above, must now include attributes and methods for managing Transition and Superimposition objects. They are kept in an Interval-IndexedCollection that allows for the quick retrieval of the Transition/Superimposition objects that are active at a particular frame.

An Aside: Interval Indexed Collections

Many collections (e.g., Vector, Hashtable) associate each element with a single index/key (e.g., an int in the case of Vector and an Object in the case of Hashtable). However, it is sometimes useful to associate each element with a closed interval (e.g., the closed interval $[0, 9]$).

One easy way to implement such a collection is to use an ArrayList of ArrayList objects, as in the SimpleIntervalIndexedCollection class. This class has the following structure:

```java
package collectionframework;

import java.util.*;

public class      SimpleIntervalIndexedCollection<E>
        implements IntervalIndexedCollection<E>
{
    private ArrayList<ArrayList<E>>    elements;
    private final Iterator<E>          EMPTY_ITERATOR;

    public SimpleIntervalIndexedCollection()
    {
        ArrayList<E>     temp;

        elements        = new ArrayList<ArrayList<E>>();

        temp            = new ArrayList<E>();
        EMPTY_ITERATOR = temp.iterator();
    }
}
```

The ensureCapacity() method ensures that the ArrayList of ArrayList objects is big enough.

```java
    private void ensureCapacity(int size)
    {
        ArrayList<E>    temp;

        for (int i=0; i<size; i++)
        {
```

```
        try
        {
            temp = elements.get(i);
        }
        catch (IndexOutOfBoundsException ioobe)
        {
            elements.add(i, new ArrayList<E>());
        }
    }
}
```

The add() method adds the element to all of the ArrayList objects in the interval.

```
public void add(E element, int left, int right)
{
    ArrayList<E>    temp;

    for (int i=left; i<=right; i++)
    {
        // Get the collection at i (or construct one)
        ensureCapacity(i+1);
        temp = elements.get(i);

        // Add the element to the collection at i
        temp.add(element);
    }
}
```

Finally, the get() method returns an Iterator that contains all of the elements that have an associated interval that includes a particular index.

```
public Iterator<E> get(int i)
{
    ArrayList<E>    temp;
    Iterator<E>     result;

    result = EMPTY_ITERATOR;

    try
    {
        temp    = elements.get(i);
    }
    catch (IndexOutOfBoundsException ioobe)
```

```
        {
            temp = null;
        }

        if (temp != null) result = temp.iterator();

        return result;
    }
```

This implementation is not space efficient since the 'outer' `ArrayList` is sparse (i.e., there are many more frames than transitions). However, relative to the amount of memory used by the frames themselves, the space wasted by this implementation is inconsequential. Hence, this implementation is adequate for this application. For other applications there are several better implementations. See, for example, the discussion of interval trees in Cormen et al. (2001).

```
        // Attributes used for transitions
        private IntervalIndexedCollection<Transition> transitions;
```

The superimpositions are kept in another `IntervalIndexedCollection`.

```
        // Attributes used for superimpositions
        private IntervalIndexedCollection<Superimposition> superimpositions;
```

`Transition` objects are managed using the following `addTransition()` method,

```
    public void addTransition(Transition t)
    {
        transitions.add(t, t.getFirstFrame(), t.getLastFrame());
    }
```

and the following `getTransition()` method.

```
    public Iterator<Transition> getTransitions()
    {
        Iterator<Transition>    result;

        result = null;
```

```
        if (frameNumber >= 0) result=transitions.get(frameNumber);

        return result;
    }
```

Superimposition objects are managed using the following addSuperimposition() method,

```
    public void addSuperimposition(Superimposition si)
    {
        superimpositions.add(si, si.getFirstFrame(), si.getLastFrame());
    }
```

and the following getSuperimposition() method:

```
    public Iterator<Superimposition> getSuperimpositions()
    {
        Iterator<Superimposition>     result;

        result = null;
        if (frameNumber >= 0) result=superimpositions.get(frameNumber);

        return result;
    }
```

Finally, an 'enhanced' VisualizationView is needed that uses the transitions and superimpositions. As it turns out, the best way to make this kind of enhancement has already been identified. In particular, recall that the VisualizationView class was designed with this kind of enhancement in mind. Specifically, VisualizationView objects actually delegate their rendering responsibilities to a VisualizationRenderer, and a VisualizationRenderer object can be decorated to add functionality. Recall, for example, that the ScaledVisualizationRenderer class can add the ability to scale the content before it is rendered. So, one need only create a decorator of a VisualizationRenderer that has the necessary enhancements. Again, in keeping with the film analogy, this decorator is called a ScreenRenderer.

The pre-rendering method must get the current Transition and Superimposition objects, and call their preRendering() methods.

```
    public void preRendering(Graphics          g,
                             Visualization     model,
                             VisualizationView view)
```

```
{
    Graphics2D                 g2;
    int                        frameNumber;
    Screen                     smodel;
    Iterator<Transition>       transitions;
    Iterator<Superimposition>  superimpositions;

    g2 = (Graphics2D)g;
    oldComposite = g2.getComposite();
    view.setDoubleBuffered(true);

    // Get information from the model
    smodel           = (Screen)model;
    transitions      = smodel.getTransitions();
    superimpositions = smodel.getSuperimpositions();
    frameNumber      = smodel.getFrameNumber();

    // Apply the transitions
    if (transitions != null)
    {
        while (transitions.hasNext())
        {
            transitions.next().preRendering(g, frameNumber);
        }
    }

    // Apply the superimpositions
    if (superimpositions != null)
    {
        while (superimpositions.hasNext())
        {
            superimpositions.next().preRendering(g, frameNumber);
        }
    }
}
```

In addition, the post-rendering method must get the current Transition and Superimposition objects, and call their postRendering() methods.

```
public void postRendering(Graphics          g,
                          Visualization     model,
                          VisualizationView view)
{
    Graphics2D                 g2;
    int                        frameNumber;
```

```
    Screen                  smodel;
    Iterator<Transition>    transitions;
    Iterator<Superimposition> superimpositions;

    g2 = (Graphics2D)g;
    g2.setComposite(oldComposite);
    view.setDoubleBuffered(true);

    // Get information from the model
    smodel          = (Screen)model;
    frameNumber     = smodel.getFrameNumber();
    transitions     = smodel.getTransitions();
    superimpositions = smodel.getSuperimpositions();

    // Apply the transitions
    if (transitions != null)
    {
        while (transitions.hasNext())
        {
            transitions.next().postRendering(g, frameNumber);
        }
    }

    // Apply the superimpositions
    if (superimpositions != null)
    {
        while (superimpositions.hasNext())
        {
            superimpositions.next().postRendering(g, frameNumber);
        }
    }
}
```

The rendering method need only delegate the `VisualizationRenderer` that it is decorating.

```
public void render(Graphics         g,
                   Visualization     model,
                   VisualizationView view)
{
    decorated.render(g, model, view);
}
```

The Screen class now needs to override the createDefaultView() method in the Visualization class so that the VisualizationView uses a ScreenRenderer. This is accomplished as follows:

```
protected VisualizationView createDefaultView()
{
    ScreenRenderer    renderer;

    renderer = new ScreenRenderer(new PlainVisualizationRenderer());

    return new VisualizationView(this, renderer);
}
```

EXERCISES

1. Are there any situations in which some frames contain sampled static content and some frames contain described static content?

2. (*Review*) The Screen class would be simpler if a Visualization only contained a single piece of content because then the Screen class would not need to use a NullIterator for the current frame (it could just use a SimpleContent object). What important functionality would be lost if this approach were used?

3. (*Review*) The rendering process in Figure 8.3 appears to be quite complicated because of the amount of delegation. Discuss the benefits that are afforded by each stage in this process.

4. Why does it make sense to use a collection of SimpleContent objects that can return a ListIterator rather than an ordinary Iterator?

5. Develop an app that can both 'play' and 'fast forward' (at different rates) a sequence of SimpleContent objects. Your app must not assume that the frames can be rendered at the fast-forward rates. Instead, it must skip frames as appropriate.

6. In Section 5.3.3 on page 141 we wrote a BufferedImageOp that creates a night vision effect. Use this BufferedImageOp to develop an app that will render any sequence of sampled.SimpleContent objects as if they were being viewed through night-vision goggles. (Hint: A well-designed system will also be able to render any sequence of sampled.SimpleContent objects in black and white or using any other BufferedImageOp).

7. Many television advertisements use frames that are black and white except for the product that they are highlighting (e.g., the iPod and its cord). Design (but do not implement) an app that can be used for this purpose with any sequence of sampled.SimpleContent

objects. Would it be easier or harder to use a sequence of `described.SimpleContent` objects? Why?

8. Create a `FrameNumberSuperimposition` class that displays the frame number superimposed on top of the frame itself. (Hint: You will need to make use of what you learned about measuring glyphs and fonts in Section 6.3.2 on page 164.)

9. Create a `StarWipe` class. (Hint: Create a basic star shape using a `Path2D` object. Then create several scaled versions of it using an `AffineTransform`. For efficiency reasons, store the different stars in a collection.)

10. Design (but do not implement) a system that can be used to highlight important yard lines (e.g., the current spot, the first-down marker) in an NFL football game.

11. Develop an improved `IntervalIndexedCollection` class. What are the worst-case asymptotic bounds on its time efficiency and space efficiency?

REFERENCES AND FURTHER READING ···

Cormen, T. H., C. E. Leiserson, R. L. Rivest, and C. Stein. 2001. *Introduction to algorithms*. Cambridge, MA: MIT Press.

Haase, C. and R. Guy. 2008. *Filthy rich clients*. Santa Clara, CA: Sun Microsystems.

Jack, K. 2007. *Video demystified: A handbook for the digital engineer*. Oxford, UK: Newnes.

Described Dynamic Visual Content

9

Like Chapter 8, this chapter is concerned with visual content that changes over time in a way that causes the perception of apparent motion. However, rather than sampling from the visual 'stream' as in Chapter 8, this chapter considers ways in which one can **describe** the way the visual 'stream' changes over time.

A natural way to design such a system is to consider the ways in which this is done in the 'real world'. With that in mind, this chapter uses the analogy of the theater (and acting). In the theater, a script (along with the stage directions it contains) is a description of how the actors in a play should perform over time, and the stage is where they perform. The stage often has one or more sets (which can loosely be defined as items in the background/foreground) and the actors often manipulate one or more props. Fortunately, the static visual content system in Chapters 4 through 7 already has many of the necessary pieces. In particular, the set and the props can, for the most part, be handled using existing components. In addition, Java can be used to write the script. Hence, this chapter focuses on encapsulating the stage and the actors. However, in keeping with the terminology used in computer animation, the actors/characters are referred to as *sprites*.

9.1 A 'Quick Start'

To incorporate described dynamic visual content, the system must:

F9.1 Manage a collection of sprites.

F9.2 Repeatedly inform each sprite that it should perform the next task in its script.

F9.3 Render the sprites.

As with described dynamic content, to satisfy these requirements the `Visualization` class must be enhanced. Also, as with described dynamic content, there are three different ways to provide the additional functionality.

 The additional functionality could be provided by adding code to the `Visualization` class. However, there is no reason that someone who is interested in static visual content should have to understand features that are required to work with dynamic visual content. Hence, this alternative adds unnecessary complexity to the `Visualization` class.

 The additional functionality could also be provided using the decorator pattern. In other words, one could create a class that decorates a `Visualization` object, delegating to it for the original functionality and adding methods that provide the new functionality. However, as before, it is hard to imagine a situation in which, at runtime, one would want to add these kinds of capabilities to a Visualization object that had been constructed earlier.

Finally, the additional functionality could be provided by creating a Stage class that specializes the Visualization class. Using this approach, the programmer must decide up front whether to use a Visualization object or a Stage object. However, since the programmer will not know whether the app requires the additional capabilities, this does not seem like a significant limitation. Hence, this seems like the best alternative.

The process of extending the Visualization class is actually quite simple. As with the Screen class (see Chapter 8), the most important part of this extension is the addition of a Metronome and the ability to respond to 'ticks.' However, unlike the Screen class, the Stage class does not use the notion of a frame since sprites might need to change their behavior at any time. Hence, the Stage works with time explicitly.

Before turning to the details of the Stage class, consider the capabilities of a Sprite. Put simply, a Sprite is an object that can respond to render() messages and transform itself in response to handleTick() messages. That is, a Sprite object must implement the methods in the TransformableContent interface and the MetronomeListener interface. Hence, the capabilities of a Sprite object can be specified as follows:

```
package visual.dynamic.described;

public interface Sprite extends event.MetronomeListener,
                                visual.statik.TransformableContent
{
}
```

An Aside: Specializing Interfaces

As you (hopefully) know, Java does not support multiple inheritance. That is, a class in Java can not extend more than one superclass. The designers of Java did not include multiple inheritance because of "all the problems it generates" (Gosling and McGilton 1996). Presumably they were concerned with the additional complexity and ambiguities that must be resolved when multiple inheritance is supported.

An interface in Java can, however, extend multiple interfaces. It is interesting to consider why the designers of Java included this feature in the language. Recall that an interface is simply a list of methods that must be included in an implementing class. When one interface extends another, the subinterface is simply adding methods to the list of methods required by the superinterface. So, what happens when a subinterface extends to superinterfaces? It is simply adding methods to two lists. Thus, the designers of Java included this feature because it can be very useful in many situations and neither adds complexity nor ambiguity.

It is now time to consider the structure of the Stage class that manages a Metronome and its associated time attributes (like the time step and whether/when it should restart). This class has the following structure:

```
package visual.dynamic.described;

import java.awt.*;
import java.util.*;

import event.*;
import visual.*;
import visual.statik.sampled.*;

public class Stage extends     Visualization
                   implements MetronomeListener
{
    private boolean             shouldRestart;
    private int                 timeStep, restartTime, time;
    private Metronome           metronome;

    public Stage(int timeStep)
    {
        this(timeStep, new Metronome(timeStep));
    }

    public Stage(int timeStep, Metronome metronome)
    {
        super();

        this.timeStep     =  timeStep;
        time              = -timeStep;
        shouldRestart     =  false;
        restartTime       = -1;
        this.metronome    = metronome;
        setBackground(Color.WHITE);

        // The first listener is notified last
        metronome.addListener(this);
    }
}
```

To make this class more flexible, it has one constructor that is passed a **Metronome** and one that is not. In most cases, the former will be used and the **Stage** will construct its own **Metronome**. There are situations in which the latter is useful, however. For example, one might want to have several **Stage** objects use the same **Metronome** in order to synchronize them.

The starting, stopping, and resetting of the **Metronome** are controlled by a few simple methods.

```
    public void setRestartTime(int restartTime)
    {
        if (restartTime < 0)
        {
            this.restartTime = -1;
            shouldRestart = false;
        }
        else
        {
            this.restartTime = restartTime;
            shouldRestart = true;
        }
    }

    public void start()
    {
        metronome.start();
    }

    public void stop()
    {
        metronome.stop();
    }
```

Of course, since the `Stage` class extends the `Visualization` class and `Sprite` objects implement the `TransformableContent` interface, it is possible to add `Sprite` objects to a `Stage` using the `add()` method it inherits. However, the `Stage` class needs an overloaded version of the `add()` method that is passed a `Sprite` object (as opposed to a `SimpleContent` object). This is because it needs to distinguish the objects that only need to be rendered (i.e., the `SimpleContent` objects) from the objects that need to both be informed of `Metronome` ticks and rendered (i.e., the `Sprite` objects). Specifically, when a `Sprite` is added to the `Stage`, the `Stage` must make it a `MetronomeListener` in addition to adding it to the `Visualization`. For the same reason, it has an overloaded version of the `remove()` method.

```
    public void add(Sprite sprite)
    {
        // Make the Sprite a MetronomeListener
        metronome.addListener(sprite);

        // Treat the Sprite as a SimpleContent and
        // add it to the Visualization
        super.add(sprite);
    }
```

```
public void remove(Sprite sprite)
{
   metronome.removeListener(sprite);
   super.remove(sprite);
}
```

Each time the `Metronome` 'ticks', it calls the `handleTick()` method in each `Sprite` object and then initiates the rendering process.

```
public void handleTick(int time)
{
   if ((shouldRestart) && (time > restartTime))
   {
      metronome.setTime(-timeStep);
   }

   repaint();
}
```

The rendering process is initiated by the `repaint()` method in the `Visualization` class, which calls the `repaint()` method in each of its associated `VisualizationView` objects. These calls, in turn, result in calls to the `VisualizationView` objects' `paint()` methods that, in turn, result in calls to the `preRendering()`, `render()`, and `postRendering()` methods. Each `Sprite` is then told to render itself.[1]

Obviously, to satisfy Requirements F9.2 and F9.3 on page 243, a class that implements the `Sprite` interface must have a `handleTick()` method and a `render()` method. Given the existing system, there are two obvious approaches.

 One alternative is to have classes that extend one of the classes that implements the `SimpleContent` interface. So, for example, a `SampledSprite` class could extend the `statik.sampled.TransformableContent` class and a `DescribedSprite` class could extend the `statik.described.TransformableContent` class. This alternative is illustrated in Figure 9.1 on the next page.

 Another alternative is to use the decorator pattern and have an `AbstractSprite` class that delegates to one of the classes that implements the `SimpleContent` interface. This design, which has two clear advantages, is illustrated in Figure 9.2 on the following page. First, it makes it possible to decorate different `SimpleContent` objects in the same way. For example, one could have a `FallingSprite` that could decorate `SimpleContent` that looks like a leaf, a raindrop, a snowflake, etc. Second, it makes it possible to associate a different `SimpleContent` object with

---

[1]The `Sprite` objects need to be able to render themselves fairly quickly. This can be a problem in some cases. See, for example, Exercise 10 on page 284

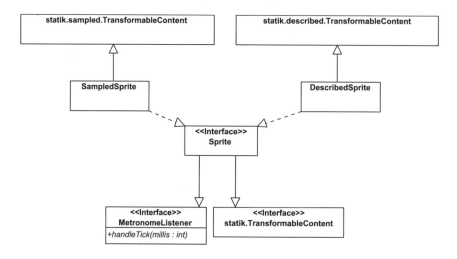

Figure 9.1 A High-Level Design That Uses Specialization

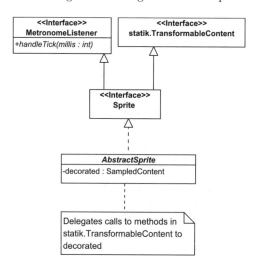

Figure 9.2 A High-Level Design That Uses the Decorator Pattern

a particular Sprite at different points in time. For example, a WalkingPersonSprite might use different sampled.Content objects to represent its legs at different points in the walking process (e.g., right leg forward, left leg forward, etc.).

The question now arises of how to incorporate a 'script' in objects that implement the Sprite interface. Or, more properly, it is time to determine how, from a design perspective, these objects should respond to handleTick() messages. Conceptually, there are a variety of different kinds of sprites. The two most popular conceptualizations, and the two that are considered here, involve (1) the use of 'rules' (i.e., rule-based sprites), and (2) the use of interpolation between known states (i.e., interpolating sprites). This kind of functionality can be added to the current high-level design in several different ways.

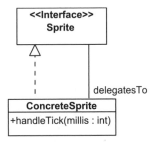

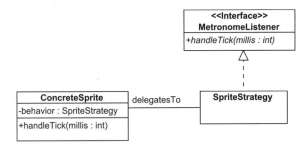

Figure 9.3   A Mid-Level Design That Uses the Decorator Pattern

Figure 9.4   A Mid-Level Design That Uses the Strategy Pattern

 One alternative is to use the decorator pattern. In this design a `ConcreteSprite` is constructed from a `Sprite`, and all messages, except `handleTick()` messages, are delegated to this decorated `Sprite`. For example, in a fish tank app, the `handleTick()` method in the `ConcreteSprite` class would provide the swimming behavior and all other messages would be delegated to the decorated `Sprite`. This design is illustrated in Figure 9.3. The biggest drawback of this design is that it is a little confusing because a `ConcreteSprite` decorates an `AbstractSprite` that, in turn, decorates a `TransformableContent` object.

 Another alternative is to use the strategy pattern. In this design, a `ConcreteSprite` (regardless of its type) delegates `handleTick()` messages to a `SpriteStrategy` object that does the actual work. For example, in a fish tank app, one might have a `ConcreteSprite` that uses a `SwimmingStrategy`. This alternative is illustrated in Figure 9.4.

 A third alternative is to use specialization. In this design, a `ConcreteSprite` class extends the `AbstractSprite` class, implementing the `handleTick()` method as appropriate. In other words, each `ConcreteSprite` class contains the specific behaviors that it requires. For example, in a fish tank app, the `handleTick()` in the `ConcreteSprite` would contain the swimming behavior. This is illustrated in Figure 9.5 on the next page.

These last two designs both have a lot to offer, but specialization seems to be the better alternative because it is simpler and it seems unlikely that the system will need to change a rule-based sprite to an interpolating sprite at runtime. Fortunately, should that need arise in the future, the necessary functionality could be added without breaking any 'legacy' code.

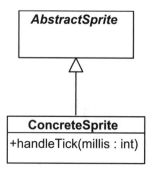

Figure 9.5 A Mid-Level Design That Uses Specialization

That is, one could use the strategy pattern in the future without breaking any 'legacy' classes that used specialization.

Given this, the AbstractSprite class has the following structure:

```
package visual.dynamic.described;

import java.awt.*;
import java.awt.geom.*;
import java.util.*;
import javax.swing.*;

import visual.statik.TransformableContent;

public abstract class      AbstractSprite
                implements Sprite
{
    protected boolean      rotationPoint, visible;
    protected double       angle, rotationX, rotationY;
    protected double       scaleX, scaleY, x, y;

    public AbstractSprite()
    {
        super();

        x     = 0.0;
        y     = 0.0;
        angle = 0.0;
        scaleX = 1.0;
        scaleY = 1.0;

        rotationPoint = false;
```

```
        rotationX    = 0.0;
        rotationY    = 0.0;
    }
}
```

It has two abstract methods, the `handleTick()` method,

```
    public abstract void handleTick(int time);
```

and the `getContent()` method.

```
    protected abstract TransformableContent getContent();
```

The former is abstract because each specialization needs to provide its own behavior. The latter is abstract because different kinds of `Sprite` objects need to provide their content in a variety of different ways.

The `AbstractSprite` class has several 'setters' that can be used to control the various transformations.

```
    public void setLocation(double x, double y)
    {
        this.x = x;
        this.y = y;
    }

    public void setRotation(double r, double x, double y)
    {
        rotationPoint = true;
        this.angle    = r;
        this.x        = x;
        this.y        = y;
    }

    public void setRotation(double r)
    {
        rotationPoint = false;
        this.angle    = r;
    }

    public void setScale(double sx, double sy)
    {
```

```
          scaleX = sx;
          scaleY = sy;
      }

      public void setScale(double s)
      {
          setScale(s, s);
      }

      public void setVisible(boolean v)
      {
           visible = v;
      }
  }
```

It also has methods for getting the bounds of the transformed and untransformed versions of the content.

```
      public Rectangle2D getBounds2D(boolean ofTransformed)
      {
          return getContent().getBounds2D(ofTransformed);
      }

      public Rectangle2D getBounds2D()
      {
          return getBounds2D(true);
      }
```

When an AbstractSprite is told to render itself, it does two things. First, if necessary, it transforms the TransformableContent it is decorating. Second, it delegates the rendering to the TransformableContent object it is decorating.

```
      public void render(Graphics g)
      {
          double                  rx, ry;
          Rectangle2D             bounds;
          TransformableContent    tc;

          if (visible)
          {
              tc = getContent();

              if (tc != null)
```

```
            {
                // Find the point to rotate around
                if (rotationPoint)
                {
                    rx = rotationX;
                    ry = rotationY;
                }
                else
                {
                    bounds = tc.getBounds2D(false);
                    rx     = bounds.getWidth()/2.0;
                    ry     = bounds.getHeight()/2.0;
                }

                // Transform
                tc.setLocation(x, y);
                tc.setRotation(angle, rx, ry);
                tc.setScale(scaleX, scaleY);

                // Render
                tc.render(g);
            }
        }
    }
```

Each specialization of the AbstractSprite class must implement the handleTick() method. As an example, consider a simple rule-based sprite that 'floats' from the top of the Stage to the bottom of the Stage. The overall structure of this FloatingSprite class is as follows:

```
import java.awt.*;
import java.awt.geom.*;
import java.util.*;

import visual.dynamic.described.*;
import visual.statik.TransformableContent;

public class FloatingSprite extends AbstractSprite
{
    private double                  maxX, maxY, x, y;
    private Random                  rng;
    private TransformableContent    content;

    public FloatingSprite(TransformableContent content,
                          double width, double height)
```

```
    {
        super();
        this.content = content;
        maxX        = width;
        maxY        = height;

        rng = new Random();

        x = rng.nextDouble()*maxX;
        y = 0.0;
        setLocation(x, y);

        setVisible(true);
    }
}
```

When a `FloatingSprite` object is constructed, it is passed the `TransformableContent` to decorate, as well as the width and height of the `Stage`.

The `getContent()` method simply returns the `TransformableContent` object that is being decorated.

```
    public TransformableContent getContent()
    {
        return content;
    }
```

The `handleTick()` method contains the 'floating' logic. The movement in the x and y directions is determined using a pseudorandomly generated number.

```
    public void handleTick(int time)
    {
        double       n;

        n = rng.nextDouble();
        if      (n < 0.80)   y += 2.0;
        else if (n > 0.90)   y -= 1.0;

        n = rng.nextDouble();
        if      (n < 0.20) x -= 1.0;
        else if (n > 0.80) x += 1.0;

        // Check if at the bottom
        if (y > maxY)
```

```
    {
        y  = 0.0;
        x = rng.nextDouble()*maxX;
    }

    setLocation(x, y);
}
```

A complete app that demonstrates the use of a `FloatingSprite` is then easy to create.

```
ContentFactory              factory;
FloatingSprite              sprite;
int                         height, width;
JPanel                      contentPane;
ResourceFinder              finder;
Stage                       stage;
TransformableContent        content;
VisualizationView           stageView;

width    = 640;
height   = 480;

finder  = ResourceFinder.createInstance(this);
factory = new ContentFactory(finder);

// The Stage
stage        = new Stage(50);
stage.setBackground(new Color(255, 255, 255));
stageView = stage.getView();
stageView.setBounds(0,0,width,height);

// The Sprite
content = factory.createContent("snowflake.png", 4, false);
sprite  = new FloatingSprite(content, width, height);
stage.add(sprite);

// The content pane
contentPane = (JPanel)rootPaneContainer.getContentPane();
contentPane.add(stageView);

// Start the dynamics
stage.start();
```

With this to whet your appetite, it is time to turn to a more complete discussion of described dynamic visual content.

9.2   Encapsulating Rule-Based Dynamics

As discussed in the motivating example (i.e., the `FloatingSprite` class above), one way to describe dynamic behavior is to provide the sprites with 'rules' that dictate how they change over time. These rules can range from the very simple (e.g., move down one pixel) to the very complicated (e.g., obey the "laws" of physics while falling), and are implemented in the `handleTick()` method.

What was neglected in the motivating example is that, in most multimedia applications, sprites need to interact either with each other or with the user. Hence, the system must:

F9.4 Allow one sprite to interact with another.

F9.5 Allow the user to interact with sprites.

Designs that satisfy these requirements are considered below.

9.2.1   Sprite Interactions

For sprites to interact with each other the system needs to be able to determine the spatial relationships between sprites. Hence, in addition to knowing the locations and dimensions of `Sprite` objects, the system needs to be able to calculate distances between points and to determine if two `Sprite` objects intersect/collide. The system already contains the functionality required for calculating distances (in the `Metric` interface discussed in Section 5.3 on page 119 and the classes that implement it). However, some attention needs to be given to the intersection/collision problem.

When both sprites are regular rectangles it is fairly easy to determine whether they intersect. To start, observe that, as illustrated in Figure 9.6, two sprites, A and B, **do not** intersect if the left-most point of A is to the right of the right-most point of B. Similarly, they **do not** intersect if the left-most point of B is to the right of the right-most point of A. In the vertical

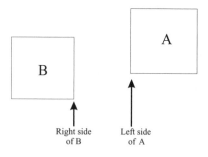

Figure 9.6   Determining Whether Rectangles Do Not Intersect

dimension, they **do not** intersect if the top-most point of A is below the bottom-most point of B. Finally, they **do not** intersect if the top-most point of B is below the bottom-most point of A. Letting `rightA`, `leftA`, `topA`, and `botA` denote the right, left, top, and bottom of A, respectively, and `rightB`, `leftB`, `topB`, and `botB` denote the right, left, top, and bottom of B, respectively, the expression to use to test whether A and B **do not** intersect is

```
(rightA < leftB) || (leftA > rightB) || (botA < topB) || (topA > botB)
```

While it might seem odd to test whether two rectangles **do not** intersect, most people find it easier to create this expression than one that allows them to test when A and B **do** intersect. (Try asking several of your friends.) One can, of course, simply negate this expression as follows:

```
!((rightA < leftB) || (leftA > rightB) || (botA < topB) || (topA > botB))
```

However, this is a little confusing and likely to be misunderstood.

Fortunately, it is easy to convert between the two using some basic propositional logic. In particular, simplifying this negation leads to the following expression that can be used to test whether A and B **do** intersect:

```
(rightA >= leftB) && (leftA <= rightB) && (botA >= topB) && (topA <= botB)
```

An Aside: Using Propositional Logic

Recall from De Morgan's laws that

$$\neg(x \vee y) \equiv \neg x \wedge \neg y.$$

Further, recall from the associative laws that

$$(p \vee q) \vee r \equiv p \vee (q \vee r).$$

and

$$(p \wedge q) \wedge r \equiv p \wedge (q \wedge r)$$

Hence,

$$
\begin{aligned}
\neg(p \vee q \vee r \vee s) &\equiv \neg[(p \vee q) \vee (r \vee s)] \\
&\equiv [\neg(p \vee q)] \wedge [\neg(r \vee s)] \\
&\equiv (\neg p \wedge \neg q) \wedge (\neg r \wedge \neg s) \\
&\equiv \neg p \wedge \neg q \wedge \neg r \wedge \neg s.
\end{aligned}
$$

Unfortunately, when the sprites are not rectangular, this technique does not work. This can be demonstrated with the simple example in Figure 9.7 on the following page. Note that

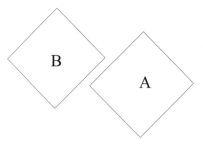

Figure 9.7 Intersection of Non-Rectangular, Convex Sprites

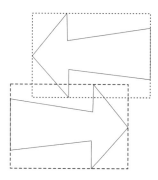

Figure 9.8 Using Bounding Boxes

the right-most point in B is farther to the right than the left-most point in A, but A and B do not intersect.

When the sprites are convex polygons one can use the *vertices* (loosely speaking, the 'corners') to determine whether two convex sprites intersect fairly easily (though algorithms for doing so are not considered in this book). However, when one (or more) of the sprites is non-convex, it can be very difficult to determine whether two sprites intersect. Hence, very often one only checks to see whether the bounding boxes of the two sprites intersect, as illustrated in Figure 9.8.

Obviously, this approach sometimes concludes that two sprites intersect when they do not. For simplicity, this book does not concern itself with this issue. One can, if necessary, implement one of several algorithms that correctly determine when two non-convex sprites intersect.[2] To implement this capability, the `Sprite` class must include an `intersects()` method.

```
public boolean intersects(Sprite s)
{
    boolean        retval;
    double         maxx, maxy, minx, miny;
    double         maxx0, maxy0, minx0, miny0;
    Rectangle2D    r;
```

---

[2]The **Area** class provides this functionality.

```
        retval = true;

        r = getBounds2D(true);
        minx = r.getX();
        miny = r.getY();
        maxx = minx + r.getWidth();
        maxy = miny + r.getHeight();

        r = s.getBounds2D(true);
        minxO = r.getX();
        minyO = r.getY();
        maxxO = minxO + r.getWidth();
        maxyO = minyO + r.getHeight();

        if ( (maxx < minxO) || (minx > maxxO) ||
             (maxy < minyO) || (miny > maxyO) ) retval = false;

        return retval;
    }
```

It is also necessary to organize the sprites that interact. This is accomplished with an abstract RuleBasedSprite class that manages a collection of 'antagonist' Sprite objects (i.e., a collection of Sprite objects that this Sprite is concerned with).

```
package visual.dynamic.described;

import java.awt.*;
import java.awt.geom.*;
import java.util.*;

import visual.statik.TransformableContent;

public abstract class RuleBasedSprite extends AbstractSprite
{
    protected ArrayList<Sprite>           antagonists;
    protected TransformableContent        content;

    public RuleBasedSprite(TransformableContent content)
    {
        super();

        antagonists = new ArrayList<Sprite>();
        this.content = content;
        setVisible(true);
```

```
        }

        public void addAntagonist(Sprite antagonist)
        {
            antagonists.add(antagonist);
        }

        public TransformableContent getContent()
        {
            return content;
        }

        public abstract void handleTick(int time);


        public void removeAntagonist(Sprite antagonist)
        {
            antagonists.remove(antagonist);
        }
}
```

As an example of how sprite interactions might be used, consider a simple fish tank app. This app has `Fish` objects that keep track of their location, their speed, and the size of the tank.

```
import java.util.*;

import visual.dynamic.described.*;
import visual.statik.TransformableContent;

public class Fish extends RuleBasedSprite
{
    protected double       initialSpeed, maxX, maxY, speed, x, y;

    private static final int      INITIAL_LOCATION = -320;
    private static final Random   rng = new Random();

    public Fish(TransformableContent content,
                double width, double height, double speed)
    {
        super(content);
        maxX = width;
        maxY = height;

        x     = rng.nextDouble()*maxX;
```

```
        y     = rng.nextInt()*maxY;

        this.initialSpeed = speed;
        this.speed        = speed;
    }
}
```

A Fish object changes its horizontal position each tick. If it moves off of the right side of the Stage, it resets its position (off of the Stage to the left).

```
    protected void updateLocation()
    {
        x += speed;

        if (x > (int)maxX)
        {
            x     = INITIAL_LOCATION;
            y     = rng.nextDouble()*maxX;
            speed = initialSpeed;
        }

        // Set the location
        setLocation(x, y);
    }
```

There are also some sharks in the fish tank that play the role of antagonists. If a Fish intersects an antagonist, it increases its speed.

```
    public void handleTick(int time)
    {
        double            initialSpeed;
        Iterator<Sprite>  i;
        Sprite            shark;

        initialSpeed = speed;

        i = antagonists.iterator();
        while (i.hasNext())
        {
            shark = i.next();
            if (intersects(shark)) speed = 20.;
        }
```

```
        updateLocation();
    }
```

Using these classes, one can create a simple app as follows:

```
        width  = 640;
        height = 480;

        finder      = ResourceFinder.createInstance(this);
        factory     = new ContentFactory(finder);
        imageFactory = new ImageFactory(finder);

        // The Stage
        stage = new Stage(50);
        stage.setBackground(Color.blue);
        content = factory.createContent("ocean.png", 3, false);
        stage.add(content);
        stageView = stage.getView();
        stageView.setBounds(0,0,width,height);

        // The Shark
        content = factory.createContent("shark.png", 4, false);
        shark = new Fish(content, width, height, 8.);
        stage.add(shark);

        // The school of Fish
        // (Use the same BufferedImage object for all Fish)
        image   = imageFactory.createBufferedImage("fish.png", 4);
        for (int i=0; i<10; i++)
        {
            content = factory.createContent(image, false);
            fish = new Fish(content, width, height, 3.);
            fish.addAntagonist(shark);
            stage.add(fish);
        }

        // The content pane
        contentPane = (JPanel)rootPaneContainer.getContentPane();
        contentPane.add(stageView);

        stage.start();
```

9.2.2 User Interaction

To satisfy Requirement F9.5 on page 256, interested `Sprite` objects must be able to observe user-generated events. To indicate that it is capable of observing such events, interested classes need to implement the `KeyListener` interface and/or the `MouseListener` and `MouseMotionListener` interfaces. In addition, a subject is needed. Fortunately, the `VisualizationView` class extends the `JComponent` class, and the `JComponent` class provides this functionality.

There is one complication, however. Since a `Visualization` (in this case, a `Stage`) might have multiple views associated with it, each listener must be added to all of the views. Hence, the `Visualization` class must be modified appropriately.[3] To that end, the `Visualization` class manages `KeyListener` objects as follows:

```
public void addKeyListener(KeyListener kl)
{
    Iterator<VisualizationView>  i;
    VisualizationView            view;

    i = getViews();
    while (i.hasNext())
    {
        view = i.next();
        view.addKeyListener(kl);
    }
}

public synchronized void removeKeyListener(
                            KeyListener kl)
{
    Iterator<VisualizationView>  i;
    VisualizationView            view;

    i = getViews();
    while (i.hasNext())
    {
        view = i.next();
        view.removeKeyListener(kl);
    }
}
```

---

[3]This functionality could be added to the `Stage` class. However, now that the need for user interaction has been identified, it's clear that all `Visualization` objects should have these capabilities.

Similarly, the `Visualization` class manages `MouseListener` and `MouseMotionListener` objects as follows:

```
public void addMouseListener(MouseListener ml)
{
   Iterator<VisualizationView>  i;
   VisualizationView            view;

   i = getViews();
   while (i.hasNext())
   {
      view = i.next();
      view.addMouseListener(ml);
   }
}

public void addMouseMotionListener(
                  MouseMotionListener mml)
{
   Iterator<VisualizationView>  i;
   VisualizationView            view;

   i = getViews();
   while (i.hasNext())
   {
      view = i.next();
      view.addMouseMotionListener(mml);
   }
}

public synchronized void removeMouseListener(
                           MouseListener ml)
{
   Iterator<VisualizationView>  i;
   VisualizationView            view;

   i = getViews();
   while (i.hasNext())
   {
      view = i.next();
      view.removeMouseListener(ml);
   }
}

public synchronized void removeMouseMotionListener(
                           MouseMotionListener mml)
{
```

```
        Iterator<VisualizationView>  i;
        VisualizationView            view;

        i = getViews();
        while (i.hasNext())
        {
           view = i.next();
           view.removeMouseMotionListener(mml);
        }
    }
}
```

This is illustrated in the `Cupola` class, a part of an amazingly addictive (and/or unbearably stupid) balloon popping game. The constructor of this class positions the sprite at the bottom left of the screen.

```
import java.awt.event.*;
import java.awt.geom.*;

import visual.dynamic.described.*;
import visual.statik.TransformableContent;

public class Cupola extends     RuleBasedSprite
                    implements MouseMotionListener
{
    private double      left, top;

    public Cupola(TransformableContent content,
                  double stageWidth, double stageHeight)
    {
       super(content);
       Rectangle2D          bounds;

       bounds = content.getBounds2D(false);
       top    = (stageHeight - bounds.getHeight());
       left   = (stageWidth  - bounds.getWidth())/2.0;

       setLocation(left, top);
    }
}
```

The `mouseMoved()` and `mouseDragged()` methods (required by the `MouseMotionListener` interface) simply store the horizontal cursor position.

```
public void mouseDragged(MouseEvent evt)
{
    mouseMoved(evt);
}

public void mouseMoved(MouseEvent evt)
{
    this.left = (double)evt.getX();
}
```

Finally, the handleTick() method positions the sprite in anticipation of the render() method being called.

```
public void handleTick(int time)
{
    setLocation(left, top);
}
```

The Balloon class, the other sprite in the game, is pretty straightforward. Its handleTick() method first checks to see whether it intersects the Cupola (which is the only antagonist). If it does, it makes the Balloon invisible. If it does not, it increases the y position.

```
public void handleTick(int time)
{
    Sprite   cupola;

    // Check for an intersection
    cupola = null;
    if (antagonists.size() > 0) cupola = antagonists.get(0);

    if ((cupola != null) && (intersects(cupola)))
    {
        speed = 0;
        setVisible(false);
    }

    // Update the location
    top += speed;

    if (top > maxY)
    {
```

```
        left    = rng.nextInt(maxX);
        top     = minY;
        speed   = rng.nextInt(10);
    }

    // Set the location
    setLocation(left, top);
}
```

9.3 Encapsulating Key-Time Dynamics

In traditional cel animation there are many different jobs, some more glamorous than others. For example, some artists are responsible for developing characters, some are responsible for drawing the important frames (called the "key" frames), and some are responsible for drawing all of the frames in between the important frames. People in this last group are referred to as "in betweeners" (or "tweeners," for short).

Tweening is particularly attractive in computerized systems because the tweening process can often be automated. With that in mind, it is clear that the system must:

F9.6 Support the description of dynamic behavior using key times and tweening.

From a design standpoint, there are two obvious alternatives to consider, both of which use a collection of `TransformableContent` objects.

One alternative is to store the attributes of the `TransformableContent` objects at each key time in the `TransformableContent` objects themselves. In other words, using this approach, each `TransformableContent` object knows its attributes (e.g., location, rotation, scaling) for each of the key times. While this seems like a natural way to proceed, it actually makes it difficult to interpolate between the key times. In particular, observe that using this approach, the system must change the attributes of one of the key-time `TransformableContent` objects at each in-between time (so that it renders itself properly). Unfortunately, the attributes of the tweened times are a weighted combination of the attributes of the surrounding key times, and these values are not immediately available.

The other way to proceed is to keep the attributes for each of the key times external to the `TransformableContent` objects themselves. In other words, using this approach, each `Sprite` has collections of attributes (e.g., a collection of locations, a collection of rotations, and a collection of scalings) that are somehow indexed by key time. In this way, the `Sprite` has easy access to all of the information it needs to calculate the attributes at the in-between times.

To that end, an abstract `TweeningSprite` class is used to manage the attributes at the key times. This class has the following structure:

```
package visual.dynamic.described;
```

```java
import java.awt.*;
import java.awt.geom.*;
import java.util.*;
import javax.swing.*;

public abstract class TweeningSprite extends AbstractSprite
{
    private    double        frac;
    private    int           currentIndex, endState, lastTime;
    private    int           nextIndex, nextKT;
    protected Vector<Integer>  keyTimes;
    protected Vector<Point2D>  locations;
    protected Vector<Double>   rotations, scalings;

    public static final int REMAIN        = 0;
    public static final int REMOVE        = 1;

    public TweeningSprite()
    {
        super();

        keyTimes  = new Vector<Integer>();
        locations = new Vector<Point2D>();
        rotations = new Vector<Double>();
        scalings  = new Vector<Double>();
        endState  = REMAIN;

        initialize();
    }
}
```

Key-time information (i.e., the location, rotation, and scaling factor at key times) can then be added as follows:

```java
    protected int addKeyTime(int keyTime, Point2D location,
                             Double rotation, Double scaling)
    {
        boolean     keepLooking;
        int         existingKT, i, index;

        existingKT  = -1;
        keepLooking = true;

        i = 0;
```

```
    while ((i < keyTimes.size()) && keepLooking)
    {
        existingKT = ((Integer)keyTimes.get(i)).intValue();

        if (existingKT >= keyTime) keepLooking = false;
        else                            i++;
    }

    if ((existingKT == i) && !keepLooking)  // Duplicate
    {
        i = -1;
    }
    else
    {
        keyTimes.insertElementAt(new Integer(keyTime), i);
        locations.insertElementAt(location, i);
        rotations.insertElementAt(rotation, i);
        scalings.insertElementAt(scaling, i);
    }

    return i;
}
```

Note that this method makes some effort to ensure that key times are properly ordered; however, it makes no guarantees. Such functionality could be added if necessary.

The tweening of the various attributes is commonly implemented using linear interpolation. Letting a_t denote the value of the attribute at the previous/current key time and a_{t+1} denote the value of the attribute at the next key time, the in-between value, $b(\lambda)$, is then given by

$$b(\lambda) = (1 - \lambda)a_t + \lambda a_{t+1} \tag{9.1}$$

where $\lambda \in [0, 1]$ denotes the interpolation fraction. In other words, b is a convex combination of a_t and a_{t+1}. Note that (9.1) implies

$$b(\lambda) = a_t - \lambda a_t + \lambda a_{t+1} \tag{9.2}$$
$$= a_t + \lambda(a_{t+1} - a_t), \tag{9.3}$$

which is the more widely used form.

9.3.1 Location and Rotation Tweening

One common practice in sprite animation is to specify the location and rotation of a sprite for different key times and to tween the remaining times. This practice is called *location tweening* (or *path following* or *trail following*) and is illustrated in Figure 9.9 on the following page.

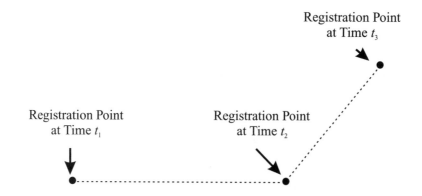

Figure 9.9 Location Tweening

Since the location consists of two values, the x/horizontal and y/vertical, both must be tweened. This is implemented as follows:

```
protected void tweenLocation(int currentIndex, int nextIndex,
                             double frac)
{
    double          x, y;
    Point2D         currentKTLocation, nextKTLocation;

    currentKTLocation = locations.get(currentIndex);
    nextKTLocation    = locations.get(nextIndex);

    x = currentKTLocation.getX() +
        frac*(nextKTLocation.getX()- currentKTLocation.getX());
    y = currentKTLocation.getY() +
        frac*(nextKTLocation.getY() - currentKTLocation.getY());

    setLocation(x, y);
}
```

Rotation tweening is a little more complicated because there are two ways to define it. One approach to rotation tweening is to use the line segment between two locations to determine the rotation angle. The other approach, called "pure" rotation tweening, is illustrated in Figure 9.10 on the next page.

Both of these approaches are implemented in the `tweenRotation()` method. The pure rotation tweening portion of this method is implemented like the `tweenLocation()` method except that, if the next angle does not exist, no tweening is performed.

```
currentKTRotation = rotation.doubleValue();
```

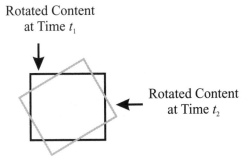

Figure 9.10 Pure Rotation Tweening

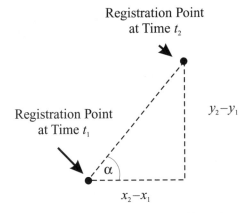

Figure 9.11 Aligned Rotation Tweening

```
        rotation = rotations.get(nextIndex);
        if (rotation == null) nextKTRotation = currentKTRotation;
        else                  nextKTRotation = rotation.doubleValue();

        r = currentKTRotation + frac*(nextKTRotation-currentKTRotation);
}
```

The aligned rotation tweening portion of this method requires a little trigonometry, as illustrated in Figure 9.11. Thinking of the current segment as the hypotenuse of a right triangle, the difference in y values defines the length of the side opposite the angle of interest (denoted by α), and the difference in x values defines the length of the adjacent side. Hence,

$$\tan(\alpha) = \frac{y_2 - y_1}{x_2 - x_1}. \tag{9.4}$$

It follows that

$$\alpha = \text{atan}\left(\frac{y_2 - y_1}{x_2 - x_1}\right). \tag{9.5}$$

This logic is implemented as follows:

```
currentKTLocation = locations.get(currentIndex);
nextKTLocation    = locations.get(nextIndex);

r=Math.atan((nextKTLocation.getY()-currentKTLocation.getY())/
            (nextKTLocation.getX()-currentKTLocation.getX()) );
```

Note that this method assumes that pure rotation tweening should be used only when rotation angles are provided.

The following `Airplane` sprite, which contains sampled static content, uses pure rotation tweening. That is, it provides rotation information for each key time.

```java
import java.awt.geom.*;
import java.awt.image.*;

import io.*;
import visual.dynamic.described.*;
import visual.statik.sampled.*;

public class Airplane extends SampledSprite
{
    public Airplane()
    {
        super();
        Content            content;
        ContentFactory     factory;

        factory = new ContentFactory(ResourceFinder.createInstance(this));
        content = factory.createContent("airplane.png", 4);
        addKeyTime(  500,    0.0, 350.0, -0.75, 1.0, content);
        addKeyTime( 2000, 100.0, 200.0, -0.30, 1.0, null);
        addKeyTime( 4000, 200.0,  50.0,  0.00, 1.0, null);
        addKeyTime( 6000, 300.0,  50.0,  0.20, 1.0, null);
        addKeyTime( 8000, 400.0, 200.0,  0.00, 1.0, null);
        addKeyTime( 8500, 500.0, 200.0,  0.00, 1.0, null);
        setEndState(REMOVE);
    }

    private void addKeyTime(int time, double x, double y,
                            double r, double s, Content c)
    {
```

```
        addKeyTime(time, new Point2D.Double(x, y), new Double(r),
                  new Double(s), c);
    }
}
```

The following `BuzzyOnMars` sprite, which contains described sampled content, also uses pure rotation tweening.

```java
import java.awt.geom.Point2D;

import visual.dynamic.described.DescribedSprite;
import visual.statik.described.*;

public class BuzzyOnMars extends DescribedSprite
{
    public BuzzyOnMars()
    {
        super();
        BuzzyStanding        buzzy;

        buzzy = new BuzzyStanding();
        addKeyTime(  500,    0.0, 380.0,  0.00, 1.0, buzzy);
        addKeyTime( 2000, 180.0, 380.0,  0.00, 1.0, null);
        addKeyTime( 4000, 180.0,  75.0,  0.20, 1.0, null);
        addKeyTime( 6000, 640.0,  20.0,  6.48, 1.0, null);
        setEndState(REMOVE);
    }

    private void addKeyTime(int time, double x, double y,
                            double r, double s, AggregateContent c)
    {
        addKeyTime(time, new Point2D.Double(x, y), new Double(r),
                  new Double(s), c);
    }
}
```

On the other hand, the following `BusOnRoute` sprite aligns itself with its direction of travel:

```java
import java.awt.geom.Point2D;

import io.*;
```

```java
import visual.dynamic.described.*;
import visual.statik.sampled.*;

public class BusOnRoute extends SampledSprite
{
    public BusOnRoute()
    {
        super();
        Content                content;
        ContentFactory         factory;
        ResourceFinder         finder;

        finder  = ResourceFinder.createInstance(this);
        factory = new ContentFactory(finder);
        content = factory.createContent("bus.png");
        addKeyTime( 0, 164, 210, content);
        addKeyTime( 1, 310, 255, null);
        addKeyTime( 2, 314, 234, null);
        addKeyTime( 3, 401, 231, null);
        addKeyTime( 4, 419, 269, null);
        addKeyTime( 5, 353, 340, null);
        addKeyTime( 6, 430, 367, null);
        addKeyTime( 7, 420, 418, null);
        addKeyTime( 8, 450, 421, null);
        addKeyTime( 9, 454, 386, null);
        addKeyTime(10, 512, 393, null);
        addKeyTime(11, 487, 338, null);
        addKeyTime(12, 554, 323, null);
        addKeyTime(13, 500, 238, null);
        addKeyTime(14, 577, 206, null);
        addKeyTime(15, 632, 155, null);
        addKeyTime(16, 480, 151, null);
        addKeyTime(19, 301,  88, null);
        addKeyTime(21, 233, 149, null);
        addKeyTime(22, 147, 181, null);
        addKeyTime(30, 164, 210, null);
        setEndState(REMAIN);
    }

    private void addKeyTime(int time, int x, int y,
                            Content content)
    {
        addKeyTime(time*1000, new Point2D.Double((double)x, (double)y),
                   null, new Double(1.0), content);
    }
}
```

Note that the bus in this example may not behave as 'desired.' In particular, if you want the bus to always be 'above' the route, you may need to reflect the bus as well as rotate it. (See Exercise 9 on page 284.)

9.3.2   Tweening Samples and Descriptions

In addition to tweening a sprite's location and rotation, one can tween what might be thought of as the visual content that makes up the sprite. Since the way in which this is done varies considerably depending on whether the `Sprite` has sampled or described content, it makes sense to have both a `SampledSprite` class and a `DescribedSprite` class.

With sampled sprites this kind of tweening involves specifying a raster for each key frame and tweening from one to the next. One way to do this is to use an object that has two component `statik.Content` objects and combine them with alpha blending. Recall from Chapter 7 that the `statik.CompositeContent` class provides these kinds of capabilities. However, it is a little easier to use a simple (i.e., nonhierarchical) collection so, to that end, it makes sense to create a `sampled.AggregateContent` class. This class has the following structure:

```
package visual.statik.sampled;

import java.awt.*;
import java.awt.image.*;
import java.util.Iterator;

public class        AggregateContent
        extends     visual.statik.AbstractAggregateContent<Content>
        implements  TransformableContent
{
    public AggregateContent()
    {
        super();
    }
}
```

The `setBufferedImageOp()` method delegates to each of the component `statik.Content` objects.

```
    public void setBufferedImageOp(BufferedImageOp op)
    {
        Iterator<Content>  i;

        i = iterator();
```

```
        while (i.hasNext())
        {
            i.next().setBufferedImageOp(op);
        }
    }
}
```

The setComposite() method, on the other hand, delegates only to the last statik.Content object, rather than all of them.

```
    public void setComposite(Composite c)
    {
        Content       content;

        content = components.getLast();
        content.setComposite(c);
    }
```

Now, it is relatively easy to implement a SampledSprite class. This class has a collection of statik.Content objects, one statik.Content object for each key time. It also has a statik.AggregateContent object that it uses to hold the tweened content.

```
package visual.dynamic.described;

import java.awt.*;
import java.awt.geom.*;
import java.awt.image.*;
import java.util.Vector;

import visual.statik.sampled.AggregateContent;
import visual.statik.sampled.Content;
import visual.statik.sampled.TransformableContent;

public class SampledSprite extends TweeningSprite
{
    private   AggregateContent    tweened;
    private   Vector<Content>     content;

    public SampledSprite()
    {
        super();

        content = new Vector<Content>();
    }
```

```
    public void addKeyTime(int keyTime, Point2D location,
                           Double rotation, Double scaling,
                           Content c)
    {
       int          index;

       index = super.addKeyTime(keyTime, location, rotation, scaling);

       if (index >= 0)
       {
          // If c is null then re-use the last Content
          if (c==null) c = content.get(index-1);

          content.insertElementAt(c, index);
       }
    }
}
```

The getContent() method performs the content tweening. It gets the content for the two key times, adds them to the statik.AggregateContent object, and sets the AlphaComposite appropriately.

```
    protected visual.statik.TransformableContent getContent()
    {
       AggregateContent        aggregate;
       Content                 currentContent, nextContent;
       float                   alpha;
       int                     current, next;
       visual.statik.TransformableContent   result;

       result  = null;
       current = getKeyTimeIndex();
       next    = getNextKeyTimeIndex();

       if (visible && (current >= 0))
       {
          currentContent = content.get(current);
          nextContent    = content.get(next);

          if ((nextContent != null) &&
              (currentContent != nextContent))
          {
             aggregate = new AggregateContent();
             aggregate.add(currentContent);
```

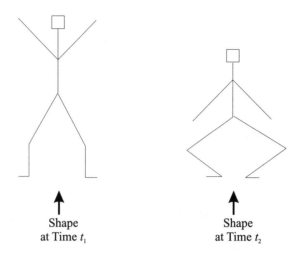

Shape
at Time t_1

Shape
at Time t_2

Figure 9.12 Shape Tweening

```
        aggregate.add(nextContent);

        // Setup alpha blending
        alpha = (float)getInterpolationFraction();

        aggregate.setComposite(
                AlphaComposite.getInstance(
                        AlphaComposite.SRC_OVER,
                        alpha));

        result = aggregate;
    }
    else
    {
        result = currentContent;
    }
}
return result;
}
```

With described sprites this kind of tweening involves specifying a shape (or shapes) for each key frame and tweening from one to the next. This is illustrated in Figure 9.12.

The most common approach to shape tweening is to tween the location of each of the points that defines the shape. In Java, this is enabled by the **PathIterator** interface that provides access to "move to" and "draw to" segments. In this way one can shape tween any arbitrary shape. With this in mind, it is important to add a `getPathIterator()` method to the `described.Content` class.

```
public PathIterator getPathIterator(boolean transformed)
{
    if (transformed)
        return transformedShape.getPathIterator(IDENTITY);
    else
        return originalShape.getPathIterator(IDENTITY);
}
```

Now, as with sample tweening, it is easier to work with a simple collection of described content objects than a hierarchical collection. Hence, rather than use the `described.CompositeContent` class it makes sense to implement a `described.AggregateContent` class. This class has the following structure:

```
package visual.statik.described;

import java.awt.*;
import java.util.Iterator;

public class      AggregateContent
      extends     visual.statik.AbstractAggregateContent<Content>
      implements TransformableContent
{
    public AggregateContent()
    {
        super();
    }
}
```

The 'setters' in this class simply delegate to the component `described.Content` objects.

```
public void setColor(Color color)
{
    Iterator<Content>  i;

    i = iterator();
    while (i.hasNext())
    {
        i.next().setColor(color);
    }
}
```

```java
    public void setPaint(Paint paint)
    {
       Iterator<Content>  i;

       i = iterator();
       while (i.hasNext())
       {
          i.next().setPaint(paint);
       }
    }

    public void setStroke(Stroke stroke)
    {
       Iterator<Content>  i;

       i = iterator();
       while (i.hasNext())
       {
          i.next().setStroke(stroke);
       }
    }
```

With this, one can implement a `DescribedSprite` class with the following structure:

```java
package visual.dynamic.described;

import java.awt.*;
import java.awt.geom.*;
import java.util.Iterator;
import java.util.Vector;

import visual.statik.described.*;

public class DescribedSprite extends TweeningSprite
{
    private    AggregateContent            tweened;
    private    Vector<AggregateContent>    content;

    public DescribedSprite()
    {
       content = new Vector<AggregateContent>();
       tweened = new AggregateContent();
    }
```

```
    public void addKeyTime(int keyTime, Point2D location,
                           Double rotation, Double scaling,
                           AggregateContent ctc)
    {
        int          index;

        index = super.addKeyTime(keyTime, location, rotation, scaling);

        if (index >= 0)
        {
            // If ctc is null then re-use the last CompositeContent
            if (ctc == null) ctc = content.get(index-1);

            content.insertElementAt(ctc, index);
        }

    }
}
```

The getContent() method gets the described static content for the two relevant key times
and then calls the tweenShape() method.

```
    public visual.statik.TransformableContent getContent()
    {
        int                 current, next;
        AggregateContent    currentCTC, nextCTC, result;


        current = getKeyTimeIndex();
        next    = getNextKeyTimeIndex();

        result = null;

        if (current >= 0)
        {
            currentCTC = content.get(current);
            nextCTC    = content.get(next);

            result     = currentCTC;

            if (currentCTC != nextCTC)
            {
                tweenShape(currentCTC, nextCTC, getInterpolationFraction());
                result = tweened;
            }
```

```
        }

        return result;
    }
```

The tweenShape() iterates over all of the component described.TransformableContent objects in the described.AggregateContent objects. For each of these, it iterates over all of the segments in the Shape and interpolates all of the points that define each segment.

```
    protected void tweenShape(AggregateContent a,
                              AggregateContent b,
                              double frac)
    {
        Color                   color;
        float[]                 coords, coordsA, coordsB;
        GeneralPath             gp;
        int                     seg;
        Iterator<Content>       iterA, iterB;
        PathIterator            piA, piB;
        Paint                   paint;
        Content                 shapeA, shapeB;
        Stroke                  stroke;


        tweened = new AggregateContent();

        coordsA = new float[6];
        coordsB = new float[6];
        coords  = new float[6];

        iterA = a.iterator();
        iterB = b.iterator();

        // Loop over all of the TransformableContent objects
        // in the AggregateContent
        while (iterA.hasNext())
        {
            shapeA = iterA.next();
            if (iterB.hasNext()) shapeB = iterB.next();
            else                 shapeB = shapeA;

            piA = shapeA.getPathIterator(false);
            piB = shapeB.getPathIterator(false);

            gp = new GeneralPath();
```

```
gp.setWindingRule(piA.getWindingRule());


// Loop over all of the segments in the
// TransformableContent object
while (!piA.isDone())
{
   seg = piA.currentSegment(coordsA);
   if (piB.isDone()) // Use the coordinates of the first shape
   {
      for (int i=0; i < coordsA.length; i++)
         coords[i] = coordsA[i];
   }
   else            // Interpolate the coordinates
   {
      piB.currentSegment(coordsB);

      for (int i=0; i < coordsA.length; i++)
      {
         coords[i] = coordsA[i] +
                   (float)frac*(coordsB[i] - coordsA[i]);
      }
   }

   // Add to the General Path object
   if     (seg == PathIterator.SEG_MOVETO)
   {
      gp.moveTo(coords[0], coords[1]);
   }
   else if (seg == PathIterator.SEG_LINETO)
   {
      gp.lineTo(coords[0], coords[1]);
   }
   else if (seg == PathIterator.SEG_QUADTO)
   {
      gp.quadTo(coords[0], coords[1], coords[2], coords[3]);
   }
   else if (seg == PathIterator.SEG_CUBICTO)
   {
      gp.curveTo(coords[0], coords[1],
                 coords[2], coords[3],
                 coords[4], coords[5]);
   }
   else if (seg == PathIterator.SEG_CLOSE)
   {
      gp.closePath();
   }
```

```
        piA.next();
        piB.next();
    }

    paint  = shapeA.getPaint();
    color  = shapeA.getColor(); // This could also be tweened
    stroke = shapeA.getStroke();

    tweened.add(new Content(gp, color, paint, stroke));
    }
}
```

EXERCISES

1. Explain the difference between described dynamic visual content (sometimes called sprite animation) and sampled dynamic visual content (sometimes called frame animation).

2. It is nontrivial to add sprite interaction to shape-tweening sprites. Describe what would be necessary to add sprite interactions to the BuzzyJumping app. In particular, describe what would need to be done to change Buzzy's behavior if he bumps into a falling balloon.

3. In the classic game *Space Invaders*, the invaders continue to move in one direction until any invader reaches the edge of the screen. Describe three different designs for incorporating this kind of behavior and compare the three designs.

4. (*Review*) Modify the FishTankApp so that it includes diagonal rays of light that lighten the content underneath them. (Hint: Make the rays partially transparent white.)

5. Modify the FishTankApp so that it includes bubbles that rise to the surface (from off the bottom of the Stage).

6. Using the FishTankApp, create a simple fishing game. The hook should track the mouse. A fish should be caught if it intersects the hook. The shark should never be caught.

7. Create a SchoolOfFishApp in which the fish exhibit schooling behavior. That is, fish that are close to each either should remain close to each other, even when scared.

8. Modify the fishing game in the previous application so that a fish is caught only when the head of the fish moves over the top of the hook.

9. Modify the BusOnRoute class so that the bus is always 'above' the route and the wheels of the bus are always on the route.

10. It can be fairly time-consuming to rotate static content (especially static content). Hence, for performance reasons, it is sometimes necessary to limit the number of rotation angles (e.g., to 45° increments) and store the rotated content. Modify the

visual.statik.sampled.Content and visual.statik.sampled.Content classes so that they support this functionality.

11. The president of the university is looking for ways to save money without reducing education quality. She heard about the work you did on Exercise 7 on page 207 and has realized that, with a little more work, she can replace most of the professors on campus with a multimedia application that simulates what they do in the classroom (i.e., make the 'movie/projector' screen go up and down). Again, you must NOT use the classes in this book. Instead, you must complete the following AnimatedFrontWall class that simulates the raising and lowering of the 'movie' screen. Specifically, complete the actionPerformed(), lowerScreen(), and raiseScreen() methods. You should assume that the other classes all work correctly. You may add attributes and/or other methods to the class if necessary.

```java
import java.awt.*;
import java.awt.event.*;
import java.awt.geom.*;
import javax.swing.*;


/**
 * A GUI component that displays the front wall of a classroom with an
 * animated "movie" screen that can be raised and lowered.  The way in
 * which this component is rendered depends on whether lightsOn is
 * true or false (simulating the lights in the room being on or off).
 */
public class AnimatedFrontWall extends    FrontWallWithScreenAndLights
                               implements MetronomeListener
{
    protected Metronome               metronome;

    /**
     * Default Constructor
     */
    public AnimatedFrontWall()
    {
        super();
        metronome = new Metronome(40);
        metronome.addListener(this);
    }

    /**
     * Start the animation of the screen lowering
     */
    public void lowerScreen()
    {
        // YOUR CODE HERE!
```

```
    }

    /**
     * Start the animation of the screen raising
     */
    public void raiseScreen()
    {
        // YOUR CODE HERE!
    }

    /**
     * Handle tick events (required by MetronomeListener)
     *
     * Specifically, this method is called by the Metronome every 40
     * milliseconds.  Each time it is called it either increases or
     * decreases the attribute amountLowered (depending on whether the
     * "movie" screen is being raised or lowered) and starts the
     * rendering process (so that the "movie" screen appears to be
     * animated).  It stops the animation when the "movie" screen is
     * either fully raised or fully lowered.
     *
     * @param millis    Milliseconds since the Metronome started
     */
    public void handleTick(int millis)
    {


        // YOUR CODE HERE!

    }
```

REFERENCES AND FURTHER READING

Davison, A. 2005. *Killer game programming in Java.* Sebastopol, CA: O'Reilly.

Gosling, J. and H. McGilton. 1996. *The Java language environment: A white paper.* http://java.sun.com/docs/white/langenv/.

Laybourne, K. and J. Canemaker. 1998. *The animation book.* New York: Three Rivers Press.

Parent, R. 2007. *Computer animation: Algorithms and techniques.* Cambridge, MA: Morgan Kaufmann.

Auditory Content

Part III deals with auditory content. It begins, in Chapter 10, with a general discussion of the physics, biology, and psychology of hearing/audition. Then, Chapter 11 considers sampled auditory content. Finally, it concludes in Chapter 12 with a discussion of described auditory content, specifically, described music.

Auditory Content

10

This chapter's study of auditory content begins with a discussion of the physics of sound. It then considers the biology of hearing and the psychology of auditory perception. Finally, it considers auditory output devices and how they can be used to present auditory content.

10.1 Sound

The word "sound" can be defined in a variety of different ways. This book uses the following definition:

....

Definition 10.1 *Sound* is a series of vibrations moving as waves (see Section 1.3) through air or other gases, liquids, or solids.

....

This definition makes it easy to answer the question "If a tree falls in the forest and there is nobody there to hear it, does it make a sound?" Using this definition of "sound," the answer is clearly, "yes."

Though sound waves can move through gases, liquids, and solids, this book is almost exclusively concerned with sound waves that move through the air. In this context, a sound wave consists of successive *compressions/condensations* and *rarefactions* of air molecules. In compressions, the air molecules are pushed closer together and, hence, the air pressure is higher. In rarefactions, the molecules are pulled farther apart and the air pressure is lower. This is illustrated in Figure 10.1 on the following page. Compressions and rarefactions are typically produced by a vibrating material called the *excitation source*. The classic example of an excitation source is a guitar string.

Whereas light waves are transverse (i.e., the wave is perpendicular to the direction of travel), sound waves are longitudinal (i.e., the wave is in the direction of travel). Note also that sound waves are *traveling waves*. That is, the air molecules disturb neighboring molecules, transferring their energy to them. In general, energy is lost during the transfer and, as a result, the wave weakens as it moves away from the source. An example of a periodic (see Chapter 1) pressure wave is shown in Figure 10.2 on the next page.

Some sources radiate sounds *omnidirectionally* (that is, the waves radiate spherically from the source), while others direct sounds in particular directions. In most environments, sound waves are both reflected and absorbed by a variety of different surfaces. There are environments in which this is not the case, however.

....

Definition 10.2 A *free field* is an environment in which there are no reflections.

....

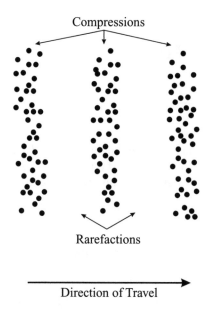

Figure 10.1   Sound Waves

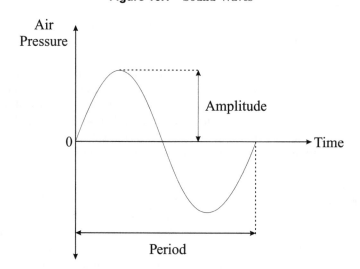

Figure 10.2   A Periodic Pressure Wave

The speed at which sound travels is a function of the medium in which the waves are propagating. The denser the medium, the greater the speed.

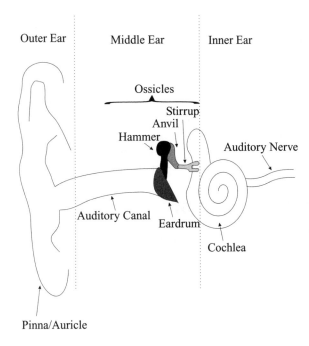

Figure 10.3   The Human Ear

10.2   Hearing

Humans sense sound using organs called ears[1] and interpret the sensation using the brain. The ear is a very complicated organ. Fortunately, the abstraction of the ear illustrated in Figure 10.3 suffices for the purposes of this book.

Sound waves are collected by the *auricle* (or *pinna*) and travel through the auditory canal to the *eardrum* (or *tympanic membrane*). The compressions and rarefactions result in a change in pressure on the two sides of the eardrum. The difference in pressure between the pressure in the auditory canal and the normal pressure on the inside of the eardrum causes the eardrum to vibrate.

The vibrations of the eardrum are transmitted through the *ossicles* (the chain of bones in the middle ear called the *hammer* [or *malleus*], *anvil* [or *incus*], and *stirrup* [or *stapes*]). As the vibrations pass from the larger bones through the sequence of smaller bones, their force is amplified.

The stirrup pushes a membrane and the movement of the membrane is transferred to the *endolymph fluid* in the *cochlea*. This causes the *basilar membrane* to move. The amplitude of the movement is different at different locations, depending on the frequency of the wave. In other words, each point on the basilar membrane is 'tuned' to a small range of frequencies. The way the basilar membrane responds to complex waves depends on the nature of the waveform.

---

[1]Note that humans hear their own voices partly by bone conduction. The voice causes the bones of the skull to vibrate, and these vibrations directly stimulate the sound-sensitive cells of the inner ear. This is part of the reason why you might not recognize a recording of your own voice.

For example, when a wave is formed from two tones with similar frequencies, some points on the basilar membrane respond to both tones.

The *organ of Corti*, which is on top of the basilar membrane, contains hairlike projections (called *stereocilia*). When the membrane vibrates, these hairs vibrate, causing a voltage difference that leads to the release of a neurotransmitter, which initiates the transmission of impulses along the *auditory nerve* to the brain. Each auditory nerve contains about 30,000 neurons that carry signals to the brain. Individual fibers in the auditory nerve are 'tuned' to particular frequencies. Hence, (there is reason to believe that) each fiber is stimulated by a particular part of the basilar membrane. It is also important to note that these fibers fire (up to 150 times per second) even in the absence of stimulation (called *spontaneous firings*).

10.3   Auditory Perception

The brain processes the output of the auditory nerve in the auditory cortex (in the temporal lobe), the frontal lobe, and the parietal lobe. The data processed by the brain are perceived in a variety of different ways.

10.3.1   Volume

Humans normally perceive differences in amplitude as differences in *volume* (or *loudness*).[2] Sound pressure levels are measured in decibels (dB), which is a logarithmic unit.

0 dB is loosely defined to be the softest sound that is audible to humans.[3] This is obviously related to the responsiveness of the neurons involved.

....

Definition 10.3 The *threshold* of a neuron is the lowest level of sound that causes a measurable change in response.

....

Different fibers in the auditory nerve have different spontaneous firing rates. The threshold varies inversely with its spontaneous firing rate.

It is important to note that continued exposure to auditory stimuli seems to lead to both *adaptation* (an apparent decrease in volume) and *fatigue* (an increase in the threshold for subsequent stimuli). The mechanisms that cause these changes in responsiveness are not well understood.

10.3.2   Pitch

The *pitch* of a sound is related to its vibration frequency; the greater the frequency, the higher the pitch. The maximum range of human hearing includes sound frequencies from about 15 Hz (i.e., 15 cycles per second) to 18 kHz (i.e., 18,000 Hz). Sounds in this range are often

---

[2]Actually, the perceived loudness of a sound depends on both its amplitude and its frequency because our ear/brain tends to amplify certain frequencies and attenuate others. *Fletcher–Munson curves* capture this effect. Hence, sound volumes are sometimes measured in *phons* and *sones*.

[3]Painful sounds are those above 120 dB. Because decibels are logarithmic, the softest audible sound is about 1 million times less intense than a sound of 120 dB.

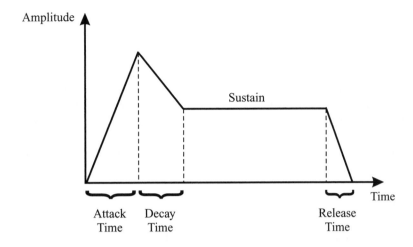

Figure 10.4 A Stylized Envelope

called *acoustic signals*. Interestingly, our perception is logarithmic, not linear. That is, people perceive the same pitch difference between 100 Hz and 200 Hz as they do between 200 Hz and 400 Hz.

10.3.3 Timbre

Two sound waves with the same pitch and volume, but produced by a piano and a trumpet, are perceived very differently. These differences are often referred to as *timbre* (pronounced tam-bur). Timbre is often defined as the attribute of sound that enables us to distinguish between two sounds that are rendered with the same loudness and pitch. Timbre is obviously a subjective notion. However, it is related to the waveform's distribution of energy at different frequencies (i.e., spectra). It is common to try and categorize timbre using an abstraction of a wave called an envelope that has four parts—an *attack*, a *decay*, a *sustain*, and a *release*. One such stylized envelope is illustrated in Figure 10.4.

10.3.4 Localization

A person's ability to locate the origin of a sound is called localization. People use several mechanisms to localize sounds. One such mechanism is the *interaural time difference*; that is, the difference in the time it takes for a sound to reach both ears. (Most people can detect a difference of about 20 microseconds.) Another such mechanism is the *interaural density difference*; that is, the difference in amplitude caused by our head interfering with the sound wave. A third mechanism that people use to localize sound is frequency filtering performed by the outer ear.

It is interesting to note that people find it more difficult to locate the origin of sounds with longer wavelengths. This is why subwoofers can be located anywhere in a room.

10.3.5 Complex Wave Forms

Two (or more) sound waves traveling through the same medium at the same time interfere with each other, creating a single complex wave. Amazingly, because of the way the basilar membrane behaves, humans have the ability to discern the original sound waves.[4]

For example, when two instruments, say a piano and a violin, generate sound waves at the same time, the sound wave that reaches a listener's ear is very complex. Yet, the listener can, in general, perceive both instruments very clearly. As another example, a listener presented with two pure tones (at the same time) can, sometimes, distinguish the two tones. This is sometimes referred to as Ohm's acoustical law.

10.3.6 Noise

Individuals find some complex waveforms pleasant and others unpleasant. The particular complex waveforms that fall into each category vary from person to person (and, even for a single person, can vary over time). As a result, everyone has probably heard a parent yell "Turn off that noise!" meaning "Turn off that complex waveform that I find unpleasant!"

In common parlance, the word "noise" means many different things. In the context of noise pollution, it usually refers to amplitude. In the context of a restaurant, it usually refers to the fact that there are many sources (e.g., many different conversations, televisions, pots and pans) of auditory content. This book uses the following definition:

....

Definition 10.4 *Noise* is a signal that is generated by a random process.

....

Interestingly, noise is often described as having different colors. *White noise* is a signal that has equal power in every band with the same width. *Red noise* is a signal that arises from a "random walk" (more formally, a signal that arises from Brownian motion).

It is possible to reduce, or even cancel/eliminate, noise using destructive interference. That is, one can produce a wave that is the inverse of the noise. Then, when the two waves are added, the noise will be eliminated. This is called *active noise cancellation*.

10.3.7 Reverberation

Except in a free field, some sound waves reach the ear directly from the source (called *direct waves*) and others reflect off of one or more surfaces before reaching the ear. This includes both *early reflections* and *late reflections*. When a reflected sound wave (with smaller amplitude because of the loss of energy) arrives at the ear after the original sound wave we perceive an echo or reverberation. (The difference between the two is usually defined in terms of the delays involved. Reverberation involves a shorter delay.) Of course, regardless of the environment, reflected waves eventually lose so much energy that they become imperceptible.

---

[4]This is not true for light waves. For example, as discussed in Section 4.3 on page 76, if two light waves of different wavelength were to interfere with each other, the observer would perceive a single color.

10.4 Auditory Output Devices

The most common auditory output device is the *conventional loudspeaker*. A loudspeaker has one or more *drivers*, each of which consists of a *diaphragm* (often a semiflexible cloth or paper with a piece of metal attached) mounted in a *basket*. The loudspeaker receives an electrical signal that turns an electromagnet on and off, causing the diaphragm to vibrate, creating pressure waves.

Electrostatic speakers use a very thin electrically conductive diaphragm mounted between two charged panels. *Planar magnetic speakers* use a thin magnetically conductive diaphragm mounted between two magnetic panels. In both of these systems the diaphragm is thin and responds very quickly. However, the range of motion is relatively small. So, these kinds of speakers accurately reproduce high frequencies but not low frequencies.

Many speakers consist of multiple drivers in a single cabinet, though some have only a single driver. The drivers are classified based on the frequencies of the sounds they produce. *Subwoofers* and *woofers* produce the lowest frequency sounds, *tweeters* produce the highest frequency sounds, and the in-between frequencies are usually referred to as the *midrange*.

The electrical signal sent to a speaker is often altered by one or more devices called *filters*. Low pass/high pass filters attenuate low/high frequencies, respectively; band pass filters attenuate frequencies outside of a given range; and bandstop filters attenuate frequencies within a range.

Auditory output systems with one speaker are often called *monophonic* or *monaural*. There are many different kinds of auditory output systems with more than one speaker, including *stereophonic* and *quadraphonic*. Systems with more than one speaker are usually said to be "more realistic" than those with just one speaker. This is because most sound sources are not located at a single point in space. For example, the sound waves produced by a band, orchestra, or choir are originating from many different locations. Systems with more than one speaker are usually better able to produce waves that have the same properties as the waves produced by these kinds of sources.

10.5 Rendering

Of course, auditory content must be presented in order to be perceived.

....

Definition 10.5 *Aural rendering* is the process of taking an internal representation of auditory content and presenting it using an auditory output device.

....

Given the nature of speakers, this involves the generation of appropriate electrical signals. On most computer systems, this process is delegated to a specialized audio/sound card.

10.6 Designing an Auditory Content System

Before turning to specific types of auditory content, it is helpful to consider the design of a system for handling auditory content in the abstract. As with the visual content system in Section 4.6 on page 88, the requirements for such a system are relatively straightforward. Specifically, the system must:

Figure 10.5 A Conceptual Model of an Auditory Content System

F10.1 Manage individual 'pieces' of auditory content.

F10.2 Manage 'aggregate' auditory content.

F10.3 Render/present auditory content.

Using the same kinds of arguments that were used to evaluate the alternative designs of the static and dynamic visual content systems, it is clear that such a system should have distinct encapsulations of the individual 'pieces,' the aggregate content, and the renderer. This is illustrated in Figure 10.5. In this design, `Content` encapsulates the individual pieces, `Audition` encapsulates the aggregate content (and plays the same role as `Visualization` in the visual system), and `AuditionView` encapsulates the renderer/presenter (and plays the same role as `VisualizationView` in the visual system). Do not be confused by the use of the word "view"—it is not meant to imply anything visual, it simply implies presentation.

Unfortunately, because of the way most audio hardware and the associated lower-level application programming interfaces (APIs) are designed, it is generally not possible to render/present sampled auditory content and described auditory content at the same time. Hence, the auditory content systems developed in the subsequent chapters will be completely independent. Nonetheless, both will be based on the conceptual model in Figure 10.5.

EXERCISES

1. Are sound waves one-dimensional, two-dimensional, or three-dimensional? Explain.

2. Explain the relationship between the period of a sound wave and its frequency.

3. (*Library Research*) Describe several different causes of hearing loss. Explain how "cochlear implant" and "middle ear implant" hearing aids differ.

4. Compare the pitch of a sound with the color of a light source. Similarly, compare the volume of a sound with the brightness of a light source.

5. How do we localize light sources? Why do we localize light sources so differently from sound sources?

6. (*Library Research*) Write a brief essay that describes how the interaural time difference can be used to localize sound. Given that people have only two ears, is it possible to use interaural time differences to localize a source in three dimensions? If you could add a third ear to your body (for this purpose), where would you put it? (Hint: You might want to start by understanding how triangulation is used in a global positioning system.)

7. Why do we have so many different notions of "noise"? What do these different notions have in common? How are the different notions of "noise" related to the physics, biology, and psychology of sound?

8. (*Library Research*) Write a brief essay that describes 5.1 channel sound systems.

9. Given your understanding of auditory noise, explain what is meant by the term "visual noise"?

10. (*Review*) Create a `NoiseOp` class that implements the `BufferedImageOp` interface. (Hint: Think about whether this class should specialize the `IdentityOp` class.)

11. (*Thinking Ahead*) Based on your knowledge of visual content, list two different ways of representing auditory content.

REFERENCES AND FURTHER READING

Kosko, B. 2006. *Noise.* New York: Viking.
Moore, B. C. J. 2003. *An introduction to the psychology of hearing.* Boston: Academic Press.
Rumsey, F. 2001. *Spatial sound.* Burlington, MA: Focal Press.
Serway, R. A., J. S. Faughn, C. Vuille, and C. A. Bennet. 2005. *College physics.* Boston: Brooks Cole.

Sampled Auditory Content

11

Recall from Chapter 5 that the sampling of static visual content involves the sampling of colors and space, and from Chapter 8 that the sampling of dynamic visual content involves sampling from all possible points in time. The sampling of auditory content, which involves two discretizations, has things in common with both. It is often referred to as *analog-to-digital* (or *A–D*) conversion.

One part of the A–D conversion process involves sampling over time.

....

Definition 11.1 *Temporal sampling* involves measuring the wave at (usually regular) discrete points in time.

....

For example, music CDs normally use a 44.1 kHz sampling rate and DVD audio normally uses a 96 kHz sampling rate. That is, music CDs contains 44,100 samples per second and the audio track of a DVD contains 96,000 samples per second. Temporal sampling is illustrated in Figure 11.1.

The other part of the A–D conversion process involves limiting the possible values taken on by each sample.

....

Definition 11.2 *Quantization* involves limiting the measured amplitudes to a discrete set of values.

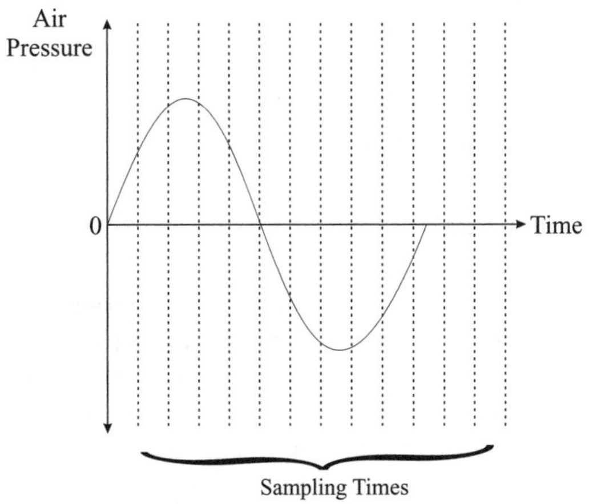

....

Figure 11.1 Temporal Sampling

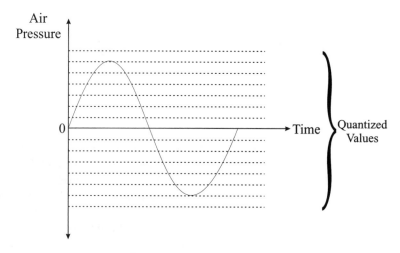

Figure 11.2 Quantization

Figure 11.3 Presentation of Sampled Audio in Java

For example, if 8 bits quantization is used, there are 256 different amplitudes and the actual amplitude is rounded or truncated to one of these 256 values. Sound wave quantization is illustrated in Figure 11.2. The most common sample size is 16 bits (which is the size used on audio CDs).

One of the most important results in this area is the *Nyquist–Shannon Sampling Theorem* that essentially says that a digital signal cannot unambiguously represent signal components with frequencies above half the sampling rate. This means that in order to reconstruct the original perfectly, the sampling rate must be greater than twice the highest frequency of the input signal. A low sampling rate tends to result in high signal frequencies appearing as lower frequencies (which is known as *aliasing*).

11.1 A 'Quick Start'

In Java, the attributes of the sampling process are encapsulated in the `AudioFormat` class. An `AudioFormat` object contains information about the number of channels (e.g., mono, stereo), the sampling rate, the quantization (i.e., the number of bits per sample), and the encoding technique (e.g., linear pulse code modulation, nonlinear mu-law).

The presentation of sampled auditory content in Java can be conceptualized as in Figure 11.3. A `Mixer` has one or more source `Line` objects and one or more target `Line` objects. The `Mixer` reads from one or more sources, processes the input, and writes to one or more targets. Most sources implement either the `SourceDataLine` interface or the `Port` interface.

Most targets implement either the TargetDataLine interface or the Port interface. Since the Mixer interface extends the Line interface, one Mixer can serve as a source for another.

A Clip object is a type of Line object that contains data that can be loaded prior to presentation. A Clip object will render its sampled auditory content when its start() method is called. Several steps must be taken to create and use a Clip object.

First, one needs to create an AudioInputStream from a File or an InputStream. As with other kinds of content, it makes sense to use the ResourceFinder class to get an InputStream.

```
// Get the resource
finder = ResourceFinder.createInstance();
is     = finder.findInputStream("/"+args[0]);

// Create an AudioInputStream from the InputStream
stream = AudioSystem.getAudioInputStream(is);
```

Second, one needs to create a Clip object using a factory method in the AudioSystem class.

```
// Create a Clip (i.e., a Line that can be pre-loaded)
clip = AudioSystem.getClip();
```

Third, one needs to load the content into the Clip. This is accomplished by calling its open method, passing it the appropriate AudioInputStream.

```
// Tell the Clip to acquire any required system
// resources and become operational
clip.open(stream);
```

Finally, one needs to start the Clip.

```
// Present the Clip (without blocking the
// thread of execution)
clip.start();
```

Note that start() method does not block the thread of execution. Hence, if you use the above fragments in an application, you will need to prevent the main thread from terminating. One way to do this is with a call to System.in.read().

With this as an overview, it is now time to turn to a more detailed discussion of a sampled auditory content system. Such a system must:

F11.1 Encapsulate signals.

F11.2 Operate on signals.

F11.3 Present/render these signals.

This chapter next discusses ways to satisfy Requirement F11.1. It then discusses ways to satisfy Requirements F11.2 and F11.3.

11.2 Encapsulating Sampled Auditory Content

Any encapsulation of sampled auditory content must include the sample points for all of the signals (i.e., one signal for monophonic, two signals for stereophonic, etc.) and information about the sampling process. Since the information about the sampling process can be stored in an AudioFormat object, all that remains is to consider ways to encapsulate samples and signals. Not surprisingly, there are many alternative designs that are consistent with the conceptual model in Figure 10.5 on page 296.

One obvious design includes a Sample class that encapsulates individual samples, a Signal class that encapsulates signals (i.e., collections of samples), and a MultiChannelSound class that contains multiple signals. Since samples and signals can both be rendered/presented, each of these classes implements a Content interface. This design is illustrated in Figure 11.4. The problem with this design is that it is overly complicated. In particular, since a sample is nothing but a numeric value, there is no reason to have a Sample class.

 A simpler design is illustrated in Figure 11.5 on the next page. In this design, samples are represented as double values and signals are represented as arrays of double values. It has two classes that implement the Content interface, the SingleChannelSound class and the MultiChannelSound class. The latter is simply a collection of the former. This is a nice design in many respects. In particular, the MultiChannel sound class can delegate many operations to its component SingleChannelSound objects. Unfortunately, this design is difficult to reconcile with many file formats that are used for storing sampled auditory content. That is, many existing file formats make it difficult to independently/sequentially construct SingleChannelSound objects and then combine them into a MultiChannelSound object.

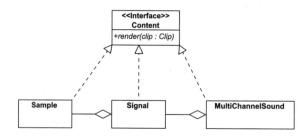

Figure 11.4 A Design with a Sample Class

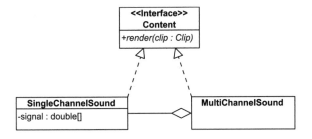

Figure 11.5 A Design with `SingleChannelSound` and `MultiChannelSound` Classes

Figure 11.6 A Simple Design

Hence, there is a better design that is even simpler. In this design, samples are again represented as `double` values and signals are again represented as arrays of `double` values. Now, however, as illustrated in Figure 11.6, the collection of signals is just a collection (e.g., a `List`) of arrays of `double` values (i.e., a collection of `double[]`). This is similar to the way in which the pixels in sampled visual content can be represented as an array (either one-dimensional or two-dimensional) of `Color` objects. Since this design is similar in spirit to the design of the `BufferedImage` class, this encapsulation of a sound is called a `BufferedSound`.

The `BufferedSound` class has the following structure:

```java
package auditory.sampled;

import java.util.*;
import javax.sound.sampled.*;

public class BufferedSound implements Content
{
    private ArrayList<double[]>  channels;
    private AudioFormat          format;
    private int                  numberOfSamples;

    private static final double MAX_AMPLITUDE       =  32767.0;
    private static final double MIN_AMPLITUDE       = -32767.0;
    private static final int    SAMPLE_SIZE_IN_BITS = 16;
    private static final int    BYTES_PER_CHANNEL   = SAMPLE_SIZE_IN_BITS/8;
}
```

To simplify the discussion that follows, this class uses sampling processes that vary only in their sampling rates; all other aspects of the process are standardized. This is evident in the explicit value constructor of the BufferedSound class.

```java
public BufferedSound(float sampleRate)
{
    format = new AudioFormat(
        AudioFormat.Encoding.PCM_SIGNED,
        sampleRate,            // Sample rate in Hz
        SAMPLE_SIZE_IN_BITS, // Sample size in bits
        0,                     // Number of channels
        0,                     // Frame size in bytes
        sampleRate,            // Frame rate in Hz
        true);                 // Big-endian or not

    channels = new ArrayList<double[]>();
    numberOfSamples = 0;
}
```

Note that when a BufferedSound is constructed, it contains no channels. Channels are added using the addChannel() method (which checks to see whether the signal to be added has the correct length).

```java
public synchronized void addChannel(double[] signal)
{
    if (numberOfSamples == 0) numberOfSamples = signal.length;

    if (numberOfSamples == signal.length)
    {
        channels.add(signal);
        updateAudioFormat();
    }
}
```

This method uses the updateAudioFormat() method to modify the AudioFormat so that it reflects the current state of the BufferedSound. This involves changing the number of channels and the frame size.

```java
private void updateAudioFormat()
{
    format = new AudioFormat(
        format.getEncoding(),          // Encoding
```

```
                 format.getSampleRate(),               // Sample rate in Hz
                 format.getSampleSizeInBits(),         // Sample size in bits
                 channels.size(),                      // Number of channels
                 channels.size()*BYTES_PER_CHANNEL,    // Frame size in bytes
                 format.getSampleRate(),               // Frame rate in Hz
                 format.isBigEndian());                // Big-endian or not
    }
```

Since some operations on two `BufferedSound` objects can be performed only if the two objects are compatible, this class has a `matches()` method that compares two `BufferedSound` objects.

```
    public synchronized boolean matches(BufferedSound other)
    {
        boolean        result;

        result = false;
        result = getAudioFormat().matches(other.getAudioFormat()) &&
                 (getNumberOfSamples() == other.getNumberOfSamples());


        return result;
    }
```

Next, this class has a method that can be used to append one `BufferedSound` object to another. This is actually a pretty simple process. In particular, if the two objects are compatible, then all that is necessary is to append the signals (channel by channel).

```
    public synchronized void append(BufferedSound other)
    {
        ArrayList<double[]>   temp;
        double[]              otherSignal, tempSignal, thisSignal;
        Iterator<double[]>    i, j;

        if (matches(other))
        {
            temp = new ArrayList<double[]>();

            i = channels.iterator();
            j = other.channels.iterator();
            while (i.hasNext())
            {
                thisSignal  = i.next();
```

```
                    otherSignal = j.next();

                    // Allocate space for the new signal
                    tempSignal = new double[thisSignal.length +
                                            otherSignal.length];

                    // Copy the current signal
                    System.arraycopy(thisSignal, 0,
                                     tempSignal, 0, thisSignal.length);

                    // Append the other left signal
                    System.arraycopy(otherSignal, 0,
                                     tempSignal, thisSignal.length,
                                     otherSignal.length);

                    // Save the longer signal
                    temp.add(tempSignal);
                }
                channels = temp;
            }
        }
```

BufferedSound objects can be constructed in a variety of different ways. As in earlier chapters, in order to keep the BufferedSound class cohesive, it makes sense to create a BufferedSoundFactory for creating BufferedSound objects. Unlike earlier chapters, there are several different ways to create BufferedSound objects.

One obvious approach is to create a pure tone by sampling from a sine wave. To this end, the BufferedSoundFactory class should include a method with the following signature:

```
public BufferedSound createBufferedSound(double frequency,
                                         int    length,
                                         float  sampleRate,
                                         double amplitude)
```

This method first allocates memory for the signal, which involves determining the number of samples from the sample rate (measured in samples/second) and the duration (in seconds).

```
        //samples =      samples/sec * sec
        n        = (int)(sampleRate * (double)length/1000000.0);

        signal   = new double[n];
```

Next, this method determines the number of radians per sample.

```
// rads/sample  = ( rads/cycle * cycles/sec)/ samples/sec
radiansPerSample = (Math.PI*2.0 * frequency) / sampleRate;
```

An Aside: Radians

A circle can be divided into any number of equal pieces. One degree is $1/360$th of a circle and one radian is $1/2\pi$th of a circle. Though many people are more comfortable with degrees (and find radians confusing) there is a good rationale for radians. In particular, since the circumference of a circle is given by $2\pi r$ (where r is the radius), the circumference of a *unit circle* (i.e., a circle with radius 1) is 2π. Hence, it makes sense to divide "one trip around" a unit circle into 2π pieces. Each such piece has an angular 'size' of 1 radian.

After that it is relatively easy to determine the signal values using the static `sin()` method in the `Math` class.

```
for (int i=0; i<signal.length; i++)
{
    // rad  =   rad/sample    * sample
    radians = radiansPerSample * i;

    signal[i] = amplitude * Math.sin(radians);
}
```

Finally, the `BufferedSound` object is constructed, initialized, and returned.

```
sound = new BufferedSound(sampleRate);
sound.addChannel(signal);
return sound;
```

Of course, the `BufferedSoundFactory` class also needs to be able to create a `BufferedSound` object from an `AudioInputStream`. This method has the following signature:

```
public BufferedSound createBufferedSound(double frequency,
                                         int    length,
                                         float  sampleRate,
                                         double amplitude)
```

The first thing this method does is convert to the pulse code modulation (PCM) encoding that is used in the `BufferedSound` class. If the `AudioInputStream` has a different encoding, it uses the `AudioSystem` class to perform the conversion.

```java
inFormat = inStream.getFormat();

// Convert ULAW and ALAW to PCM
if ((inFormat.getEncoding() == AudioFormat.Encoding.ULAW) ||
    (inFormat.getEncoding() == AudioFormat.Encoding.ALAW)   ) {

    pcmFormat = new AudioFormat(
                    AudioFormat.Encoding.PCM_SIGNED,
                    inFormat.getSampleRate(),
                    inFormat.getSampleSizeInBits()*2,
                    inFormat.getChannels(),
                    inFormat.getFrameSize()*2,
                    inFormat.getFrameRate(),
                    true);

    pcmStream = AudioSystem.getAudioInputStream(pcmFormat,
                                                inStream);
}
else // It is PCM
{
    pcmFormat = inFormat;
    pcmStream = inStream;
}
```

Next, this method creates a buffer to hold the raw bytes and reads them from the `AudioInputStream`.

```java
// Create a buffer and read the raw bytes
bufferSize = (int)(pcmStream.getFrameLength())
                * pcmFormat.getFrameSize();

rawBytes = new byte[bufferSize];
pcmStream.read(rawBytes);
```

After that it converts the raw bytes.

```java
// Convert the raw bytes
if (pcmFormat.getSampleSizeInBits() == 8)
```

```
{
    signal = processEightBitQuantization(rawBytes, pcmFormat);
}
else
{
    signal = processSixteenBitQuantization(rawBytes, pcmFormat);
}
```

Finally, this method processes the channel or channels, converting each sample from an `int` to a `double`.

```
sound = new BufferedSound(pcmFormat.getSampleRate());

// Process the individual channels
if (pcmFormat.getChannels() == 1)  // Mono
{
    sampleLength = signal.length;
    monoSignal   = new double[sampleLength];

    for (int i=0; i<sampleLength; i++)
    {
        monoSignal[i]  = signal[i]; // Convert to double
    }
    sound.addChannel(monoSignal);
}
else                               // Stereo
{
    sampleLength = signal.length/2;
    leftSignal   = new double[sampleLength];
    rightSignal  = new double[sampleLength];

    for (int i=0; i<sampleLength; i++)
    {
        leftSignal[i]  = signal[2*i];
        rightSignal[i] = signal[2*i+1];
    }
    sound.addChannel(leftSignal);
    sound.addChannel(rightSignal);
}
```

While using a `double[]` rather than an `int[]` uses extra memory, it makes it easier to operate on signals using floating point arithmetic. One could, obviously, easily modify the `BufferedSound` class so that it uses `int` values instead.

The exact process used to convert the raw bytes depends on whether the signal uses an

8-bit quantization or a 16-bit quantization. 8-bit quantization is the simpler case since the class need only be concerned with whether the samples are signed or not. If the samples are signed, the raw bytes can be used. If not, each raw byte needs to have 128 subtracted from it to flip the sign.

```
private int[] processEightBitQuantization(
                              byte[]       rawBytes,
                              AudioFormat format)
{
    int         lsb, msb;
    int[]       signal;
    String      encoding;


    signal = new int[rawBytes.length];
    encoding = format.getEncoding().toString();

    if (encoding.startsWith("PCM_SIGN"))
    {
       for (int i=0; i<rawBytes.length; i++)
          signal[i] = rawBytes[i];
    }
    else
    {
       for (int i=0; i<rawBytes.length; i++)
          signal[i] = rawBytes[i]-128;
    }

    return signal;
}
```

If 16-bit quantization is used, the class must worry about the byte order. This method has the following signature,

```
private int[] processSixteenBitQuantization(
                              byte[]       rawBytes,
                              AudioFormat format)
```

and uses the following local variables:

```
    int         lsb, msb;
    int[]       signal;
```

```
signal = new int[rawBytes.length / 2];
```

If the stream is big-endian then the first byte is the high-order byte and the signal is processed as follows:

```
if (format.isBigEndian())  // Big-endian
{
    for (int i=0; i<signal.length; i++)
    {
        // First byte is high-order byte
        msb = (int) rawBytes[2*i];

        // Second byte is low-order byte
        lsb = (int) rawBytes[2*i+1];

        signal[i] = msb << 8 | (255 & lsb);
    }
}
```

Otherwise, the second byte is the high-order byte and the signal is processed as follows:

```
else                          // Little-endian
{
    for (int i=0; i<signal.length; i++)
    {
        // First byte is low-order byte
        lsb = (int) rawBytes[2*i];

        // Second byte is high-order byte
        msb = (int) rawBytes[2*i+1];

        signal[i] = msb << 8 | (255 & lsb);
    }
}
```

(See the discussion of bit masks on on page 116.) With this, it is easy to create a `BufferedSound` object from a file.

```
public BufferedSound createBufferedSound(String name)
                    throws IOException,
```

```
                                        UnsupportedAudioFileException
    {
        AudioInputStream          stream;
        InputStream               is;

        is     = finder.findInputStream(name);
        stream = AudioSystem.getAudioInputStream(is);

        return createBufferedSound(stream);
    }
```

Before concluding this section it is important to note that, except for one vague reference, **this discussion has ignored file formats**. This is completely consistent with the approach used in the chapters on visual content. That is, this book ignores storage issues—not because they are unimportant but because they are the topic of many other books. In Java, audio file formats are encapsulated by the `AudioFileFormat` class. Common file formats include `.aiff`, `.au`, `.mp3`, `.snd`, and `.wav`.

11.3   Operating on Sampled Auditory Content

It should be clear that one can operate on sampled auditory content in much the same way that one can operate on sampled visual content (see Chapters 5 and 8). However, with auditory content it makes sense to consider both operations with one source signal (i.e., unary operations) and operations with two source signals (i.e., binary operations). So, since the discussion of operating on static sampled visual content in Section 5.3 on page 119 started with a discussion of the `BufferedImageOp` interface, it makes sense to start here with a discussion of both a `BufferedSoundUnaryOp` interface,

```
package auditory.sampled;

public interface BufferedSoundUnaryOp
{
    public BufferedSound filter(BufferedSound src,
                                BufferedSound dest);
}
```

and a `BufferedSoundBinaryOp` interface,

```
package auditory.sampled;

public interface BufferedSoundBinaryOp
{
```

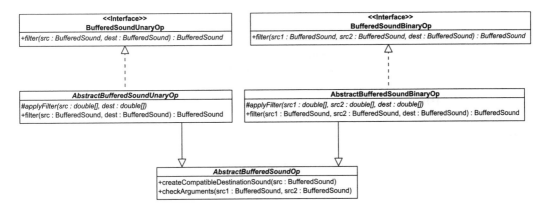

Figure 11.7 Operating on Sampled Auditory Content

```
public BufferedSound filter(BufferedSound src1, BufferedSound src2,
                            BufferedSound dest)
                throws IllegalArgumentException;
}
```

both of which include `filter()` methods (as does the `BufferedImageOp` interface).

In general, classes that implement these interfaces will operate on the signals independently. Hence, it makes sense to create abstract implementations of these interfaces that implement the `filter()` method and iteratively call an `applyFilter()` method, passing it the array of `double` values for each signal. Further, since both of these classes need to create compatible destination `BufferedSound` objects and check the compatibility of `BufferedSound` objects, they should inherit these capabilities from a common parent. This leads to the design illustrated in Figure 11.7.

Implementing this design is relatively easy. The `AbstractBufferedSoundOp` class has a method for checking compatibility,

```
protected void checkArguments(BufferedSound a, BufferedSound b)
                            throws IllegalArgumentException
{
    if (!a.matches(b))
        throw(new IllegalArgumentException("Argument Mismatch"));
}
```

and a method that creates compatible destination `BufferedSound` objects.

```
public BufferedSound createCompatibleDestinationSound(
                                BufferedSound src)
```

```
{
    BufferedSound        temp;
    float                sampleRate;
    int                  channels, length;

    channels   = src.getNumberOfChannels();
    length     = src.getNumberOfSamples();
    sampleRate = src.getSampleRate();

    temp = new BufferedSound(sampleRate);

    for (int i=0; i<channels; i++)
    {
        temp.addChannel(new double[length]);
    }

    return temp;
}

protected void checkArguments(BufferedSound a, BufferedSound b)
                            throws IllegalArgumentException
{
    if (!a.matches(b))
        throw(new IllegalArgumentException("Argument Mismatch"));
}
}
```

The `AbstractBufferedSoundUnaryOp` class is a specialization of the `AbstractBuffered-SoundOp` that has a `filter()` method that is passed source and destination `BufferedSound` objects, extracts the signals, and calls an `applyFilter()` method that operates on them.

```
public BufferedSound filter(BufferedSound src,
                           BufferedSound dest)
{
    Iterator<double[]>   source, destination;

    // Construct the destination if necessary; otherwise check it
    if (dest == null)
        dest = createCompatibleDestinationSound(src);

    // Get the source channels
    source     = src.getSignals();

    // Get the destination channels
    destination = dest.getSignals();
```

```
        // Apply the filter
        applyFilter(source, destination);

        return dest;
    }
```

This `applyFilter()` method extracts the channels and calls a method (with the same name) that operates on each channel.

```
    public void applyFilter(Iterator<double[]> source,
                            Iterator<double[]> destination)
    {
        while (source.hasNext())
        {
            applyFilter(source.next(), destination.next());
        }
    }
```

The method that operates on an individual channel must be implemented by concrete children and, hence, is abstract.

```
    public abstract void applyFilter(double[] source,
                                     double[] destination);
```

The `AbstractBufferedSoundBinaryOp` class does the same thing for operations with two sources. It has a convenience method that is used to determine whether the two source `BufferedSound` objects are compatible.

```
    protected void checkArguments(BufferedSound a,
                                  BufferedSound b)
                                  throws IllegalArgumentException
    {
        if (!a.matches(b))
            throw(new IllegalArgumentException("Argument Mismatch"));
    }
```

It has a `filter()` method that is passed `BufferedSound` objects.

```java
    public BufferedSound filter(BufferedSound src1,
                                BufferedSound src2,
                                BufferedSound dest)
                      throws IllegalArgumentException
    {
      Iterator<double[]>  source1, source2, destination;


      // Check the properties of the two source sounds
      checkArguments(src1, src2);

      // Construct the destination if necessary; otherwise check it
      if (dest == null)
          dest = createCompatibleDestinationSound(src1);
      else
          checkArguments(src1, dest);


      // Get the source channels
      source1     = src1.getSignals();
      source2     = src2.getSignals();

      // Get the destination channels
      destination = dest.getSignals();


      // Apply the filter
      applyFilter(source1, source2, destination);

      return dest;
    }
```

This method calls an `applyFilter()` method that is passed all of the channels.

```java
    public void applyFilter(Iterator<double[]> source1,
                            Iterator<double[]> source2,
                            Iterator<double[]> destination)
    {
      while (source1.hasNext())
      {
        applyFilter(source1.next(), source2.next(), destination.next());
      }
    }
```

The version of the `applyFilter()` method that is passed the individual signals must be implemented by concrete children.

```
public abstract void applyFilter(double[] source1,
                                 double[] source2,
                                 double[] destination);
```

With these abstract classes, it is now possible to consider actual operations. These operations can be divided into two broad categories: *filters* (which involve the transformation of a set of samples 'around' the current sample) and other operations. The easiest place to start is with the latter.

11.3.1   Addition

One of the simplest binary operations is *addition*, which simply involves the pointwise addition of the samples. It can be implemented as follows:

```
package auditory.sampled;

public class AddOp extends     AbstractBufferedSoundBinaryOp
{
    public void applyFilter(double[] source1, double[] source2,
                            double[] destination)
    {
        for (int i=0; i<source1.length; i++)
        {
            destination[i] = source1[i] + source2[i];
        }
    }
}
```

The result of an addition operation can often be somewhat surprising to the uninitiated. With that in mind, it is useful to consider some examples. Consider a sample of a sine wave with a frequency of 100 Hz, a sampling rate of 10 kHz, and a length of 100,000 microseconds as illustrated on the left side of Figure 11.8 on the following page and a sample of a sine wave with a frequency of 200 Hz, a sampling rate of 10 kHz, and a length of 100,000 microseconds as illustrated on the right side of Figure 11.8 on the next page.

The addition of these two samples (which are said to be *harmonics*) is illustrated in Figure 11.9 on the following page. Note that the peaks and troughs of the 100 Hz wave correspond to the even-numbered peaks and troughs in the 200 Hz wave. Hence, the amplitudes of these peaks and troughs are doubled in the result. However, around the odd-numbered peaks

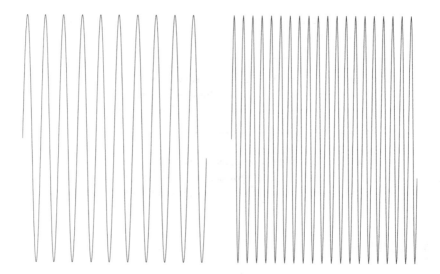

Figure 11.8   A 100 Hz Sine Wave (left) and 200 Hz Sine Wave (right)

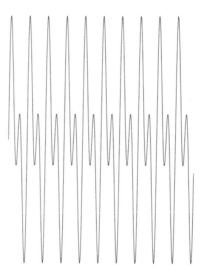

Figure 11.9   The Result of Adding 100 Hz and 200 Hz Sine Waves

in the 200 Hz wave, smaller values (centered around 0) from the 100 Hz wave will be added. This is what gives rise to the wave in Figure 11.9.

As another example, suppose the 100 Hz sample above is added to a sample of a sine wave with a frequency of 105 Hz, a sampling rate of 10 kHz, and a length of 100,000 microseconds as illustrated in Figure 11.10 on the next page. In this case, the addition of the two yields the wave illustrated in Figure 11.11 on the following page. This result, which is an example of

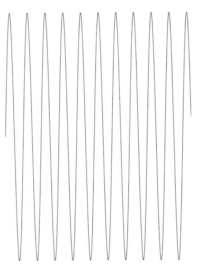

Figure 11.10   A 105 Hz Sine Wave

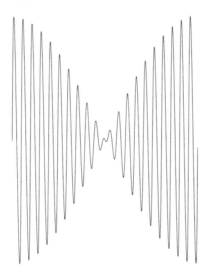

Figure 11.11   The Result of Adding 100 Hz and 105 Hz Sine Waves

beating or *phasing*,[1] is more difficult to intuit. However, if you work through a small example by hand, you should be able to convince yourself that it is true.

---

[1]When the result of the addition is "pleasing to the ear," as when several violins play approximately the same pitch, this is, instead, referred to as chorusing.

11.3.2 Reversal

One of the simplest unary operations, and one that arises in popular music from time to time, is sample reversal. This operation can be implemented as follows:

```java
package auditory.sampled;

public class ReverseOp extends    AbstractBufferedSoundUnaryOp
{
    public void applyFilter(double[] source, double[] destination)
    {
        int       length;

        length    = source.length;

        for (int i=0; i<length; i++)
        {
            destination[i]  = source[length-1-i];
        }
    }
}
```

The most famous example of this operation is probably the (supposed) use of it by the Beatles in the song "Revolution Number 9." More recently, this operation was applied to the song "Join the Navy" in an episode of *The Simpsons*.

11.3.3 Inversion

Another simple unary operations is inversion. This operation can be implemented as follows:

```java
package auditory.sampled;

public class InvertOp extends    AbstractBufferedSoundUnaryOp
{
    public void applyFilter(double[] source, double[] destination)
    {
        int       length;

        length    = source.length;

        for (int i=0; i<length; i++)
        {
            destination[i]  = -source[i];
```

```
        }
    }
}
```

As discussed in Chapter 10, the most common use of inversion is wave cancellation using destructive interference. However, if you play with the inversion filter, you will see that cancellation is much more complicated than it might seem at first glance.

11.3.4 Filters

Filters are distinguished from each other in several different ways. *Causal* filters use only sample points 'before' the current point, whereas *noncausal* filters can use sample points 'after' the current point. (Note that noncausal filters can be used only in post-processing, they cannot be applied in real time.) *Finite* filters use only the source whereas *infinite* filters use both the source and the destination. Linear filters only combine the sample points in a linear fashion (that is, using addition and multiplication by constants). Finally, *time-invariant* filters do not change over time whereas *adaptive* filters do. This chapter is primarily concerned with infinite and finite linear causal filters.

Letting d denote the destination, s denote the source, and w and v denote weights, an *infinite, linear, causal filter* is a filter than can be expressed as follows:

$$d_i = \sum_{k=0}^{n} s_{i-k} w_k + \sum_{j=0}^{m} d_{i-j} v_j \text{ for all } i.$$

In contrast, a *finite, linear causal filter* (which is also called a *finite impulse response* or FIR filter) is a filter that can be expressed as follows:

$$d_i = \sum_{k=0}^{n} s_{i-k} w_k \text{ for all } i.$$

A FIR filter with $n = 5$ is illustrated in Figure 11.12 on the next page. Conceptually, for each sample in the source (denoted by index i) the appropriate weights are applied, the resulting values are added, and the sum is stored in the appropriate location in the destination. Then, the weights are moved one position to the right and the process is repeated. You should be able to see the similarity between filters and the convolutions used to operate on sampled visual content in Section 5.3.1 on page 127.

The `FIRFilter` class, which needs to manage an array of `double` values that contains the weights, has the following overall structure:

```
package auditory.sampled;

public class FIRFilter
{
```

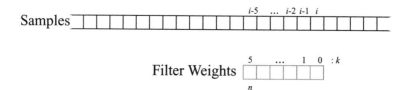

Figure 11.12   A FIR Filter

```
private double[]     weights;

public FIRFilter(double[] weights)
{
   this.weights = new double[weights.length];
   System.arraycopy(weights, 0, this.weights, 0, weights.length);
}
}
```

The getWeight() method simply returns the appropriate weight (or the value 1).

```
public double getWeight(int index)
{
   double    weight;

   weight = 0.0;
   if ((weights == null) && (index == weights.length-1))
   {
      weight = 1.0;
   }
   else if ((index >=0) && (index < weights.length-1))
   {
      weight = weights[index];
   }

   return weight;
}
```

The getLength() method simply returns the number of weights.

```
public int getLength()
{
   int    length;
```

```
        length = 0;
        if (weights != null) length = weights.length;

        return length;
    }
```

The `FIRFilter` class can now be used to create an `FIRFilterOp` that implements the `BufferedSoundUnaryOp` interfaces. This class has the following structure:

```
package auditory.sampled;

public class FIRFilterOp extends AbstractBufferedSoundUnaryOp
{
    private FIRFilter          fir;

    public FIRFilterOp(FIRFilter fir)
    {
        this.fir = fir;
    }
}
```

It implements the `applyFilter()` method in the obvious way. It simply copies the first $n - 2$ samples and calculates the weighted sum for the other samples.

```
    public void applyFilter(double[] source, double[] destination)
    {
        double     weight;
        int        length, n;

        n          = fir.getLength();
        length     = source.length;

        // Copy the first n-2 samples
        for (int i=0; i<n-1; i++)
        {
            destination[i]  = source[i];
        }

        // Filter the remaining samples
        for (int i=n-1; i<length; i++)
        {
            for (int k=0; k<n; k++)
            {
```

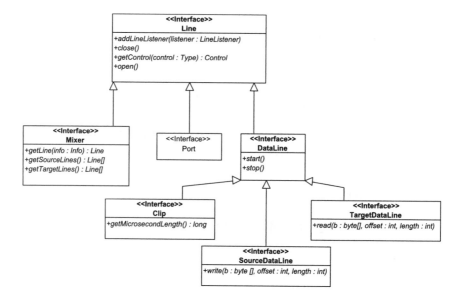

Figure 11.13   The Java Sound API

```
        weight        = fir.getWeight(k);

        destination[i]  += source[i-k]  * weight;
      }
    }
  }
```

Presenting Sampled Auditory Content

Sampled auditory content is presented/rendered and 'recorded' in Java using an object that implements the Line. As illustrated in Figure 11.13, there are several specializations of the Line interface, some of which are used for presenting/rendering, some for 'recording', and some for mixing (i.e., combining the input/output from multiple Line objects). For the purposes of this discussion, the most important such objects are those that implement the Clip interface, which can present/render auditory content that is completely in-memory.

Mirroring the design of the system that renders sampled static visual content (see Section 5.4 on page 143), it makes sense to include the capabilities for rendering/presenting sampled auditory content in a Player class. This class has the following overall structure:

```
package auditory.sampled;

import java.util.*;
import javax.sound.sampled.*;
```

```
public class BoomBox implements LineListener
{
    private Content        content;
    private Clip           clip;
    private final Object   sync = new Object();

    public BoomBox(Content content)
    {
        this.content = content;
    }
}
```

This class needs to implement the **LineListener** interface since it needs to be informed when the **Clip** stops. Since other objects might also want to be informed of these kinds of events, this class maintains its own collection of **LineListener** objects that it forwards the events to.

```
private Vector<LineListener> listeners = new Vector<LineListener>();
```

This collection is managed as follows:

```
public void addLineListener(LineListener listener)
{
    listeners.add(listener);
}

public void removeLineListener(LineListener listener)
{
    listeners.remove(listener);
}
```

Since this class implements the **LineListener** interface it must have an **update()** method. This method forwards all events. It also processes **LineEvent.Type.STOP** events by closing the **Clip** and removing itself as a **LineListener**. (As discussed below, it adds itself as a **LineListener** when it starts the **Clip**.)

```
public void update(LineEvent evt)
{
    Enumeration     e;
    LineEvent.Type  type;
    LineListener    listener;
```

```
        synchronized(sync)
        {
            // Forward the LineEvent to all LineListener objects
            e = listeners.elements();
            while (e.hasMoreElements())
            {
                listener = (LineListener)e.nextElement();
                listener.update(evt);
            }

            // Get the type of the event
            type = evt.getType();

            // Process STOP events
            if (type.equals(LineEvent.Type.STOP))
            {
                sync.notifyAll();
                clip.close();
                clip.removeLineListener(this);
                clip = null;
            }
        }
    }
}
```

The start() method in the BoomBox class is passed a boolean to indicate whether it should block the calling thread of execution.

```
    public void start(boolean block)
            throws LineUnavailableException
    {
    }
```

As in the system that renders sampled static visual content (see Section 5.4 on page 143), the BoomBox delegates the actual rendering to the Content object. So, the start() method constructs a Clip object, adds the BoomBox as a LineListener, and tells the Content object to start rendering.

```
    Clip                clip;

    clip = AudioSystem.getClip();
    clip.addLineListener(this); // So the calling thread can be informed
```

```
content.render(clip);
```

Recalling that the `start()` method in the `Clip` class does not block, this method can, if desired (i.e., if the parameter `block` has the value `true`), wait until the `Clip` stops (and calls the `update()` method).

```
synchronized(sync)
{
    // Wait until the Clip stops [and notifies us by
    // calling the update() method]
    if (block)
    {
        try
        {
            sync.wait();
        }
        catch (InterruptedException ie)
        {
            // Ignore
        }
    }
}
```

Note that all of this code is in a `synchronized` block that uses the `Object` named `sync` as its monitor to prevent changes to the listeners while the `Content` is being rendered.

It is now important to consider the actual rendering (in the `BufferedSound` class). Since the `Clip` class renders/presents `short` values, the `BufferedSound` class has a method that forces an amplitude to fit in 2 bytes. The simplest way to accomplish this is with truncation.

```
private short scaleSample(double sample)
{
    short     scaled;

    if        (sample > MAX_AMPLITUDE) scaled=(short)MAX_AMPLITUDE;
    else if (sample < MIN_AMPLITUDE) scaled=(short)MIN_AMPLITUDE;
    else                                 scaled=(short)sample;

    return scaled;
}
```

The `render()` method that will actually present/render the `BufferedSound` has the following signature:

```
public synchronized void render(Clip clip)
                        throws LineUnavailableException
```

This method first creates an array to hold the amplitudes. This process is complicated by the fact that, in the PCM encoding, the different channels are interleaved. For example, when there are two channels, the first sample in the first channel is followed by the first sample in the second channel. They are followed by the second sample in the first channel and the second sample in the second channel. Hence, the number of bytes required is the number of samples per channel times the number of bytes per channel times the number of channels. With that in mind, the following process is used to allocate the necessary amount of memory:

```
size    = channels.size();
length = getNumberOfSamples();
frameSize  = format.getFrameSize();

// bytes              samples/channel *  bytes/channel     *  channels
rawBytes = new byte[length            *  BYTES_PER_CHANNEL *     size];
```

The interleaving of the samples is handled as follows:

```
channel  = 0;
iterator = channels.iterator();
while (iterator.hasNext())
{
    signal = iterator.next();
    offset = channel * BYTES_PER_CHANNEL;

    for (int i=0; i<length; i++)
    {
        scaled = scaleSample(signal[i]);

        // Big-endian
        rawBytes[frameSize*i+offset]   = (byte)(scaled >> 8);
        rawBytes[frameSize*i+offset+1] = (byte)(scaled & 0xff);

        // Little-endian
        // rawBytes[frameSize*i+offset+1] = (byte)(scaled >> 8);
        // rawBytes[frameSize*i+offset]   = (byte)(scaled & 0xff);
    }
    ++channel;
}
```

11.5 Controlling the Rendering of Sampled Audio

One can control audio playback in a number of ways. The specifics vary from Line to Line and from Mixer to Mixer. In general, one gets a Control object from a Line object and then calls the setValue() method. The different controls are encapsulated in the Control.Type class. Examples include the gain control and the balance control.

EXERCISES

1. Briefly describe the two steps used when digitizing sound waves.

2. Using what you know about convolutions and convolution kernels, are there edge effects associated with FIR filters? If so, how might one deal with them? If not, why do they not arise?

3. (*Library Research*) Write a brief essay that describes, in general, what is involved in *noise reduction*.

4. What is the effect of applying a FIR filter with $n = 0$ and $w_0 = 2$?

5. Using the discussion of reflected sound waves in Chapter 10, design and implement a FIR filter that creates an echo/reverberation effect.

6. Using your understanding of sampled visual content, construct a filter that 'blurs' sampled auditory content. When might you want to use such a filter?

7. (*Library Research*) What is the *Doppler effect*?

8. Using your answer to Exercise 7, create a DopplerFilter that simulates the Doppler effect. (Hint: To create an increase in frequency, you can drop some samples from the signal. To create a decrease in frequency, you can duplicate some samples. To simulate the Doppler effect, the rate at which you drop/duplicate must change.)

9. Can you construct a 'visual echo'? Why or why not?

10. What are the differences/similarities between adding two sine waves before rendering them and rendering the two on different channels?

11. Modify the BalloonApp so that it plays a popping noise when a Balloon pops.

12. The president of the university really likes the work you did on Exercise 11 on page 285 but thinks it would be more interesting if you could listen to her talking while the screen goes up and down. Again, not using the classes in this book, write an application that will render one sampled audio clip while the screen is going down and another while it is going up.

13. Design and implement a BoomBoxApp. It must include play, stop, pause, and rewind buttons. (Note: The rewind button must render the content in reverse.)

14. Modify the `BoomBoxApp` you created in Exercise 13 on the page before so that it includes a 'toggle button' that can be used to turn an echo effect on and off.

15. Create a `MashUpApp` that, given a collection of sampled auditory content, will create and render a mash-up. That is, it must randomly select portions of the sampled auditory content and render them. (Note: This is not a random playlist. The `MashUpApp` must not render complete 'songs'; it must render parts of 'songs' that are selected at random, without pausing in between.)

REFERENCES AND FURTHER READING

Kientzle, T. 1997. *A programmer's guide to sound.* Reading, MA: Addison-Wesley.
Lindley, C. 1999. *Digital audio with Java.* Upper Saddle River, NJ: Prentice Hall.
Pohlmann, K. 2005. *Principles of digital audio.* New York: McGraw-Hill.

Described Auditory Content (Music)   12

Described auditory content can be divided into three different categories—described speech, described sounds, and described music. This chapter is exclusively about described music, which usually involves a way to 'name' frequencies, a way to describe the duration of individual sounds, a way to describe the 'voice' or 'instrument,' and a way to describe the loudness of those sounds.

12.1   A 'Quick Start'

This chapter uses the *Musical Instrument Digital Interface* (MIDI) to **present** described auditory content. MIDI was designed as a protocol for passing musical events between electronic instruments and sequencers (devices that stored musical events). Today, many sound cards include hardware for MIDI input/output (I/O) and synthesis. Those that don't almost always include a software implementation of a synthesizer.

The hardware portion of the MIDI specification is of little interest here; the software portion concerns the MIDI data protocol. MIDI data can be streamed (in real time) or sequenced (i.e., stored and preloaded). The original MIDI protocol, the wire protocol, deals with data being sent over a MIDI cable from one device to another. It does not include timing information—data are presented when received. The standard MIDI files protocol is designed to overcome the timing limitations in the wire protocol. These files consist of *tracks* that typically contain the notes that a single instrument should play and when those notes should be played. There are three types of standard MIDI files. Type 0 intermingles all of the tracks or staves (that comprise a complete score). Type 1 separates the tracks or staves; only the first contains tempo and time signature information. Type 2 also separates the tracks or staves but includes the tempo and time signatures in each. (*General MIDI*, an extension to the original specification, includes 16 families of instruments with 8 instruments in each family.) In order to get an overall feeling for the way in which MIDI works, this chapter begins with a discussion of the way in which one can present the information contained in a MIDI file.

The Java API for MIDI is in the package `javax.sound.midi`. MIDI events are encapsulated in the `MidiEvent` class. Each `MidiEvent` object contains a `MidiMessage` and timing information (called a `tick`). `MidiEvent` objects are grouped together into a `Track` object, and `Track` objects are grouped into a `Sequence` object. This is illustrated in Figure 12.1 on the following page.

The easiest way to read and write sequences of MIDI events is with a `Sequencer` object. To use a `Sequencer`, one must: create a `Sequence` from a `File` or an `InputStream`, create a `Sequencer`, open the `Sequencer`, associate the `Sequence` with the `Sequencer`, and start the `Sequencer`.[1] This process is demonstrated in the following simple application:

---

[1]Individual tracks in a sequence can be muted (by calling the `Sequencer` object's `setTrackMute()` method).

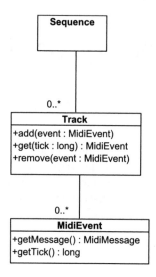

Figure 12.1   The Sequence, Track, and MidiEvent Classes

```java
import java.io.*;
import javax.sound.midi.*;

public class MidiPlayer
{
    public static void main(String[] args) throws Exception
    {
        Sequencer           sequencer;
        Sequence            seq;

        seq = MidiSystem.getSequence(new File(args[0]));

        sequencer = MidiSystem.getSequencer();
        sequencer.open();

        sequencer.setSequence(seq);
        sequencer.start();
    }
}
```

With this background, it is now time to address some of the issues involved in representing and presenting described auditory content (i.e., described music) in more detail. Clearly, such a system must:

★🎵 **F12.1** Encapsulate a description of music.

F12.2 Present/render this description.

This chapter next discusses ways to satisfy Requirement F12.2. It then discusses ways to satisfy Requirement F12.1.

12.2 Presenting/Rendering Described Auditory Content

Described auditory content is rendered using a synthesizer. There are, in general, two different ways to generate the appropriate electrical signals. In one, a *soundbank* is used. That is, the synthesizer has a database of 'sounds' (e.g., samplings of different instruments producing different tones) that it uses to produce the electrical signal. In the other, the synthesizer constructs the electrical signals from continuous waves. Just as there was no need to worry about the difference between raster visual output devices and vector visual output devices, there is no reason to worry about the differences between these two types of synthesizers.

Java encapsulates MIDI synthesizers in the `Synthesizer` class. A `Synthesizer` controls a set (typically with 16 members) of `MidiChannel` objects that encapsulate 'voices.' It takes several steps to create and initialize a `Synthesizer` object. First, one must obtain a `Synthesizer` object by calling the `MidiSystem.getSynthesizer()` method. Second, one must get a `Soundbank` object (e.g., by calling the `Synthesizer` object's `getDefaultSoundBank()` method). Third, one must call the `Synthesizer` object's `loadAllInstruments()` method (passing it the `Soundbank` object). Finally, one must get the `MidiChannel` objects by calling the `Synthesizer` object's `getChannels()` method.

A `Synthesizer` object can be used to render notes in two different ways.

One way to render notes requires the use of `MidiMessage` objects. Using this approach, the program must first obtain a `Receiver` object by calling the `Synthesizer` object's `getReceiver()` method. Then the program must construct a `ShortMessage` object that turns the note on. After that, the program must call the `Receiver` object's `send()` method (passing it the `ShortMessage` object). Fourth, the program must wait the appropriate amount of time. Fifth, the program must construct a `ShortMessage` object that turns off the note. Finally, the program must call the `Receiver` object's `send()` method (passing it the `ShortMessage` object).

The other way to play notes is to use the `MidiChannel` directly. Using this approach, the program must first call the `MidiChannel` object's `noteOn()` method. Then, the program must wait the appropriate amount of time. Finally, the program must call the `MidiChannel` object's `noteOff()` method.

The second method is used here because it is simpler and provides all of the necessary functionality.

12.3 Encapsulating Described Auditory Content

Frequencies, the atomic unit of described music, are commonly 'named' using letters and modifiers. "A" is the name commonly given to the frequencies 55 Hz, 110 Hz, 220 Hz, 440 Hz,

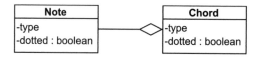

Figure 12.2 A Design of Described Auditory Content That Leads to Code Duplication

880 Hz, 1760 Hz, etc. (Note that the octaves are multiples of powers of 2. That is, $55 \cdot 2^0$, $55 \cdot 2^1$, $55 \cdot 2^2$, $55 \cdot 2^3$, etc. This is because of our logarithmic perception of pitch, as discussed in Section 10.3.2 on page 292.) Loosely, the frequencies in a single octave are denoted by the letters A–G followed by either a sharp indicator (i.e., a ♯ character), which denotes a half-step or half-tone up, or flat indicator (i.e., a ♭ character), which denotes a half-step or half-tone down. More specifically, an octave consists of the notes A, A♯, B, C, C♯, D, D♯, E, F, F♯, G, and G♯. (Note that E and F are, by convention, only a half-step apart, as are B and C.) Clearly, multiple *notes* can actually refer to the same frequency (for example, A sharp and B flat). Such notes are often called *enharmonics*.

Durations are commonly given as multiples/fractions of a base duration, or *beat*. Common durations are whole notes, half notes, quarter notes, eighth notes, and sixteenth notes. So, for example, if a whole note lasts for 800 milliseconds, then an eighth note lasts for 100 milliseconds. A standard duration can be 'dotted' to indicate that it should be increased by 50%. So, if a whole note lasts for 800 milliseconds, then a dotted eighth note lasts for 150 milliseconds. *Triplets* are notes that are grouped in sets of three (i.e., the three notes evenly divide an integral number of beats).

In some theories of music, a *chord* is multiple notes that are presented at the same time.[2] In others, the notes in a chord need not be presented together (as, for example, in a *broken chord*). This book assumes that the notes in a chord must be presented at the same time and must have the same duration (since, if needed, broken chords can be represented as individual notes). The design and implementation of a `BrokenChord` class is left as an exercise (see Exercise 9 on page 360).

There are several different ways to encapsulate described auditory content, all of which are consistent with the conceptual model in Figure 10.5 on page 296. They all involve notes and chords that play the role of the `Content` and collections of `Content` objects that play the role of the `Audition`. These designs have different advantages and disadvantages.

 One possible design has a `Note` class and a `Chord` class that is an aggregation of multiple `Note` objects. This design is illustrated in Figure 12.2. The shortcoming of this design is that it will probably result in code duplication. That is, both the `Note` class and the `Chord` class will certainly include code for managing the duration and may contain other duplicate code as well.

 Alternatively, one could add an `AbstractContent` class that contains the members that the `Note` and `Chord` classes have in common (for example, the `type` attribute and the `dotted` attribute). This design is illustrated in Figure 12.3 on the next page. This design is pretty

---

[2]Some definitions require that a chord consist of more than two notes, referring to two notes presented together as a *dyad—idxfootnote* or *vertical/harmonic interval*.

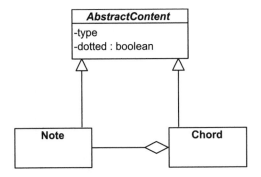

Figure 12.3   An Inflexible Design of Described Auditory Content

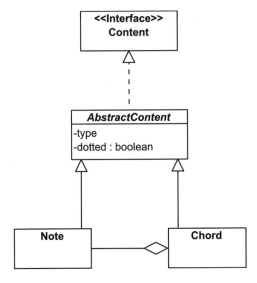

Figure 12.4   A More Flexible Design of Described Auditory Content

good, but is inflexible because it makes it difficult to add other kinds of content. Specifically, it makes it difficult to add content that is not a specialization of the AbstractContent class.

 The design in Figure 12.3 can be made more flexible by adding a Content interface. This is illustrated in Figure 12.4. The advantage of this design is that it enables one to create other classes that implement the Content interface without having to specialize the AbstractContent class. So, for example, if one had to create a BrokenChord (or Arpeggio) class, those classes could implement the Content interface without having to specialize the AbstractContent class.

 The introduction of the Content interface naturally leads to the consideration of a design that uses the composite pattern. In other words, one should also consider a design in which the Chord class contains a collection of Content objects rather than a collection of Note objects. This is illustrated in Figure 12.5 on the following page. Using this design, a Chord

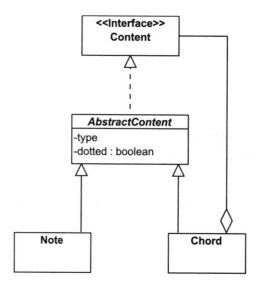

Figure 12.5   A Design of Described Auditory Content Using the Composite Pattern

could contain both Note objects and Chord objects. While this is a very elegant solution, it is not consistent with the way the term "chord" is normally used in music theory. Hence, the design in Figure 12.4 on the page before seems like the best alternative.

Recall that the design of the described visual content system in Chapter 6 included existing interfaces and classes. That is not the case here. Specifically, there is nothing comparable to the Shape interface. Hence, a class that implements the **Content** interface can and should include all of the functionality necessary for a piece of described auditory content to render itself, including a render() method.

Note also that it is not very useful to think about static auditory content. That is, in all applications of interest, the auditory content is going to change over time. At a minimum, one will almost always need to be able to make described auditory content inaudible after a certain amount of time. Hence, the **Content** interface should include a **setAudible()** method. (This method is similar to the setVisible() method in the **AbstractSprite** class in Chapter 9.)

Even taking all of this into account, the **Content** interface is fairly straightforward. It includes methods for getting the duration of the content, for making the content audible or not, and for rendering the content (regardless of whether it is audible or not).

```
package auditory.described;

import javax.sound.midi.*;

public interface Content
{
    public abstract int  getType();
```

```
        public abstract boolean isDotted();

        public abstract void render(MidiChannel channel);

        public abstract void setAudible(boolean audible);
}
```

The overall structure of the **AbstractContent** class is also fairly simple. It contains a type attribute and a dotted attribute. It also has attributes to indicate whether it is currently audible and currently being rendered/played.

```
package auditory.described;

import javax.sound.midi.*;

public abstract class        AbstractContent
                implements Content
{
    protected boolean                    audible, dotted, playing;
    protected int                        type;

    public AbstractContent()
    {
        this(1, false);
    }

    public AbstractContent(int type, boolean dotted)
    {
        this.type     = type;
        this.dotted   = dotted;
        this.audible  = false;
        this.playing  = false;
    }
}
```

The 'getters' are straightforward,

```
    public int getType()
    {
        return type;
    }
```

```
public boolean isDotted()
{
    return dotted;
}
```

as are the 'setters.'

```
public void setAudible(boolean audible)
{
    this.audible = audible;
}

protected void setDotted(boolean dotted)
{
    this.dotted = dotted;
}

protected void setType(int type)
{
    this.type = type;
}
```

The basic functionality required for rendering is also pretty simple. If the Content should be audible and is not playing, then it should start playing. On the other hand, if it should not be audible and it is playing, then it should stop playing. Hence, the render() method is implemented as follows:

```
public void render(MidiChannel channel)
{
    if      ( audible && !playing)
    {
        playing = true;
        startPlaying(channel);
    }
    else if (!audible &&  playing)
    {
        playing = false;
        stopPlaying(channel);
    }
}
```

Each concrete extension of the AbstractContent class must implement the startPlaying()

and stopPlaying() methods that are used by the **render()** method. Hence, these methods are abstract.

```
    protected abstract void startPlaying(MidiChannel channel);

    protected abstract void stopPlaying(MidiChannel channel);
```

With the **AbstractContent** class as a parent, the **Note** class need only add/manage attributes related to the frequency. For simplicity, the **Note** class implemented here ignores enharmonics. Specifically, it includes sharps but not flats.[3]

```java
package auditory.described;

import javax.sound.midi.*;

public class   Note
       extends AbstractContent
{
    private boolean            sharp;
    private char               pitch;
    private int                midiNumber;

    public Note()
    {
        this('C', false, 0, 1, false);
    }

    public Note(char pitch,   boolean sharp, int octave,
               int type, boolean dotted)
    {
        super(type, dotted);

        this.pitch = Character.toUpperCase(pitch);
        this.sharp = sharp;
        midiNumber = MidiCalculator.numberFor(pitch, sharp, octave);
    }
}
```

The startPlaying() and stopPlaying() methods use the **MidiChannel** for the actual rendering.

---

[3]This decision will certainly upset most people who have studied music theory as they would argue that there is a difference between a C♯ and a D♭. However, the inclusion of only sharps greatly simplifies the exposition.

```
    protected void startPlaying(MidiChannel channel)
    {
        channel.noteOn(midiNumber, 127);
    }

    protected void stopPlaying(MidiChannel channel)
    {
        channel.noteOff(midiNumber, 127);
    }
```

Note that this class uses the following `MidiCalculator` class to calculate a MIDI number from the other attributes. It simply determines the offset from middle C and sets it to 60 (which is the MIDI value of middle C). So, for example, the D above middle C, which is two notes above middle C, has a MIDI number of 62. Similarly, the D♯ above middle C has a MIDI value of 63. For simplicity, this class treats B♯ (which has the same MIDI number as C) and E♯ (which has the same MIDI number as F) as special cases.

```
package auditory.described;

public class MidiCalculator
{
    public static int numberFor(char    pitch,
                                boolean sharp,
                                int     octave)
    {
        int    midiBase, midiNumber;


        // Handle special cases (B# and E#)
        if ((pitch == 'B') && sharp)
        {
            pitch = 'C';
            sharp = false;
        }
        else if ((pitch == 'E') && sharp)
        {
            pitch = 'F';
            sharp = false;
        }

        // Calculate the MIDI value
        midiBase = 60;
        if      (pitch == 'A') midiNumber = midiBase +  9;
```

```
            else if (pitch == 'B') midiNumber = midiBase + 11;
            else if (pitch == 'C') midiNumber = midiBase +  0;
            else if (pitch == 'D') midiNumber = midiBase +  2;
            else if (pitch == 'E') midiNumber = midiBase +  4;
            else if (pitch == 'F') midiNumber = midiBase +  5;
            else if (pitch == 'G') midiNumber = midiBase +  7;
            else                    midiNumber = -1;  // Rest

            if (sharp) midiNumber = midiNumber + 1;

            midiNumber = midiNumber + (octave * 12);

            return midiNumber;
        }
    }
```

Note that a MIDI number of –1 is used to indicate a *rest*, a duration of silence (i.e., a 'silent' note).

A `Chord` is little more than a collection of `Note` objects along with methods that ensure that they are rendered simultaneously. The `Note` objects are stored in an `ArrayList` (though they could be stored in an unordered collection) and managed as follows:

```
package auditory.described;

import java.util.*;
import javax.sound.midi.*;

public class       Chord
       extends      AbstractContent
{
    private ArrayList<Note>        notes;

    public Chord()
    {
        this(1, false);
    }

    public Chord(int type, boolean dotted)
    {
        super(type, dotted);

        notes = new ArrayList<Note>();
    }

    public void addNote(Note note)
```

```
        {
            notes.add(note);
        }
    }
}
```

The startPlaying() method iterates through all of the Note objects and starts them playing. While each of the individual Note objects could, mistakenly, have different type and dotted attributes, this method ensures that they are all the same each time they are played. This might seem unnecessary but, since objects may have external references to the Note objects, potential inconsistencies could arise.

```
    protected void startPlaying(MidiChannel channel)
    {
        Iterator<Note>     i;
        Note               note;

        i = notes.iterator();
        while (i.hasNext())
        {
            note = i.next();
            if (note != null)
            {
                note.setType(type);
                note.setDotted(dotted);
                note.startPlaying(channel);
            }
        }
    }
```

Similarly, the stopPlaying() method iterates through all of the Note objects and stops them.

```
    protected void stopPlaying(MidiChannel channel)
    {
        Iterator<Note>     i;
        Note               note;

        i = notes.iterator();
        while (i.hasNext())
        {
            note = i.next();
            if (note != null)
            {
```

Figure 12.6 Eight Measures of "Ode to Joy"

```
            note.stopPlaying(channel);
      }
   }
}
```

Auditory content is most frequently described using music notation that consists of one or more *staffs* (a set of five horizontal lines) that contain multiple measures (delimited by *bar lines*), each of which contains multiple notes (that indicate both the pitch and the duration).[4] The end of a song is usually indicated with a double bar line. An example of this notation, for eight measures of Beethoven's "Ode to Joy" (in D major) is given in Figure 12.6. The first four notes of the violin part are the quarter notes F, F, G, and A. The first three notes of the piano part, on the other hand, are a half note D, and quarter notes G and A.

While this method of describing music is both extraordinarily powerful and visually appealing, it is difficult to use as input. Hence, it makes sense to use a description that uses `String` objects instead. The notation used here consists of a comma-delimited `String` with a field for the 'name' including an optional `'#'` character, the octave (with 0 being the octave that contains middle C), and the type of the note (i.e., 1 for whole, 2 for half, 4 for quarter, etc.), which includes an optional `'.'` character.

The first eight measures of the violin part of "Ode to Joy" is represented using this notation in Figure 12.7 on the following page. (This figure uses a multicolumn format to save space. The dots indicate a continuation.) Note that the last measure includes an `'R.'` This indicates a rest; that is, a time during which nothing is being played.

---

[4]The distance (i.e., the number of lines and spaces on the staff) between two notes is called the *interval*. The distance includes the two notes. So, the interval between A and C is 3. The distance between two notes played at the same time is called a *harmonic interval* whereas the distance between two notes played at different times is called the *melodic interval*.

```
            .              .              .
            .              .              .
            .              .              .
F#,-1,4      D ,-1,4      F#,-1,4      D ,-1,4
F#,-1,4      D ,-1,4      F#,-1,4      D ,-1,4
G ,-1,4      E ,-1,4      G ,-1,4      E ,-1,4
A ,-1,4      F#,-1,4      A ,-1,4      F#,-1,4

A ,-1,4      F#,-1,4.     A ,-1,4      E ,-1,4.
G ,-1,4      E ,-1,8      G ,-1,4      D ,-1,8
F#,-1,4      E ,-1,2      F#,-1,4      D ,-1,4
E ,-1,4                   E ,-1,4      R , 0,4
            .              .              .
            .              .              .
            .              .              .
```

Figure 12.7   Eight Measures of the Violin Part of "Ode to Joy"

In order to avoid reducing the cohesiveness of the Note class, the functionality for creating Note objects from this String notation is in the NoteFactory class.

```java
package auditory.described;

import java.util.*;

null
public class NoteFactory
{
    public static Note parseNote(String s)
    {
        boolean         dotted, sharp;
        char            pitch, sharpChar;
        int             duration, octave, octaveEnd;
        Note            theNote;
        String          durationString, octaveString, token;
        StringTokenizer st;

        st = new StringTokenizer(s, ", ");

        try
        {
            token = st.nextToken();

            // Determine the pitch
            pitch = token.charAt(0);
```

```
        // Determine if this is a sharp or a natural
        sharp = false;
        if (token.length() == 2)
        {
            sharpChar = token.charAt(1);
            if (sharpChar == '#') sharp = true;
        }

        // Detemine the octave (relative to middle C)
        octaveString = st.nextToken();
        octave       = Integer.parseInt(octaveString);

        // Determine the duration (which has an arbitrary length)
        dotted         = false;
        durationString = st.nextToken();
        if (durationString.endsWith(".")) dotted = true;
        duration = (int)Double.parseDouble(durationString);

        // Construct a new Note
        theNote = new Note(pitch, sharp, octave, duration, dotted);
    }
    catch (NoSuchElementException nsee)
    {
        theNote = null;
    }

    return theNote;
    }
}
```

The static `parseNote()` method in this class is passed a `String s` and returns a `Note` object (or null). It uses a `StringTokenizer` to tokenize the `String` at the commas. The logic it uses to process each token is straightforward.

12.4   Operations on Described Audio

The most interesting operation that can be performed on described audio is *transposition*. To understand transposition you first have to understand scales.

An *ascending scale* is a sequence of notes that starts and ends on the same note, moving up in a consistent way. A *major scale* is a scale that uses the T-T-S-T-T-T-S pattern when ascending (where T denotes a tone or whole step and S denotes a semitone or half step). A *minor scale* is a scale that uses the T-S-T-T-S-T-T pattern when ascending. For example, the C-Major scale is

```
C   D   E   F   G   A   B   C
  T   T   S   T   T   T   S
```

To construct the F-Major scale, start with

```
F   G   A   B   C   D   E   F
  W   W   W   H   W   W   H
```

and then add sharps or flats to adjust for the desired pattern:

```
  W   W   H   W   W   W   H
F   G   A   Bb  C   D   E   F
```

A song that uses the notes from a particular scale is said to be in the *key* of that scale. Transposition is an operation that changes a song from one key to another.[5]

Since the representation used here does not include a *key signature*; that is, all notes include explicit sharps/flats, transposition can be performed directly on the MIDI numbers. The design and implementation of transposition functionality is left as an exercise (see Exercise 8 on page 360).

12.5   Design of a Described Auditory Content System

All that remains is to consider the `Audition` and `AuditionView` components of the conceptual model in Figure 10.5 on page 296. To that end, it is important to consider the ways in which collections of notes and chords are organized.

Notes are commonly grouped into durations of equal length, called *measures*. The *time signature* indicates how many beats are in each measure (in the 'numerator') and which type of note gets a whole beat (in the 'denominator'). So a 4/4 time signature indicates that there are 4 beats per measure and a quarter note gets a full beat whereas a 3/8 signature indicates that there are 3 beats per measure and an eighth note gets a full beat.

A collection of notes/chords ordered over time that is intended to be played by a single instrument (or sung by a single voice) is often called a *part* (as in "four-part harmony"). Further, a collection of parts (for different instruments/voices) is referred to as a *score*. The overall speed of a score is referred to as its *tempo*, which is typically measured in beats per minute.

Note that, unlike the `Sprite` objects in Chapter 6, `Note/Chord` objects become relevant sequentially over time. That is, since they are rendered sequentially, every `Note/Chord` object needn't be told about every tick of the `Metronome`. Instead, the `Part` should respond to

---

[5] *Modulation* is a key change that occurs within a song.

handleTick() messages and determine which Note/Chord needs to be rendered. With this in mind, there are two alternatives to consider.

In one alternative, each Part has its own Metronome object and renders its content (independently) in its own thread of execution. The shortcoming of this approach is that the different Part objects may not stay synchronized because the timing of handleTick() messages is not precise. That is, one Metronome may not generate handleTick() messages at the same time as another; hence, the Note objects in different Part objects that should be played at the same time may not be.

A better approach is to have a single Metronome object that synchronizes the Part objects. Using this approach, all of the Part objects listen to the same Metronome object. The handleTick() method in each Part object then needs only to determine which Note/Chord objects needs to be rendered.

Since these are high-level design alternatives, they do not consider the details of the design of the Part class. Not surprisingly, there are alternatives to consider here as well.

One possible design of a Part class includes an attribute for the instrument. The shortcoming of this design is that one cannot have the same Part object rendered using different instruments. That is, one cannot have the same Part object rendered by, say, both a trombone and a trumpet.

Alternatively, a Part object can be told what instrument to use when its render() method is called. That is, its render() method can be passed a MidiChannel object (that is associated with an instrument). Since this adds a little flexibility at no 'cost' it seems like the better alternative.

These two decisions lead to the overall design illustrated in Figure 12.8 on the next page. The Part and Score classes play the role of the Audition in Figure 10.5 on page 296. A Part has an ordered collection of Content (i.e., Note and Chord) objects and a Score is a collection of Part objects. The Orchestra class plays the role of the AuditionView and owns the single Metronome object that synchronizes the rendering. The Orchestra object responds to the handleTick() message by instructing the Score to render itself. The Score object delegates the rendering to each of it's component Part objects that, in turn, delegate to their Content objects.

The Part class is relatively easy to implement. It stores the different Content objects in an ArrayList (since they need to be ordered), the numerator and denominator of the time signature in two double values, and the number of milliseconds per measure and the stop time in int values.

```
package auditory.described;

import java.util.*;
import javax.sound.midi.*;

import event.*;

public class Part implements MetronomeListener
```

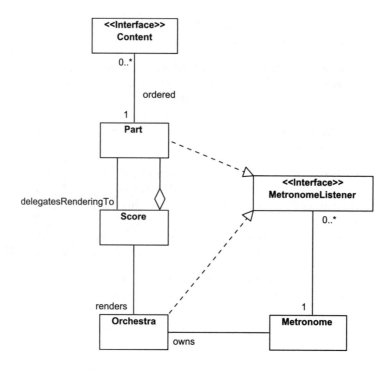

Figure 12.8   A Described Auditory Content System

```
{
    private ArrayList<Content>      sounds;
    private double                  timeSignatureDenominator,
                                    timeSignatureNumerator;
    private int                     millisPerMeasure, stopTime;
    public Part()
    {
        sounds      = new ArrayList<Content>();
    }
}
```

It has an `add()` method for adding `Content` objects.

```
    public void add(Content c)
    {
        if (c != null) sounds.add(c);
    }
```

It also has the following 'setters':

```
    public void setTempo(int millisPerMeasure)
    {
       this.millisPerMeasure = millisPerMeasure;
    }


    public void setTimeSignature(int numerator, int denominator)
    {
       this.timeSignatureNumerator   = numerator;
       this.timeSignatureDenominator = denominator;
    }
```

The upbeat() method gets the Part ready. (This name comes from the move that a conductor makes to get an orchestra/choir ready.) It makes use of several 'class globals' for convenience.

```
    private Content              currentContent,
                                 previousContent;
    private Iterator<Content>    iterator;
    private Metronome            metronome; // Not Owned
```

The upbeat() method initializes these 'class globals' and adds the Part object as an observer of the Metronome (that is owned by the Orchestra).

```
    public void upbeat(Metronome metronome)
    {
       this.metronome   = metronome; // For later removal

       iterator         = sounds.iterator();
       currentContent   = null;
       previousContent  = null;
       stopTime         = -1;

       metronome.addListener(this);
    }
```

The handleTick() method in the Part class determines whether the current Content object has been playing the appropriate amount of time (using the number of milliseconds per beat and the number of beats). If so, it makes the current Content inaudible and retrieves the next Content object.

```
public void handleTick(int millis)
{
    double    beats, millisPerBeat, type;

    if (iterator == null)
        throw(new IllegalStateException("No upbeat()"));

    if (millis >= stopTime)
    {
        if (currentContent != null)
            currentContent.setAudible(false);

        if (iterator.hasNext())
        {
            previousContent = currentContent;
            currentContent  = iterator.next();

            // This calculation needn't really be done each iteration
            millisPerBeat = 1.0/(double)timeSignatureNumerator *
                            millisPerMeasure;

            beats         = (1.0/(double)currentContent.getType()) *
                            (double)timeSignatureDenominator;

            if (currentContent.isDotted()) beats = beats * 1.5;

            stopTime = millis + (int)(beats * millisPerBeat);

            currentContent.setAudible(true);
        }
        else
        {
            metronome.removeListener(this);
        }
    }
}
```

Finally, the `render()` method in the `Part` class delegates to the previous and current `Content` objects, which will turn themselves on or off as necessary.

```
public void render(MidiChannel channel)
{
    if (previousContent != null)
        previousContent.render(channel);
```

```
            if (currentContent  != null)
                currentContent.render(channel);
        }
```

The `String` representation of a `Part` includes one or more 'lines' containing `String` representations of `Note` objects and a 'footer line' containing an `'X.'` Not surprisingly, the processing of these `String` representations is handled by a `PartFactory`. The `createPart()` method in this class reads one line at a time and delegates the processing of each line to the `parseNote()` method in the `NoteFactory` class.

```java
package auditory.described;

import java.io.*;

public class PartFactory
{
    public static Part createPart(BufferedReader in)
                    throws IOException
    {
        Note                    note;
        Part                    part;
        String                  line;

        part = new Part();

        while ((line = in.readLine()) != null &&
               (!line.equals("X"))                      )
        {
            if (!line.equals(""))
            {
                note = NoteFactory.parseNote(line);
                if (note != null) part.add(note);
            }
        }

        return part;
    }

    public static Part createPart(String filename)
                    throws IOException
    {
        BufferedReader          in;

        in = new BufferedReader(new FileReader(filename));
```

```
        return createPart(in);
    }
}
```

The `Score` class is really just a collection of `Part` objects, each of which has an associated `String` representation of an instrument. However, since a `Score` object delegates rendering to its component `Part` objects, it must keep track of the `MidiChannel` that each `Part` is supposed to use. This information is kept in two `Hashtable` objects that are managed as follows:

```java
package auditory.described;

import java.util.*;
import javax.sound.midi.*;

import event.*;

public class Score
{
    private Hashtable<Part, MidiChannel>    channelTable;
    private Hashtable<Part, String>         parts;
    private int                             timeSignatureDenominator,
                                            timeSignatureNumerator,
                                            millisPerMeasure;
    public void addPart(Part part, String instrument)
    {
        parts.put(part, instrument);
    }

    public Enumeration<Part> getParts()
    {
        return parts.keys();
    }

    public String getInstrumentName(Part part)
    {
        return parts.get(part);
    }

    public void removePart(Part part)
    {
        parts.remove(part);
    }
}
```

This class also has the following obvious 'setters':

```
public void setChannel(Part part, MidiChannel channel)
{
   channelTable.put(part, channel);
}

public void setTempo(int millisPerMeasure)
{
   this.millisPerMeasure = millisPerMeasure;
}

public void setTimeSignature(int numerator, int denominator)
{
   this.timeSignatureNumerator   = numerator;
   this.timeSignatureDenominator = denominator;
}
```

The upbeat() method in the Score class calls the upbeat() and setter methods in the component Part objects.

```
public void upbeat(Metronome metronome)
{
   Enumeration<Part>            e;
   Part                         part;

   e = parts.keys();
   while (e.hasMoreElements())
   {
      part      = e.nextElement();
      part.upbeat(metronome);
      part.setTimeSignature(timeSignatureNumerator,
                            timeSignatureDenominator);
      part.setTempo(millisPerMeasure);
   }
}
```

Similarly, the render() method in the Score class gets the appropriate MidiChannel for each component Part and then delegates.

```
public void render()
{
```

```
        Enumeration<Part>              e;
        MidiChannel                    channel;
        Part                           part;

        e = parts.keys();
        while (e.hasMoreElements())
        {
            part      = e.nextElement();
            channel   = channelTable.get(part);
            part.render(channel);
        }
    }
}
```

The Orchestra class manages the MIDI system and synchronizes the rendering. It has the following overall structure:

```
package auditory.described;

import java.io.InputStream;
import java.net.URL;
import java.util.*;
import javax.sound.midi.*;

import event.*;
import io.*;

public class Orchestra implements MetronomeListener
{
    private Hashtable<String, Instrument>      instruments;
    private Metronome                          metronome;
    private MidiChannel[]                       channels;
    private Score                              score;
}
```

The constructor in the Orchestra class has the responsibility for creating the collections of Instrument and MidiChannel objects and populating them with information from and about the MIDI system. It also has the responsibility for creating and initializing the Metronome.

```
public Orchestra(Score score) throws MidiUnavailableException
{
    this(score, new Metronome(10));
}
```

```
public Orchestra(Score score, Metronome metronome)
                            throws MidiUnavailableException
{
    Instrument[]    loaded;
    Soundbank       soundbank;
    Synthesizer     synthesizer;

    this.score     = score;
    this.metronome = metronome;
    metronome.addListener(this);

    instruments  = new Hashtable<String, Instrument>();

    synthesizer = MidiSystem.getSynthesizer();
    synthesizer.open();
    soundbank = synthesizer.getDefaultSoundbank();

    if (soundbank == null) soundbank = findSoundbank();

    synthesizer.loadAllInstruments(soundbank);

    channels     = synthesizer.getChannels();

    loaded = synthesizer.getLoadedInstruments();
    for (int i=0; i<loaded.length; i++)
    {
        instruments.put(loaded[i].getName(), loaded[i]);
    }
}
```

The start() method initializes the MIDI system, assigns voices/instruments to channels, and initializes the different Score object. It also starts the Metronome.

```
public void start()
{
    Enumeration<Part>           e;
    Instrument                  instrument;
    int                         i;
    MidiChannel                 channel;
    String                      name;
    Patch                       patch;
    Part                        part;
```

```
      e = score.getParts();
      i = 0;

      while (e.hasMoreElements())
      {
         part       = e.nextElement();
         name       = score.getInstrumentName(part);
         instrument = instruments.get(name);

         // Have the channel use the appropriate instrument
         if (instrument == null)
         {
            channels[i].programChange(0, 0);
         }
         else
         {
            patch = instrument.getPatch();
            channels[i].programChange(patch.getBank(),
                                      patch.getProgram());
         }
         score.setChannel(part, channels[i]);

         score.upbeat(metronome);
      }


      // Start the metronome
      metronome.start();
   }
```

Finally, the handleTick() method sends the render() message to the Score object. It then checks to see whether it is the only MetronomeListener and stops the Metronome if it is.

```
   public void handleTick(int millis)
   {
      score.render();

      if (metronome.getNumberOfListeners() == 1)
      {
         metronome.stop();
      }
   }
```

The `String` representation of a `Score` includes a 'header line' with the time signature and the tempo. Also, each `String` representation of a `Part` is preceded by a 'header line' that contains the instrument/voice to use for that `Part`. Again, it makes sense to create a `ScoreFactory` class to process the `String` representation of `Score` objects.

```java
package auditory.described;

import java.io.*;
import java.util.StringTokenizer;
import javax.sound.midi.MidiUnavailableException;

import io.*;

public class ScoreFactory
{
    private ResourceFinder        finder;

    public ScoreFactory()
    {
        finder = ResourceFinder.createInstance();
    }

    public ScoreFactory(ResourceFinder finder)
    {
        this.finder = finder;
    }

    public Score createScore(InputStream is)
                     throws IOException,
                            MidiUnavailableException
    {
        BufferedReader        in;
        int                   denominator, numerator, tempo;
        Note                  note;
        Part                  part;
        Score                 score;
        String                line, voice;
        StringTokenizer       st;

        in = new BufferedReader(new InputStreamReader(is));

        // Read the time signature and tempo
        line        = in.readLine();
        st          = new StringTokenizer(line, ",/");
        numerator   = Integer.parseInt(st.nextToken());
        denominator = Integer.parseInt(st.nextToken());
```

```
        tempo        = Integer.parseInt(st.nextToken());

        score = new Score();

        score.setTimeSignature(numerator, denominator);
        score.setTempo(tempo);

        while ((voice = in.readLine()) != null)
        {
            part = PartFactory.createPart(in);
            score.addPart(part, voice);
        }

        return score;
    }

    public Score createScore(String filename)
                    throws IOException,
                            MidiUnavailableException
    {
        InputStream             is;

        is = finder.findInputStream(filename);

        return createScore(is);
    }
}
```

This class delegates most of the actual processing to the **PartFactory** class.

EXERCISES

1. The MIDI file format is, not surprisingly, much more powerful than the **String** representations used here. Do the **String** representations used here have any advantages?

2. (*Library Research*) Write a brief essay on alternatives to MIDI.

3. Compare the rendering of described auditory contents with the rendering of described static visual content.

4. The first seven MIDI notes of the "James Madison University Fight Song" are 60, 62, 64, 60, 65, 64, 60 (with durations of 200, 300, 600, 400, 400, 300, 300 milliseconds). Complete the following application so that it plays these seven notes. (Note: You must NOT use the classes from this book.)

```java
import javax.sound.midi.*;

/**
 * Plays the first 7 notes of the JMU Fight Song
 *
 */
public class FightSong
{
    private static MidiChannel       channel;

    /**
     * The entry point
     *
     * @param args  Command-line args (0 for instrument)
     */
    public static void main(String[] args) throws Exception
    {
        int             instrument;
        MidiChannel[]   channels;
        Soundbank       defaultSB;
        Synthesizer     synthesizer;

        // Parse the command-line argument
        instrument = Integer.parseInt(args[0]);

        // Create and open a MIDI synthesizer

        // YOUR CODE HERE!


        // Get the sound bank, load the instruments,
        // and get the channels
        defaultSB = synthesizer.getDefaultSoundbank();
        synthesizer.loadAllInstruments(defaultSB);
        channels   = synthesizer.getChannels();
        channel    = channels[0];

        // Change the instrument
        channel.programChange(0,  instrument);

        // Play the first seven notes
        play(60, 300);
        play(62, 300);
        play(64, 600);
        play(60, 400);
```

```
        play(65, 400);
        play(64, 300);
        play(60, 300);
    }


    /**
     * Play the given note (60 is middle C) for the
     * given amount of time
     *
     * @param note    The note
     * @param millis The amount of time (in milliseconds)
     */
    private static void play(int note, int millis) throws Exception
    {
        // YOUR CODE HERE!
    }
```

5. Without using the classes from this chapter, write an app that will play the notes A–G when the corresponding keys are pressed on the keyboard.

6. The president of the university agrees that the work you did on Exercise 12 on page 330 is a little annoying. So, again not using using the classes in this book, write an application that will render one described audio clip while the screen is going down and another while it is going up. The rendering of the auditory content must stop when the screen stops and must continue while the screen is moving.

7. Given what you know about described music, describe how a system for described speech might work.

8. Design and implement the functionality required for transpositions. (Hint: Start by thinking about different ways of adding this functionality to the **Note** and **Chord** classes.)

9. Design and implement a **BrokenChord** class.

10. Design and implement an **OrchestraApp** that includes play, stop, pause, and fast-forward buttons. (Note: The fast-forward button must render the content at twice the normal speed.)

11. Modify the design of the classes in this chapter so that the **OrchestraApp** you created in Exercise 10 could include reverse and fast-reverse functionality (both of which render the auditory content).

REFERENCES AND FURTHER READING

Roads, C. 1996. *The computer music tutorial.* Cambridge, MA: MIT Press.
Messick, P. 1997. *Maximum MIDI: Music applications in C++.* Greenwich, CT: Manning.
Schmeling, P. 2005. *Berklee music theory book 1.* Boston: Berklee Press.

Index